THE
DAVIS
CUP

THE
DAVIS
CUP

CELEBRATING 100 YEARS
OF INTERNATIONAL TENNIS

RICHARD EVANS

FOREWORD BY
JOHN McENROE

EBURY PRESS
LONDON

First published in Great Britain in 1998

1 3 5 7 9 10 8 6 4 2

Copyright © ITF Limited 1998

Ebury Press
Random House, 20 Vauxhall Bridge Road, London SW1V 2SA

Random House Australia Pty Limited
20 Alfred Street, Milsons Point, Sydney, New South Wales 2061, Australia

Random House New Zealand Limited
18 Poland Road, Glenfield, Auckland 10, New Zealand

Random House South Africa (Pty) Limited
Endulini, 5A Jubilee Road, Parktown 2193, South Africa

Random House UK Limited Reg. No. 954009#

www.randomhouse.co.uk

A CIP catalogue record for this book is available from the British Library

ISBN 0 09 186565 4

Printed and bound in Italy by New Interlitho S.p.a. Milan

Papers used by Ebury Press are natural, recyclable products
made from wood grown in sustainable forests.

CONTENTS

FOREWORD

Dwight Davis had a genius of an idea. The fact that the Davis Cup still plays such an important role in the world game 100 years after that first match between the United States and Britain at the Longwood Cricket Club suggests that Davis was absolutely right in his belief that this most individualistic of sports could take on another dimension.

There had already been 24 Wimbledons by the time Davis organised the first official team match between two nations. In tournament play the ego is rampant and every player is thinking 100 per cent about himself. But get a group of guys together, call them 'USA', 'France' or 'Sweden', wave a flag and suddenly everyone has different responsibilities. How you interact with your team mates becomes almost as important as how you play.

This is one of the reasons why I always enjoyed Davis Cup so much. That may surprise people who only saw McEnroe the intense individualist playing his singles matches. But they might have overlooked the fact that I was often on the doubles court with Peter Fleming, who was a friend as well as a partner. It was good to be on court sharing the highs and lows with somebody else because singles, as it implies, is a very lonely game.

But Davis Cup is not just about camaraderie. It has also achieved what Dwight Davis set out to achieve. It has brought countries together through sporting contact, often in the face of political opposition. And, in the early years, it gave them the incentive to make those long journeys which are so commonplace and easy for us now.

How these journeys were financed and undertaken, helping to make tennis the truly international sport it is today, forms part of the story that follows.

Personally, the Davis Cup offered me more immediate pleasure than almost anything else I accomplished in my career. My parents had brought me up to believe that it was an honor to be asked to play for and represent your country, and that is why I find it so strange – and so disheartening – that some of my compatriots seem to find it a burden.

Naturally I will always remember my 6 hour 22 minute victory over Mats Wilander in St Louis. And I will never forget my Davis Cup début in doubles, playing with Brian Gottfried against Chile just after an earthquake had hit Santiago. Maybe that was a warning from the gods. Quite a few of my subsequent matches were afflicted with seismic rumblings, although not the final against France in Grenoble which was special for a variety of different reasons. For a start, it was the only time we won the Cup on foreign soil during my era; there was also the unique relationship between our captain Arthur Ashe and the new French star Yannick Noah. Just 11 years before, Arthur had discovered Yannick in the Cameroons during a State Department sponsored tour of French-speaking Africa. I know Arthur was proud of the way his young protégé developed.

But, strangely perhaps, it was my very last match, a doubles like the first, that gave me as much satisfaction as anything. I played in partnership with Pete Sampras against Switzerland in the 1992 Final at Fort Worth, Texas. Pete and I came back from two sets to love down, but even that wasn't what made it special. After so many years being the number one player on the team, I was just a doubles player again, no longer the main guy, a squad member like any other, who needed all the help he could get. And the team was great with me. They knew I was struggling off court as well as on – my first marriage had just broken up – and when I was able to contribute something and saw how Pete reacted to my desire and my commitment, it made everything very worthwhile and very memorable.

I hope you enjoy this detailed history of a unique competition. Whether it is played at Kooyong or Casablanca, a World Group Final or a first round in the Euro/African Zone, Davis Cup offers tennis players the rare chance of experiencing the thrill of playing for your team mates and your country.

John McEnroe

INTRODUCTION

WE ALL HAVE IDEAS. Some see the light of day, for a minute, a week, a year. Few get past a startled dinner companion. But the idea Dwight Davis had amidst the dying embers of the 19th century enters the 21st having spanned a century and encircled the globe. That was some idea.

The task of encapsulating the story of a sporting competition that has become a symbol for the game of tennis as well as a means of reaching out across frontiers was a daunting but highly pleasurable one. I have always considered the Davis Cup to be as good a sporting contest as has yet been devised. There has been no need to change the format because the symmetry is perfect. While retaining the one-on-one nature of tennis combat, the Davis Cup embraces the need for co-operation between members of a team – an essential ingredient that has examined the character and motivation of some huge stars and asked them questions that were not always easy to answer.

The least easy aspect of the author's task was sifting through 100 years of matches and deciding what to leave out. There are players who have toiled long and hard for their country who should be mentioned here and are not. The selection process is always painful. Mostly it is the story of the more recent years that has been given less detail because the 1980s and 1990s are well chronicled in John Barrett's excellent annual *World of Tennis* and, in more recent years, in the *Davis Cup Yearbook* that the ITF is now publishing. It is the early decades of the century that will fade away unless they are documented in detail, because the books and publications from which I worked are available to no more than a handful of collectors. In this respect, I am grateful to Alan Chalmers, the tennis antiquarian, for making some of his rarer books available to me.

My thanks also, of course, to all my colleagues in the tennis writing business and those players, captains and coaches who have given me the benefit of their thoughts and memories. Valerie Warren and her staff at the Wimbledon Library have been kind

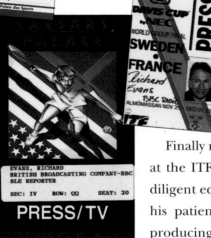

enough to open up their archives, as has Regine Tourres at the French Tennis Foundation at Roland Garros. I am indebted to them as, indeed, I am to all the authors who are listed in the bibliography, especially Nancy Kriplen whose fascinating biography of Dwight Davis is being published shortly. However, I must add a special word of gratitude to Alan Trengove, whose coverage of this sport spans a greater time frame than any of us, for his mammoth work on the Davis Cup which acted as an invaluable guide through the highways and byways of this most international of competitions. I have also enjoyed the collaboration and enthusiasm of Barry Williams who has been making the Davis Cup Centenary film, a companion piece to this book.

Finally my thanks to Christopher Stokes and Alun James at the ITF for their confidence, Barbara Travers for her diligent editing, and Julian Shuckburgh at Ebury Press for his patience. Our successors should have no problem producing the next volume 100 years from now. Contrary to what some people think, there will still be books in the year 2100 – and Dwight Davis' idea will still be a good one.

RICHARD EVANS, 1998

CHAPTER ONE

THE BEGINNING

The lights go on in St. Louis and the Davis family make
their fortune.... Young Dwight learns to play lawn tennis and
escort the belles of the ball.... An idea is born out West

O NE HUNDRED YEARS AGO, a rich young man raised in a landlocked city in the middle of America had an idea that would eventually straddle the globe. Like so many before and after him, he would arrive at his ultimate goal – in this case the furtherance of international comradeship and understanding – by utilising the tools of a personal passion. For Dwight F. Davis this happened to be a game, a relatively new and untested game called Lawn Tennis.

Davis had been born in St. Louis, Missouri in 1879 – two years after the All England Club had staged its first Championships at Wimbledon. Now, as the old century and its Victorian values prepared to give way to the more flamboyant Edwardian age, Davis was at Harvard completing an education that would take him to such heights as US Secretary for War while nurturing a talent that would make him one of the best exponents of the art of lawn tennis in America.

Dwight Davis was never going to go down in history as one of the greats but, in an article of the utmost prescience, the *Boston Herald* of 13th January, 1900, announcing the offer of a 'perpetual challenge cup' stated, 'when the effects of his generosity are evident in years to come, his rank for this will be even higher than his ability as a player will some day assure him.'

There would have been those amongst Davis's contemporaries who would have scoffed at such high flown predictions for what some of them affectionately referred to as 'Dwight's little pot.' Davis himself later expressed amazement at how quickly and universally his idea had been seized on by the world's sporting community for his original idea had been relatively modest. He simply thought it time that lawn tennis should embrace some form of international team competition and, to further this end, had put forward a suggestion to the United States National Lawn Tennis Association that a challenge should be thrown open to the British Isles with a view to staging a match between the two nations.

Dr James Dwight, the father of American tennis who had founded the national association 18 years before, was immediately attracted to Davis's idea; partially, it must be assumed, because he himself had been thinking in terms of an international team competition for tennis for some years. In fact, in a fit of generosity that might have hinted at the first shadow of professionalism waving over the sport, Dr Dwight had even offered to pay the travel expenses of top English players if they would agree to play in the United States in 1897. It was an offer that obviously gave him pause. 'I own that I have always had doubts of the propriety of paying expenses of players,' he admitted before adding, 'However we are willing to go to the extent named.'

Phew! The good Doctor must have felt a bead of perspiration on his brow after such radical thinking. The offer was never taken up and it was, no doubt, with some relief that he was able to embrace someone else's idea less than three years later. When the *Boston Herald* had first written of Davis's offer in January, the name of the donor was still being held secret and it was only revealed after the Executive Committee of the USNLTA met in New York on 21st February. Chaired by Dr Dwight, the committee comprised the treasurer Richard Stevens; Oliver S. Campbell, a former national singles champion; Palmer Presbrey who was the association's secretary and Dwight Davis himself. The publication *Golf & Lawn Tennis* noted that the following entry was made in the minutes:

'Voted, to accept the International Cup offered to the Association and it was also voted that the appreciation of the Association be expressed to the donor.'

So while an Englishman named Rowland Rhodes was employed by Durgin's silverware manufacturers in Concord, New Hampshire, to create a bowl that would become one of the most illustrious sporting trophies the world had ever known, Dr Dwight wrote a letter to the secretary of the LTA in London.

Dear Sir,

I beg to call your attention, as Secretary of the LTA, to an experiment which we are making that will, I hope, increase the interest in lawn tennis. One of our players here has offered us a Cup, to be a sort of International Challenge Cup. I enclose the conditions in a rough form. I trust that we shall both take a deep interest in them for many years to come.

I am very anxious that some of your better players should make us a visit this summer, and I hope that, should they come, your Association will see its way to challenge for the Cup. You can easily understand that we thought it necessary to require the governing Association of a country to make the challenge to prevent a series of stray challenges from players good and bad who might be coming to spend a month here. In yachting, the expense prevents the possibility of too much competition for the right to challenge. In lawn tennis it would be different.

I hope, as I said before, that the scheme will prove a success. It might do a great deal for the game here, and possibly even with you it might be a help. In any case I trust you will do what you can to give us a lead in the matter.

Please accept my sincere sympathy and good wishes in your present troubles! *(Undoubtedly a reference to the Boer War.)* I have eaten your salt too often not to feel very strongly for the anxiety that you all must feel.

Yours,

James Dwight,

Pres. USNLTA Assoc.

Many people have good ideas and yet find it very difficult to get them acted upon. More rarely still do they see them bear fruition in a short space of time. Yet a letter, sent by ship across the wintry Atlantic in the last days of the first February of the century, was not only received with enthusiasm but its suggestion acted upon with a speed that would leave many organisers of sports events breathless even today. It was less than six months later that Dwight Davis, representing the United States, and Ernest Black, representing a British team that had arrived after an eight-day sea voyage rather than a three and a half hour flight on Concorde, would walk on court at the Longwood Cricket Club in Boston to play the first ever rubber for an international challenge trophy that was already being referred to as the Davis Cup.

No one knew what they were starting but there is little doubt that everyone present that day would have been amazed had they been able to foresee the extent of mighty sporting competition that was being unleashed. One hundred years later the Davis Cup has not only survived the social changes of history's most turbulent and progressive century but has embraced no fewer than 131 nations. For millions of sports enthusiasts around the globe, Davis Cup means tennis. So who was this man, this Dwight Filley Davis?

———

Davis was born in St Louis, Missouri, some 40 years after his grandfather, Sam Davis had arrived in what was then a frontier river town in the 1830s. It was a rough place but, for a young man with ambition, one that offered a faster route to fortune than the well established cities back east. Curiously, grandfather Davis came from Brookline, Massachusetts, the Boston suburb of which the re-located Longwood Cricket Club is now a part. Tennis names and places were, obviously, in his grandson's stars.

1844

By the time Dwight's father was born in 1844, Sam was busy establishing himself in a trading firm that would eventually carry his name. The field for merchandising dry goods was so fertile that, less than 30 years later, John Davis would find himself taking over the company when his father returned to Boston to run that end of the business. As testament to the family's new found prosperity, Samuel C. Davis & Co. built a five-storey building that not only was powered by its own electrical generator in the basement but which boasted five elevators. Immediately, it became the 'best lighted building in the city' as one journal described it, which was a major advantage for those buyers choosing from fabrics of satin, gingham and worsted. Items such as sewing baskets, ribbons, buttons, hooped skirts and perfume were being dispatched to 25 midwestern states as well as California and when baby Dwight arrived in 1879, the firm had spread farther afield, opening branch offices in New York, Paris, Manchester and even Aachen in Germany. But this alone did not build the family fortune. John Davis founded a bank and became a director of several others. And his brilliantly lit building was not the only piece of real estate he owned. By the time grandfather Davis died in 1882, John's property holdings

1882

in St Louis alone were estimated at over $1 million. Before young Dwight could hold a tennis racket, he had to put down the silver spoon.

Not that Dwight or his two older brothers were allowed to wallow in the family's new found wealth. The Davis' remained thrifty with their money, preferring to save sufficiently to be able to donate to charities and institutions, like John Davis's own school, Washington University. Dwight began his schooling at the preparatory school affiliated with the University called Smith Academy. He was a classmate of Henry Eliot, the older brother of T.S. Eliot whose grandfather had founded Smith. Dwight Davis may not have had the kind of imagination that extended to Old Deuteronomy and Mr Mistoffelees but when T.S. Eliot followed him through the Academy before heading for Harvard and Oxford, it was clear Smith boys knew how to spread their wings.

Dwight was in his final year at Smith and just 14 years old when his father died suddenly of a kidney ailment. By the time the will was published, with the deceased's fortune to be divided equally between his wife and three sons, it was generally agreed that John Davis had been the richest man in Missouri.

During the otherwise sad summer of 1894, just a few months after his father had passed away, Dwight first tried his hand at the game of tennis. He and his mother, Maria, had escaped the humidity of high summer by the Mississippi by taking a holiday at the fashionable Oceanside Hotel near Magnolia in Massachusetts. Walks on the beach and chatting to friends on the vast verandah that stretched for one sixth of a mile was probably fine for a young widow but a strapping teenager needed something more demanding to occupy his time. Tennis was the obvious answer. Oceanside was, in fact, one of the resorts stretching up along the coast northeast of Boston that included Nahant where, just 20 years before, James Dwight had become either the first or second person – Mary Outerbridge at Staten Island may have had stronger claims – to have introduced the game of lawn tennis to America.

So tennis was not merely the fashionable thing to do in New England but it was sufficiently demanding to occupy the attention of an intelligent and serious young man like Dwight Davis. A left hander, he hit his first tennis ball on one of the two clay courts that had been laid the previous year at the nearby Essex County Club. Fascinated, Davis continued to play throughout the vacation and, the following year, was sufficiently advanced to enter a tournament at the Hotel Wentworth in New Hampshire. It was run by George Wright, whose son Beals would become a longtime rival, colleague and friend. Davis lost in the first round of the singles and his initial partnership with Beals was even less auspicious. They lost in a preliminary round of the doubles.

Davis was not one to be deterred by temporary setbacks, however. He looked around him and realised that there were very few competitors who really knew what they were doing. Tennis was such a young sport that the list of true practitioners of the art in America would not have filled a draw. In fact, 50 of the 82 entries for the National Championships at Newport, Rhode Island were making their first appearance in the event in that summer of 1895. Davis stood out, not for the power of his serve but for his ability to order champagne. He was probably the only millionaire amongst them. Not that the corks would pop too often. Davis was more likely to spend his money on philanthropic pursuits, like creating parks so that children could play games back home in St Louis – or donating sporting trophies.

But such things were far from his mind as he grappled with this new obsession. First he had to master the rudiments of a game that was harder than it looked. He failed to qualify for his first Nationals but, a year later, had become good enough to take a set off Robert Wrenn, a former champion.

1896

It was not until he went up to Harvard in the autumn of 1896 that he was able to study the game in detail and practise it with the kind of dedication that turns ordinary players into exceptional ones. To help him, he had three young men of similar inclination in Holcombe Ward, Malcolm Whitman and Beals Wright. Whitman, who had already broken into the nation's top ten, was beating them easily when they practiced at the Longwood Cricket Club because, it was quickly realised, of a far superior serve. So they worked at this, developing expertise at the kind of twist serve that would eventually so confound the English. It lifted their status as tennis players but, in Davis's case at least, did little for their ranking in the class room. In fact Davis's grades had become so bad that he was asked to repeat his sophomore year.

His father would probably have had something to say about this had he been alive but at least through sporting promotion he was able to deflect attention from academic relegation. By 1889 he was good enough to fight his way through to the finals of the Nationals at the Newport Casino where his name is now enshrined in the Tennis Hall of Fame, not, of course for this feat alone – as the *Boston Herald* was so quick to foresee – but for the donation of a cup. A straight set loss to Whitman did nothing to dampen his enthusiasm and, low grades or not, he used the next year's summer vacation to set off across the country in the company of Ward, Whitman and Wright to help spark greater interest in a game that was just beginning to lose its initial appeal. New ideas are often hard to maintain in America where something different always seems to create greater interest and, partially due to tennis being regarded as a passing fad, the number of clubs affiliated to the USNLTA had dropped from a peak of 106 to 44 by 1885.

Quite apart from the adventure involved, Davis and his friends felt that a series of matches against the best players from the West Coast would do something to re-focus attention on the sport and they were encouraged in this aim by Beals Wright's father, George. A talented cricketer who had also played shortstop for the Cincinnati Reds, the older Wright had a vested interest in creating more good publicity for the game because he ran a sporting goods firm, Wright and Ditson, which announced itself as 'the largest makers of lawn tennis supplies in the world' – one of those claims that

RIGHT: DWIGHT DAVIS – THE MAN WITH THE IDEA.

would have probably been nearer the truth had 'world' been replaced by 'America'. Nevertheless, George Wright was keen enough to act as a kind of manager and father figure to the young swells who arrived in Monterey, California after a week on the train. Matches were played at the Del Monte Hotel where one of the ball boys was a red headed youngster who would later be largely responsible for attracting 14,000 people to Forest Hills for the USA's victory over Australasia in the Davis Cup Challenge of 1914. He was Maurice McLoughlin, soon to be known as the California Comet. But before McLoughlin would be able to represent his country, the man for whom he was chasing balls would have to think of the idea. And, according to Davis himself, it was on that trip, which included further matches in Oregon, Washington and British Columbia, that the idea first began to percolate. Some seven years later, Davis replied to an enquiry from the editor of *American Lawn Tennis* in this fashion:

1899

> *'The plans for the competition were outlined in the fall of 1899, immediately after the return of the tennis team which visited California and other western states. This trip resulted in great benefit to the interests of lawn tennis in the west, and the idea came to me at the time that an international competition would be of the greatest possible benefit to the game throughout the whole of the United States and abroad.'*

It is hard to argue with those words from the man himself but that did not prevent a certain Englishman by the name of Charles A. Voigt from suggesting otherwise. Voigt's version draws on an earlier occurrence at a tournament he had attended three years before. The tournament was called Niagara-on-the-Lake and even if the following account holds little water, it paints such a colourful, first-hand picture of life on the American tennis circuit just before the end of the century that it is too good to pass up. Writing in *Lawn Tennis and Badminton* in July 1912, Voigt says:

> *'At Niagara-on-the-Lake, on the Canadian border, "Eddie" Fischer introduced me to Dwight Davis, who – if I remember right – had then just left one of the big schools to enter Harvard University, where he won the Inter-Collegiate singles and doubles (and the U.S. Doubles Championship at Newport with H. Ward) in 1899. The Niagara tournament was managed by Scott Griffin, of Toronto – now, I believe, one of the directors of the Canadian Pacific Railway in London – and a merrier, or more enjoyable meeting I have never been present at. A daily little paper called "The Lark" – devoted solely to the tournament and its players – appeared every*

morning, and to fill its pages with topical matter "Scottie" Griffin and Parmly Paret frequently sat up until the small hours of the morning, after the revelries of the evening.

All the visiting players lived in an annexe, from the windows of which they used to roll down into the Lake and the Niagara river. I still have vivid recollections of my swim across one morning, when, in mid-stream, my legs were carried one way and my arms another by strong counter-current of different temperature. But I struggled on and reached the opposite shore in safety. Every occurrence was chronicled next day in "The Lark," no matter how trivial. Mr. George Wright, of Boston, had brought his eldest boy Beals along, then a little chap who would play wearing a high collar. "The Lark" mentioned all this, and also frequently had occasion to refer to the "evening strolls in the shrubberies" of Dwight F. Davis with the belle of the place.

I remember there was great rivalry over her favours, but neither Whitman's blonde curls, nor Wrenn's fascination, nor young Beals Wright's spotless high collar, (he, too, was in the running), nor Scott Griffin's diamonds (to "cut diamonds" was a larkish expression for cocktails and other liquid refreshments) nor the bookays of honey-suckle which a foreign "Count" laid at her feet, could cope successfully with Dwight Davis. He cut out all the others easily and won a love set. "Who on earth is this young sport?" I remember enquiring one evening of Fischer, and Paret, as the couple passed out of the ballroom on to the hotel balcony and from thence wandered off into the moonlit gardens. "Why that's our young multi-millionaire, Dwight Davis, of St. Louis," was the reply. So rarely had I had the good fortune of meeting a millionaire who played lawn tennis and such a young one into the bargain, that my first observation was: "A millionaire, is he? If so, why don't you people get him to do something for the game? Put up some big prize, or cup?" I verily believe that passing remark laid the foundation to the Davis Cup! We had just been discussing the possibilities of international visits and matches, and I had ventured to observe that, if properly put before the Associations of the two countries, the affair would no doubt soon become a fait accompli. *Next morning "The Lark" recorded scraps of the conversation. Davis read and heard about it, and so did all the others, and when the matter was seriously brought up again a few years later Dwight Davis came forward and offered to present a trophy for international competition. And this is the true history of how the Davis Cup originated.'*

Well, maybe. It is obviously quite possible that words from *The Lark* were still singing in Davis's ears on the train back from the West Coast and that the success of the trip had merely made him realise the pertinence of Voigt's suggestion. It is not of paramount importance. The fact is that Davis had the will and the wherewithal to make it happen and it was an idea that, sooner or later, had to bear fruition.

What Voigt's observations do tell us is something about the character of the man himself. Dwight Davis was, by all accounts, a quiet, reserved individual, not given to flamboyant, eye-catching gestures, except, perhaps, with the power and authority of his game on a tennis court. But that, apparently, did not prevent him from holding the attention of the belle of the ball. His riches would not have been the sole attraction. He had a commanding presence, probably made all the more attractive by virtue of it being understated. As the manner in which he progressed through life to high positions of State indicate, he was a leader who exuded authority and that is always sexy.

Despite his youth, Dr Dwight and other leaders of American tennis were certainly eager to consider his ideas and, as we have seen, accepted with alacrity his suggestion concerning an international team competition. Once that was decided – and the challenge accepted from overseas – the next task was to create the actual cup.

———

Davis and Dr Dwight were not related although it is an odd coincidence that the Cup's founder should carry the name of one of the founders of the sport itself in the United States as well as having, in his family tree, the name of Tilden. Again, he was unrelated to Bill Tilden who would do more than anyone to popularise tennis in America in the 1920s. Davis's grandmother was Caroline Tilden and his father, John, was given Tilden as his middle name.

CHAPTER TWO

THE CUP

*Davis places an order with silversmiths in Boston.... An Englishman
is recruited to design the silver bowl*

1887

I F YOU HAD MONEY TO BURN IN BOSTON at the turn of the century, you headed for the smart striped awnings of Shreve, Crump Low Co. at the corner of Tremont and West Streets. A silver brooch for m'lady? A silver tea pot? No problem. Sporting trophies were often on sale, too, as Dwight Davis would have known when he placed the order for a cup to be made for an international tennis competition.

Shreve's did not make it themselves, of course, but they dealt with only the most exclusive manufacturers and selected a firm in Concord, just across the New Hampshire border, the William B. Durgin Company. Not nearly as large a concern as Tiffany's, Durgin's were, nonetheless, renowned for the quality of their products. Old William Durgin wanted nothing to do with new fangled ideas, like silver plating other, less precious metals. He dealt exclusively in the best – solid silver.

Although the son of a New Hampshire farmer, Durgin became known as something of an Anglophile in as much as he recruited many of his staff from England. In fact, in 1887 he travelled to England himself and advertised for craftsmen and designers. One of those who replied was a 22-year-old from Newcastle-under-Lyme called Rowland Rhodes. Already a graduate of what was to become the Royal College of Art, Rhodes had returned north to teach in Preston when he read of Durgin's offer – ten dollars a week and passage paid.

That was all the incentive this adventurous young man needed. After two years working in Concord, he was off, back across the Atlantic to Paris where he worked as a labourer in a foundry to familiarise himself with the techniques of metal casting. Then he enrolled at the Julien Academy and, before returning to Durgin's, was sufficiently successful to have one of his life-size plaster works, 'Youth's First Recognition of Love' exhibited at the Grand Salon in Paris in 1892.

Obviously a man of considerable talent, the red-bearded Englishman quickly made his mark back in Concord. To celebrate Grover Cleveland's election as President, silver manufacturers were invited to submit designs for the new White House silverware. Rhodes won the honour for Durgin's with his intricate Chrysanthemum pattern.

By now Rhodes was anxious to have his own studio and, in 1893, he came to an amicable arrangement with his employer that enabled him to move to New York and work half the week at Durgin's Manhattan establishment and half at his own studio on East 13th Street. But customers for sculpture during President Cleveland's administration were rare. Rhodes might have ensured that the President's table glittered for White House dinners but most ordinary folk were happy that their own table simply had food on it. Money was scarce and, after two years, Rhodes was forced to return to Concord where a patient fiancee finally got her wandering beau to walk up the aisle.

However marriage did not quell the Englishman's wanderlust and there were plans to work and study in Italy as the new century approached. But hard as he worked to improve as a sculptor and engraver, it was the order Durgin's received from a certain Dwight Davis for a silver trophy that would prove to be Rowland Rhodes's enduring masterpiece.

In retrospect, one can only commend Shreve's decision to choose Durgin's as manufacturers of the cup for the fashion of the time leaned towards the kind of flamboyance that could have turned Dwight's little pot into an ornament of laughable extremes. One tennis trophy made for High Rock Club in New York State was based on the Last of the Mohicans, complete with Indian war feathers decorating the rim. That sort of thing could have meant the demise of the Davis Cup. Instead Rhodes opted for a design of classical restraint that will be admired at the end of this new century as warmly as it was at the start of the last.

In her meticulously researched biography of the Cup's founder, Nancy Kriplen describes how Rhodes set about his work:

'Under Rhodes's practised pencil, the design for the new sporting trophy began to take shape. Squared lines across the top of a piece of white drawing paper marked off the general dimensions of the bowl. Small dots, placed precisely with callipers, staked out the general swell of the side curves. Instead of a smooth rim, the top edge would be gently scalloped by a dramatic Georgian border of clusters of primroses and acanthus leaves, that traditional bit of shrubbery favoured as a decorative detail by English silver designers.

ABOVE: ROWLAND RHODES' CREATION NOW SITS ON TOP OF A PLINTH CARRYING THE NAMES OF
THE WINNING NATIONS ON SILVER PLAQUES. THIS WAS EXPANDED DURING WAYNE REID'S
TENURE AS AUSTRALIAN FEDERATION PRESIDENT IN THE EARLY 1970S.

*The primrose motif would be repeated around the bottom third of the bowl, this time combined
with tiny buds and tendrils, with all descending into a sea foam effect around the foot, or base,
of the bowl. Circling the foot would be more clusters of small flowers connected with gentle waves
or scrolls. And how much silver would be required?*

*In pencil, at the top of the drawing, were preliminary calculations: 186 oz plus 30 for a total
of 216. Also written in pencil was the number 414, the Durgin file number for this piece.'*

Soon, the project was lifted from the paper and took its place amongst all the other items being created in Durgin's factory in the middle of Concord – terrapin forks, asparagus tongs and bon-bon dishes. Dwight's pot must have been one of the larger objects being moulded by expert silversmiths on a spinning wooden form but it was not prized as something special at the time. A few years later when a newspaper article listed items of which the Durgin company was particularly proud – a silver prayer book cover for the dowager Queen of Italy amongst them – there was no mention of something called the Davis Cup.

And yet when it stood, glinting in the sunshine of the century's first summer – 13 inches high and 18 inches across at the top – no one could deny that it was a beautiful object. It is not recorded if its maker ever saw the cup again but Rowland Rhodes's spirit no doubt lives on within it for the silver bowl he crafted with such care has fulfilled all his dreams of voyages to far away places – travelling in style, revered and admired as it sits courtside while men battle to deliver it to their nation for a precious 12 months. The Davis Cup – designed by Rowland Rhodes.

CHAPTER THREE

THE FIRST MATCH

An invitation is accepted.... By way of Liverpool and Niagara, the British
team arrives.... Twist serves and sagging guy ropes confound the visitors

THE DISTANT RAMIFICATIONS OF WAR RUMBLED ON behind the first Davis Cup contest which had been so hastily arranged for the beginning of August 1900 in Boston. The Boer War was still in progress in South Africa and although neither of Britain's best two players, Reginald F. Doherty and his brother Laurie, were in the army, they found reasons to absent themselves from the tie. It appears that the LTA made attempts to emphasise the weakness of the team they were sending to America because F.R. Burrows, a renowned referee and chronicler of the game, has been quoted as offering the excuse that 'several good players were absent at the front.' In fact, only one, Dr W.V. Eaves, was thought to be serving there.

The Americans seemed to have more legitimate excuses. William Larned and Robert Wrenn had both been in Cuba with Teddy Roosevelt's Rough Riders in 1898 and both had suffered from the experience. Although Larned was to go on to win the United States national title seven times, he was not physically fit enough to compete in 1900 while Wrenn, a four-time champion, contracted yellow fever while fighting the Spanish and was never a real force again.

So it was a young and largely untested team that the United States sent out to meet the British in a tie that would grow in historic significance as the competition itself spread throughout the sporting world. Malcolm Whitman, whose home was in Brookline, was the eldest at 23 and would play No 1 singles. Davis, the No 2, had just turned 21 a month before the tie while his doubles partner from South Orange, New Jersey, Holcombe Ward, was also 21. They were a close knit group of privileged young men, excited at the prospect of creating something new for their sport. The British, on the other hand, set out on a journey largely of the unknown. A few other players had crossed the Atlantic before them – C.G. Eames being the first in 1889. He was followed amongst others by two prominent Irishmen who were both to win Wimbledon, Dr Joshua Pim and H.S. Mahony. But they had travelled as individuals. Never before had Britain, or any other country, mustered a tennis team.

The enterprise might have had a more auspicious start. Despite pleas from the Lawn Tennis Association for tennis players to see the trio dubbed 'The Dauntless Three' off in a style befitting such an adventure at Euston Station, no more than a handful of well-wishers were present to wave goodbye to what, in any case, turned out to be daunt-less two. Arthur W. Gore, the 32-year-old Wimbledon champion of the previous year, and Herbert Roper Barrett, a 26-year-old London solicitor, were to rendezvous with the third man, Earnest Black, 27, a tall Scot who lived in the north of England, at Liverpool, before embarkation. For Roper Barrett injured pride was put into sharp relief when he crushed a finger in the compartment door as the boat train puffed its way north. If the throbbing had eased after nine days at sea, little was done to restore buffeted pride when the Cunard's *Campania* docked in New York. Here the accounts of the British team's reception vary. Most historians, including S. Wallis Merrihew writing in 1928, seem to think that the USNLTA had failed to get its act to together and only 'Mr Steven's manservant' was there to greet them. Nancy Kriplen, however, seems to have unearthed evidence that they were met by Ollie Campbell who had won the US National title three times in the early 1890s.

If this was true, it seems less likely that such panic would have set in when Gore, Roper Barrett and Black decided that a little tourism should take precedent over the task in hand and set off for the Canadian border to gaze in predictable astonishment at Niagara Falls. Up in Boston no one seems to have been informed of a decision taken with all the formality of the age, as recorded by Roper Barrett. 'Having had no partic-ular facilities offered us for practice,' he wrote, 'it was unanimously decided, Gore being in the chair, that we should forthwith visit Niagara.'

And forthwith they did, to be confronted by a scene of cascading water and spi-ralling mist that left Roper Barrett virtually at a loss for words. 'The Falls,' he admitted, 'beggar description.' His descriptive powers had recovered by the time he came to offer an opinion on the conditions under which the tie would be played but more of that it in a moment. To be fair to Dr Dwight and his committee, the hospitality was not found to be wanting when the Dauntless Three finally turned up, much to their host's relief, in Boston. Given that they had docked in New York on Saturday, August 4 and yet still managed to get to Boston less than 48 hours later suggests that either the train

ABOVE: DWIGHT DAVIS WITH 23-YEAR-OLD MALCOLM WHITMAN ON THE LEFT OF THE PICTURE
AND 21-YEAR-OLD HOLCOMBE WARD – THE HARVARD TRIO WHO ACCEPTED THE FIRST
CHALLENGE FOR DWIGHT'S 'LITTLE POT'.

service was extremely speedy or that they did not linger long in Niagara. Either way, there was no time to spare because the matches had been brought forward a day from the originally scheduled start of Wednesday, August 8 in deference to Roper Barrett who had informed the Americans ahead of time that he had to begin his return journey on the following Saturday – just one week after he had arrived.

'I often laugh to myself,' he admitted later, 'over the fact that I journeyed some 6,800 miles to play 30 games.'

Roper Barrett was only used in the doubles so, in effect, he had spent 18 days at sea for one match at what he described as 'considerable inconvenience and personal expense.' Set alongside what it takes to get a top tennis player to fly the Atlantic in supersonic first-class comfort today one should, perhaps, be grateful for Roper

Barrett's sacrifice although the man himself was obviously proud to represent his country. The word duty was not far from his mind when he added, 'There was no one else to represent England and I felt I had to go.'

Despite the absence of the Doherty brothers and the somewhat makeshift feel of the visiting team, the British were still considered favourites. At this stage of the game's development, a certain inferiority complex existed amongst the American tennis fraternity. The game, after all, was still in its infancy compared to Britain where Wimbledon had already established itself as a highlight of the sporting summer. Nevertheless some local writers in Boston, ever keen to score points off the English, suggested that the result might not be a foregone conclusion. Fred Mansfield, writing in the *Boston Globe,* called the team's late arrival 'ill-advised' and added delicately, 'While it would be manifestly unfair to attribute to the visitors any undue confidence in winning, their lack of reasonable training on American courts to adequately prepare themselves for the international matches is suggestive.'

Suggestive of what? Defeat? The *Brookline Chronicle* was much more confident and direct. 'There is not the slightest doubt that our team of doubles will win and little fear that the singles men will fall.'

There were technical and meteorological grounds for making such a brave prediction. Firstly, the Americans had been developing the twist serve into a fine art and when it reared and kicked, the English were left groping in astonishment. Secondly, the length of the grass would have made the courts slower than Gore and his colleagues were accustomed to even before the rain arrived to dampen the end of Monday's practice session and wipe out Tuesday's scheduled start. Ike Chambers, a former Nottinghamshire bowler who had been employed as groundsman at the Longwood Cricket Club for 16 years, used the best of his knowledge to make the courts playable but, even when the sun shone on Wednesday morning, the result was never going to be anything better than a sticky wicket.

Nevertheless the match was on and Longwood was about to write another piece of sporting history. Although the site was moved shortly afterwards to the nearby suburb of Chestnut Hill, the original club stood on the corner of Longwood and Brookline Avenues a little nearer downtown Boston. It might have been somewhat daunting for the Dauntless Three had they discovered that the club had been named by an admirer of Napoleon. The 600-acre estate had been developed by the Sears family and it was on a visit to Paris in 1811 that David Sears fell under the little Emperor's spell. On learning that the house Napoleon lived in while exiled on St Helena was called Longwood, Sears took the name for his own estate.

Originally built for cricket in 1877, the club made sure it kept up with the fast changing times by adding grass tennis courts a year later. And it was on these courts that Dwight Davis and Earnest Black began the first set of the first match in the first tie ever played under the nomenclature 'Davis Cup'.

After the rain, Wednesday had turned out hot and sunny and there were parasols amongst the twelve hundred spectators attired in all the regalia required to present oneself at a fashionable occasion in Boston in 1900. And already the Davis Cup was fashionable. The matches against the British had caught the imagination of the city's well-heeled social set and while the women in their long, frilly frocks sought shade under the lone canopy that lined one side of the Centre Court, the men sat and sweltered in their jackets, high collars and ties, protected only by straw boaters.

Soon after 2.00pm on 7th August, Black threw up the ball to serve and Davis, the donor of the Cup, inadvertently donated the first point, hitting the return out. Black, sporting a thickly sculptured moustache that matched both his name and physique, began well and took the first set 6–4. But Davis, who had every reason to be feeling extra tension – it was, after all, his cup, his idea, and they were his friends in the crowd – quickly settled down and began utilising the twist serve he had practised so diligently with Whitman and Ward on those very courts. The American levelled the match by taking the second set 6–2 and, after a far harder struggle, the third 6–4. As John McEnroe was to prove all over again so many years later, a great serve is a great serve in any hand but if it is delivered from the left side it can – for reasons that no physicist has yet been able to explain – become even more deadly. Davis was left-handed and Black found himself quite unable to counter the acute angles that were being sliced at him. The ball seemed to lose its shape as it spun off Davis's racket and skidded away off the still damp grass. In the stands, Roper Barrett shook his head in amazement. He had never seen anything like it. To the glee off the gallery, Davis rounded off the fourth set 6–4, having dropped his serve only once after the opening set.

Meanwhile, on an adjoining court, the second singles between Malcolm Whitman and Arthur Gore had got underway. It did not last long. Not only was Gore as bamboozled by Whitman's serving as Black had been by Davis's but he found the greasy ground more difficult and frequently slipped in pursuit of wide shots. Unlike the Americans who wore spikes, the British were only equipped with ordinary, smooth-soled plimsolls. This seriously handicapped one of Gore's greatest assets, his speed, and Whitman soon felt confident enough to attack the net at will. Dominating the match, he took it 6–1, 6–3, 6–2.

The doubles was scheduled for the following day with the reverse singles to follow on the Friday. If ever there was an example of not needing to change a good idea, this formatting of a Davis Cup tie must stand as a good example. Despite the problem of a having two 'dead' rubbers on the final day should one country win the first three, no one has seriously challenged the original concept and consequently the format of two singles, one doubles and two reverse singles over three days has remained unchanged for 100 years.

One thing that has changed is the American propensity to take breaks as early as the second set. At Longwood, Davis and Whitman disappeared into the little clubhouse for a rubdown after the second set – a practice which the British accepted with good grace. This apparent desire to break the flow – so starkly highlighted in basketball and grid-iron football – has remained an interesting difference between the way Americans and other nations play their sports. Today television is cited as a compelling reason for con-tinuous breaks in the action so that more commercials can be crammed into the broadcast. The American networks have always been at their wits' end over how to serve up soccer to a US audience and have seriously suggested breaking the game into quarters rather than halves. But there was no television in 1900. The Americans just wanted to stop. Surely it cannot have been through fatigue. Although it was not until the arrival of Anthony Wilding a few years later that a tennis player undertook serious physical conditioning, men were not weaklings in those days. Dwight Davis's father might have installed an elevator in St Louis but most people walked up stairs and sim-ply walked a great deal more than they do today. And, with fewer self-help appliances, their bodies were used to greater strenuous usage. Surely young men in their prime could not have been fatigued after 40 minutes' tennis?

The difference was noted in the press after the first day's play. In trying to be com-plimentary to a team that was, at 0–2, in serious trouble, writers commented on how the British kept the game moving and 'did not take any elaborate care of themselves between the sets.'

They were not able to take care of themselves in the doubles either. A contemporary view of what happened is ably recounted in the *Sportsman*.

RIGHT: HERBERT ROPER
BARRETT'S TEAM MIGHT NOT
HAVE ENJOYED THE CONDITIONS
AT LONGWOOD BUT THE DINNER
SEEMS TO HAVE BEEN A GREAT
SUCCESS AND AFTERWARDS ALL
HANDS WERE STILL STEADY
ENOUGH TO SIGN THE MENU.

'The Americans' style of play was totally different to ours. Davis is left-handed and, to return his service, means standing well outside the doubles line and playing the ball back handed. It is impossible to drive on account of Ward's position, but more particularly on account of the screw, the only possible return being a backhand lob. Imagine the feelings of the Englishmen when this further surprise was sprung on them? Where was Barrett's forehand drive and where was Black's splendid backhand return? Useless, absolutely useless, both of them. Not only did the ball screw but it rose about 4ft high in the shape of an egg. The game devolved into a question of who lost a service, and finally, in the first set at 4 all, Barrett lost his and the American secured it 6–4.'

Davis and Holcombe Ward ended up beating Black and Roper Barrett 6–4, 6–4, 6–4 and so ensured that Dwight's little pot would not be starting its travels just yet. The British were hoping to retrieve some lost pride on the Friday and Gore certainly did his best, only succumbing to Davis 9–7 in the first set and battling furiously to hold his own in the second which had reached nine-all when the day's suffocating heat was broken by a torrential thunderstorm. With the outcome of the Cup no longer in question, it was decided to cancel the rest of the tie as Gore and Black had made commitments to play on Long Island at Southampton the following day while Roper Barrett was due to sail for home.

So the occasion turned social with a splendid dinner given by members of the Longwood Cricket Club at the Somerset Club, then as now, an exclusive retreat for the Brahmins of Beacon Hill. While the guests feasted on clams, Filets of Sea Bass au Vin Blanc and Yellow Leg Plover Salad, cordial speeches were made by hosts and visitors alike before the British trio hopped on the night train to New York.

It was only later that the Americans discovered what the British thought about the conditions under which they had been asked to play. In his account of the tie, Roper Barrett wrote,

'The ground was abominable. The grass was long. Picture yourself a court in England where the grass has been the longest you ever encountered; double the length of that grass and you have the courts as they were at Longwood at that time. The net was a disgrace to civilised lawn tennis, held up by guy ropes which were continually sagging, giving way as much as 2 or 3 inches every few games and frequently requiring adjustment. As for the balls, I hardly like to mention them. They were awful – soft and mothery-looking – and when served with the American twist came at you like an animated egg-plum. I do not exaggerate. Neither Beals Wright nor Holcombe Ward nor Karl Behr can make the balls used at Wimbledon break as much as these did. They not only swerved in the air, but in hitting the ground broke surely 4 to 5 feet. Our team was altogether at a disadvantage. We had never experienced this service before and it quite nonplussed us. The spectators were most impartial and the female portion thereof not at all unpleasant to gaze upon.'

It was comforting to note that Roper Barrett did not have his eye on the ball all the time and that there were pleasing aspects to his historic trip. And although the *Sportsman,* no doubt trying to live up to its name, regretted the excuses that were made for the British team, suggesting that such excuses were 'neither dignified nor just', George Wright was one American who did not try to hide from the inadequacies of the conditions. Wright told S. Wallis Merrihew some years later that he had tried to warn the Longwood people about the state of the nets, posts and turf adding, 'The courts had been a good deal worn in the Longwood tournament of a fortnight before and the rain made them still worse. It is a matter of regret that the fixtures of the court were not better. In the great press of preparation for the matches, at short notice, they had been neglected.'

It had, indeed, been a rush but a worthwhile one. The experiment, despite the various problems, had been a success and obviously the idea of an international team competition had a future. Not an immediate one because the following year, with the Dohertys still unable to make the journey, Britain called off its challenge. However another team set off on the high seas in 1902 intent on revenge.

CHAPTER FOUR

EARLY CHALLENGES

The action moves to New York.... Finally the Dohertys arrive and the
British captain gambles.... The Cup begins its travels...and Smith of Stroud
helps to keep it in England

WITH THE DOHERTY BROTHERS UNAVAILABLE ONCE AGAIN, a British challenge for the Davis Cup fizzled out in 1901 and it was not until the following year that the competition was resumed. Finally, with the two men who were considered indispensable to the success of the team agreeing to sail for America, the LTA arranged to meet the United States for a second time.

Dr Joshua Pim, somewhat portly now in the twilight of a career that had seen him win Wimbledon in 1893 and 1894, was added to the team that would be captained by W.H. Collins, the President of the LTA. There were, apparently, fears over the Dohertys' stamina for Reggie, the older and taller of the two – hence 'Big Do' as opposed to 'Little Do' – had been ill the previous year and it was thought that the experienced Doctor would provide ballast to a team based on the exquisite skills and styles of these two remarkable but somewhat frail brothers.

The Dohertys, Londoners who were educated at Westminster School and later went undefeated in Varsity tennis during their days at Cambridge, were almost solely responsible for the resurgence in the popularity of lawn tennis after another remarkable pair of brothers, Williams and Earnest Renshaw had faded from the scene in the 1880s. Their run of success at Wimbledon had begun in 1897 and continued until 1906 – four consecutive titles for Big Do and then five on the trot for Little Do neatly divided by the first of Arthur Gore's titles in 1901 when he beat Reggie in the final.

Nor was their skill reserved for grass courts. With their good looks, Edwardian charm and gracious sportsmanship they quickly became the stars of the social scene on the Riviera during the fashionable winter months when European royalty and their acolytes cloistered themselves around the watering holes of Monte Carlo, Beaulieu, Nice and Cannes. Such was their dominance on the red clay of the Cote d'Azur that

ABOVE: AFTER LOSING THE FIRST MATCH IN 1900, BRITAIN REFUSED TO COMPETE AGAIN UNTIL THESE TWO BROTHERS, H.L. AND R.F. DOHERTY, WERE AVAILABLE TO MAKE THE SEA VOYAGE TO AMERICA – WHICH THEY DID IN 1902.

no name other than Doherty appeared on the honours board of the Monte Carlo championship for the first ten years of the tournament's existence. Between 1897 and 1906 Reggie won six titles and Laurie four.

How much longer Reggie would have gone on dominating the game had he not suffered from chronic dyspepsia and other debilitating illnesses it is impossible to judge but no one who saw him or his brother play were left in any doubt as to their status in the game. One of their contemporaries, George Hillyard described their style as being 'so easy and effortless that they made the game look so simple. It is probable, indeed almost certain, that the majority of spectators failed to realise the pace they were getting on the ball or how exceedingly awkward they were making things for their opponents.'

Writing from the greater perspective of the 1940s, John Olliff, a player who went on to become one of the London *Daily Telegraph*'s long line of distinguished tennis correspondents, offered this opinion of the Doherty's status: 'I infer... that the doubles game has improved but I can find no evidence to support a similar advance in technique of singles play. On the contrary, I can find plenty of evidence to suggest that Tilden alone reached the Doherty standard in singles.'

So it was no wonder that the LTA were not going to allow the ship to sail without them. This, however, did not mean that, once in America, they would both be selected to play. Captain Collins, in fact, caused a furore by opting for Reggie Doherty and the 33-year-old Dr Pim for the singles, leaving Laurie to partner his brother in the doubles. In hindsight, it was not a clever choice.

This second Davis Cup encounter was to be played at the Crescent Athletic Club at Bay Ridge on the outskirts of Brooklyn where the well appointed clubhouse looked out over New York Bay. The occasion was unique for two reasons. Firstly, for the only time on record, it was decided to play the doubles on the last day after all four singles had been completed and secondly the public were allowed in free. Interest would have been high in any case but this gesture ensured huge crowds and no less than 10,000 turned out on the final day, which was a Saturday, to watch the doubles even though the contest had already been decided.

The British had excited interest immediately on arrival with some impressive practice sessions up at Longwood but Joshua Pim was not able to translate that form into match play, not even when a night's sleep gave him time to recover from losing the first two sets 6–1, 6–1 to Malcolm Whitman. An enormous thunderstorm had curtailed play for the day and although Whitman, trying to finish off things too quickly on the resumption the following morning lost the third 1–6, he overwhelmed the good doctor 6–0 in the fourth. In the second singles, which was being played concurrently, Bill Larned, restored to full health again after his exertions in Cuba, seemed poised for victory when he led Reggie Doherty by two sets to love overnight. But it was windier on the Friday morning and Larned found the advancing Englishman harder to pass at the net. Doherty, serving far better than the previous day, came all the way back to win 6–4 in the fifth.

1902

RIGHT: A SELF-MADE PLAYER IN AN AGE WHEN FEW KNEW HOW TO PLAY TENNIS PROPERLY, DWIGHT DAVIS WORKED HARD AT HIS GAME.

All four players were back on court after lunch and long before the sun had set over Manhattan, the American team had ensured that Dwight Davis, who would only play doubles in this tie, would keep his cup. Britain's hopes rested on Doherty for Pim was not expected to be a match for Larned and, indeed, lost in straight sets. But Whitman brought off a stunning victory over Big Do by 6–1, 7–5, 6–4. One of the game's earliest scribes, Parmly Paret offered this excellent technical insight into the first big upset in Davis Cup history.

'Whitman was clearly the better player on the form of the day. He never showed the speed of his adversary, nor the Englishman's skill at underhand volleying and half-volleying, but in nearly every other particular he was a shade better than Doherty. Speed against him was of little advantage and Doherty declared after the match that he thought Whitman played better against speed than slower play and that he intentionally slacked off his ace... Whitman varied his service and seldom tried to kill off the ground unless a clean pass was open to him and he seldom risked a smash unless the ball was short of the service line. He managed to keep Doherty constantly on the move, however; and the ever-varying direction of his attack kept working the Englishman out of position...'

If the 10,000 people packing the grounds on the Saturday were hoping for more American glory, they were to be disappointed. In the doubles a fresh Laurie Doherty played the steady game which allowed Reggie to go for broke, hitting most of the winners and most of the errors in a match that, according to Paret, hung on the eventual extinction of Davis's hurricane serve which finally blew itself out. The Dohertys won 3–6, 10–8, 6–3, 6–4 to serve notice that things might not be as easy in the future.

On returning home Collins had some explaining to do over his selection of 'the doctor', as he called him but insisted that he had been taking into account the vagaries

ABOVE: THE DUEL AT LONGWOOD IN 1903 BETWEEN TWO TEAMS OF BROTHERS HAS NEVER
BEEN REPEATED IN A FINAL – THE DOHERTYS ARE ON THE RECEIVING END OF A ROBERT WRENN
SMASH HERE WITH GEORGE WRENN RACING BACK TO COVER. THE BRITISH CAPTAIN,
W.H. COLLINS, ALSO SIGNED THE PHOTOGRAPH.

of New York weather in August. 'They don't seem to realise that the Americans had
fresh men for the doubles and if H.L. Doherty had played singles on the first two
days... he might have been a rag on the third.'

It is a dilemma that has never gone away and one that Davis Cup captains from
Collins to Gullikson have been pondering ever since. But, even though the British captain was mistaken on this occasion, an equally important aspect of the trip had happier
results. This time there were no complaints from the visitors. 'Captain Collins and his
men made a fine impression,' wrote S. Wallis Merrihew. 'The playing conditions, so
severely criticised two years before, received nothing but praise from the visitors.'

By the time Collins brought the British back to Boston a year later for a third challenge, interest in Dwight Davis's idea of international competition between nations was
spreading through continental Europe. Early in 1903, Charles A. Voigt was writing in
the American journal, *Lawn Tennis,* about the number of countries wanting to become
involved – France, Belgium, Denmark, Sweden and Holland were all mentioned. It

1903

would not be long before the Davis Cup ceased to be an annual tea party between the British and their American cousins.

But first there was another tie to be played – one that soon set the standards for the sort of risk-taking in selection and on-court drama that would come to typify this extraordinary competition in the years to come.

The retirement of Whitman and of Davis himself ensured that there would be changes in the United States line-up. As the American champion, Larned would hold his place but the selectors sprang a surprise by overlooking the claims of Beals Wright and Holcombe Ward who were ranked three and four behind Whitman and opting for the former national champion Robert Wrenn who, like Larned, had been poorly since his return from Cuba. But Wrenn insisted that he was feeling well enough to play again at the highest level so America took the court with two of Roosevelt's Rough Riders in the saddle – happily without their horses. Wrenn's brother, George, was chosen to partner him in the doubles which meant that, for the first and only time in the history of either Challenge Rounds or Finals two pairs of brothers would face each other across the net.[1]

Collins's task in selecting the British team was made infinitely more complicated when Reggie Doherty injured his arm playing an exhibition match at Nahant. A day before the tie was due to start, a Boston doctor told Big Do that the injury could clear up in 24 hours but that there was a risk of his being sidelined for weeks if he tried to play immediately. Collins went to Larned, who was player captain of the US team, and asked if he could substitute Doherty with his reserve H.S. Mahony for the first singles and play Big Do two days later. But even at this early stage of the competition, the rules had been laid down very clearly. Dr Dwight had received advice from no less a personage than Richard Olney, who was at the time the Secretary of State for President Cleveland, when he wrote the rules of the Davis Cup which did not allow temporary substitution for an injured player. Nor, indeed, do they now.

So Collins, who was obviously not afraid of making controversial decisions, opted to forfeit the opening singles rubber in the hope that Doherty would not only have recovered in time to play the reverse singles but also would be fit enough to partner Laurie Doherty in the doubles a day earlier. As gambles go, this was worthy of Dostoevsky and it is not recorded what Mahony, a somewhat fearsome-looking Irishman with a pen-

[1]The only other occasion in which even one set of brothers played doubles in a Final tie was at Gothenburg in 1987 when Vijay and Anand Amritraj lost to Mats Wilander and Joakim Nystrom, Sweden beating India 5-0.

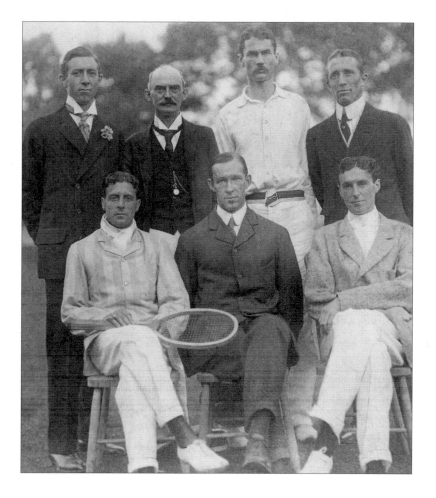

ABOVE: THE WORLD'S FIRST DAVIS CUP STARS – STANDING LEFT TO RIGHT, GEORGE WRENN,
BRITISH CAPTAIN W.H. COLLINS, H.S. MAHONY AND ROBERT WRENN. LAURIE AND REGGIE
DOHERTY ARE SEATED EITHER SIDE OF BILL LARNED.

chant for wearing mismatching socks, had to say about it. But fortune favoured a brave
captain in this instance and, unlike his more cautious selection at Bay Ridge twelve
months before, allowed Collins to return home in triumph.

But not before a piece of good fortune had come Britain's way in a dramatic finale
to this second Davis Cup tie to be held at the Longwood Cricket Club where the playing conditions had been improved considerably since 1900. With his brother
defaulting to Larned, Laurie Doherty had levelled the first day's singles by easily defeating Wrenn and then, with his brother, who showed no great discomfort after some
fortuitous rain delays, got the better of the Wrenns 6–3 in the fourth to give the British

a 2–1 lead. As was the custom at that time, the reverse singles were played simultane-
ously and Collins was to comment on what he called 'the refinement of cruelty to
tennis lovers' when he described the scene afterwards.

*'There was nothing between the two courts but the umpire's ladder and it was very disconcerting
to players when perhaps they were trying to time a well-placed lob, to hear the roars of applause
fired across their court at the neighbouring match. They had not only the anxiety of their own
match on their shoulders but could not help following the state of affairs in the other.'*

And the state of affairs in both contests was as tense as the spellbound crowd could
bear. On one court Bob Wrenn and Reggie Doherty were all tied up at three-all in the
fifth while next door William Larned and Laurie Doherty, after an equally undulating
encounter that had seen Doherty sweep through the third set 6–0 only to lose the
fourth 6–2, were also finely balanced at four-all in the decider.

If some in the crowd had been keeping an eye on the elegance of the Wrenn-Big Do
duel, they were suddenly riveted by an eruption on the other court. On break point
down at 4–4, Little Do had served and come in. Larned seeing his chance, took it with

aplomb, passing beautifully down the line.
There was no doubting that Larned's shot was
in but as soon as the umpire, Fred S.
Mansfield, called the score for the United
States 5–4, which would have left Larned serving for the match, Doherty asked whether his
own service had been in. Mansfield looked
up to verify the call with his service linesman.
But he wasn't there. He had left to catch a
boat. The said gentleman was, apparently, a
Longwood player who had agreed to take
the line on the understanding that he
would be relieved in time to catch a boat
for Nantasket Beach. At the appointed
time, he had left and no one had noticed.

LEFT: THE CLASSICAL STYLE OF LAURIE DOHERTY, SEEN
HERE PLAYING WITH HIS BROTHER AT LONGWOOD.

So Doherty's serve might well have been out, rendering Larned's pass useless.

So Mansfield reverted to what would become a time-honoured ritual and called for the referee who happened to be none other than Dr Dwight. After some discussion, which was listened to avidly by the players on the adjoining court, Dr Dwight decided to call a let and have the point replayed.

Doherty served; won the point; held for 5-all and proceeded to win the next two games and the match. There were those in the gallery who, not unreasonably, felt that Wrenn was affected by all this because, despite the obvious discomfort Big Do was feeling with his arm, the elder Doherty came through, too, taking the fifth set 6–4 to give the British Isles, as they were called, a 4–1 victory.

They were still talking about it more than twenty years later. Just before his death in 1926, Larned told Wallis Merrihew that he did not think that Dr Dwight's decision was justified and that he felt the service had been good. He pointed out, too, that under the rules Mansfield had the power to make a decision from the chair. However Merrihew had heard second-hand that Mansfield was inclined to agree with Doherty and thought the serve had probably been a fault. Ah, line decisions! Was it in or was it out? 'Twas ever thus.

So, at the third attempt the British got to take the Cup back to the country of its actual maker. Rowland Rhodes, presumably, would have considered that fitting. It would, however, be a well-travelled piece of silver by the time it returned to its original home.

1904

In 1904, the coffers of the USNLTA were so depleted that they were unable to raise the money to send a team to London. But that did not leave the British Isles without opposition for European nations had woken up to the untold potential of international tennis based on a team format. Even though Austria, keen to play, also had to default through lack of funds, France and Belgium were ready and willing and met for the right to challenge the British at Wimbledon. Despite the presence of the outstanding Max Decugis in their team, the French were beaten by their neighbours. Neither side could claim home court advantage for the tie was played on grass at Worple Road, thus becoming the first Davis Cup tie to be played in Britain. In the Challenge Round, the Dohertys led Britain to a 5–0 victory over Belgium although only Laurie played the singles. Big Do had virtually retired from singles play and contented himself with partnering his brother in the doubles while Frank Riseley played second singles.

The following year, the USNLTA, still with no more than a few hundred dollars in its bank account, discovered a man of vision and determination in Frederick G. Anderson who was a former Canadian champion. Then living in New York and sitting on the association's executive committee, Anderson pledged to raise enough money to send an American team to England. Richard Olney, now former Secretary of State, lobbed in $100 and Wallis Merrihew, presumably as hard up as the average scribe, came up with a well received $2.00.

With Anderson whipping up other contributions there was money enough to get the team on the boat. It consisted of Holcombe Ward, William Larned, Beals Wright and William J. Clothier who would succeed Wright as American champion in 1906. This time it was Belgium's turn to default, leaving just four challengers. The two semi-

BELOW: HOLCOMBE WARD SHOWS A TOUCH OF ECCENTRICITY IN HEADGEAR AS HE POSES WITH HIS COLLEAGUES ON THE US TEAM OF 1905 – BEALS WRIGHT, PAUL DASHIEL, BILL LARNED AND (SEATED) WILLIAM CLOTHIER SNR.

finals involving the USA and France and Australasia and Austria were played at the Queen's Club at Barons Court in London in the second week of July, 1905. The Americans and the Australasians came through, neither conceding a match and, in the final played a week later, Larned and Wright led their team to a 5–0 victory that was a great deal closer than the score suggests. It was the first serious test for the two players, Norman Brookes and Anthony Wilding, who would put their faraway nations on the tennis map so soon afterwards, and although they lost, everyone realised they would be heard from again.

Two days later, the eyes of the tennis world – still tiny in relative terms but gaining recognition from a wider public – turned to Wimbledon where a shock lay in store for the Americans in the Challenge Round. They were beaten 5–0 by the holders despite leading in one rubber by two sets to love and in another by two sets to one. The most thrilling encounter occurred on the first day when Laurie Doherty somehow survived an initial onslaught from Holcombe Ward the like of which, relates Wallis Myers, had never been seen before on the Centre Court. The British writer described it as 'an electrical display.' He went on: 'With a deft turn of a pliable wrist, Ward intercepted every one of Doherty's returns.'

However Doherty, with four Wimbledon titles already under his belt was, by now, a competitor of great experience. He held steady despite losing the first two sets until, as Myers describes it, 'Ward began to hoist signals of distress; his sprints to the net became less frequent, his hand lost much of its cunning, he resorted to lobbing and some of it was short enough for Doherty to smother. The end came painfully with a love set. It was almost a tragedy.'

Not for the British. By the end of the day a Davis Cup débutant for Britain, Sydney H. Smith had used his fearsome forehand to give his team a 2–0 lead with a four-set win over Larned. The Americans had tried to drill into Larned the need to play to Smith's backhand but it didn't work. In fact afterwards the Americans were heard to mutter that Smith had no need of a backhand because he ran round onto his forehand all the time. 'Smith of Stroud' as he was known didn't play tennis very long but, by the time he retired little over a year later, he had won all four of his Davis Cup singles and lost only two sets.

Reggie Doherty, now completely retired from singles play, re-appeared to partner his brother in the doubles and won what Myers described as a 'great match' 8–6 in the fifth. The Cup would remain in Britain. Indeed it was not required to travel 12 months later

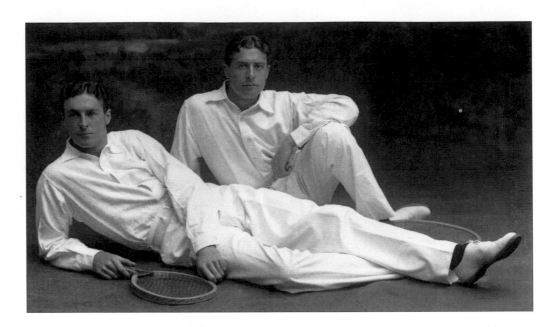

ABOVE: A CLASSIC POSE FOR THE DOHERTYS WHO REVIVED INTEREST IN THE GAME OF LAWN
TENNIS WITH THEIR CHARM, ELEGANCE AND TALENT.

1906

either when the same British team handed the Americans an even more comprehensive
5–0 beating. But in that year of 1906 bad luck struck the United States team even before
they boarded the SS *Celtic* for the transatlantic crossing. Beals Wright, still in the kind of
form that – in many people's opinion – should have seen him selected for the previous
year's singles, was definitely scheduled to be chosen this time until he did something silly
with a toothbrush. Having stayed overnight at the Crescent Athletic Club before board-
ing, he tried to push the cork of a bottle of Vichy water in with the end of his brush and
the neck broke. A finger on his right hand was badly cut and became infected at sea.
Only rapid hospital treatment on arrival in London saved his life.

So Raymond Little played second singles for the States but struggled to get games
off Smith in the opening rubber. The Doherty brothers made the Challenge Round
safe for Britain with a hard fought four set win over Ward and Little and so bowed out
of Davis Cup play. For British tennis it was the end of a era. Tragically neither lived very
long. On Laurie's death at the age of 43, following that of Reggie at the age of 36 *The
Times* wrote: 'It can be said of them that they played an English game in the spirit in
which Englishmen think that games should be played.' Not a bad epitaph.

CHAPTER FIVE

THE WILDING YEARS

*Wilding and Brookes form an Australasian alliance.... Foes march
arm-in-arm in Melbourne.... The Cup resides on Mabel's sideboard...and
with the War comes tragedy*

WHILE THE UNITED STATES AND BRITAIN were getting the show on the road – an un-signposted path at first that showed few signs of turning into a global highway – an athletic young man of 17 was winning his first tennis tournament on the other side of the world. Anthony W. Wilding was attending school in Christchurch, New Zealand and playing at the adjacent Cranmer Square Club. It was 1900 and, in the final of the Province of Canterbury Championships, Wilding beat one of his father's doubles part-ners, R.D. Harman, over five sets, having trained for the tournament 'as if for a Marathon race during the previous six weeks.'

By the end of the decade Wilding and his Australian partner Norman Brookes would have expanded the horizons and the frontiers of the Davis Cup to an extent that Davis himself could never have foreseen. Wilding would also have taken the first steps towards changing the very nature of the sport. Even though Davis and the three W's at Harvard had spent time practising their skills, it was not until Wilding arrived at Cambridge in 1902 that anyone had tried to hone their body into the perfect athletic vehicle with which to play the game. Even by today's standards, this handsome, impos-ing figure who had followed the Dohertys as one of international sport's first heart-throbs, could have been described as a fitness fanatic.

What Wilding managed to cram into the next 14 years would have left men of any age breathless. On roads frequently unmade for motorised traffic, he would criss-cross Britain and Europe on his motorcycle, dashing from Edinburgh to Baden-Baden and up to Hamburg, rackets strapped to the back, ready to leap off his machine after hours in the saddle and play anyone at tennis. Along the way he would accumulate friends – kings, prime ministers and Hungarian counts amongst them – as easily as he collected tennis titles, the one with diffident charm, the other with a combination of skill and athleticism. Wallis Myers, his biographer and friend, encapsulated Wilding's passion for motor traction in one memorable sentence: 'The open road was his highway, oil his food, distance his victim and speed his god.'

Tony Wilding was not the greatest player of his age but his dedication and, dare one suggest it, his professionalism made him the most successful. He ruled Wimbledon for four years between 1910 and 1913 and, even more importantly for the popularity of his sport in the antipodes, he joined up with Norman Brookes to take the Davis Cup into another hemisphere.

No one had to sell the Davis Cup to Wilding. It appealed to him instantly as Myers explains: 'This cosmopolitan interest in an annual competition, which generated friendship and fostered mutual understanding, which was always a clean and wholesome tournament free from any taint of private interest, inspired his zeal and sympathy. Between them, Wilding and the Davis Cup did much for lawn tennis and, through its medium, something for sporting chivalry and all that it implies in the world at large.'

It was, however, family interests that found Wilding on a train, heading away from a Davis Cup tie in 1906 before the fifth rubber had been decided. Australasia were playing the United States at Newport in Wales and, although Wilding had won both his singles, his team were without Brookes who had not made the journey that year. In his place, L.O.S. Poidevin, who was living in England at the time and played more cricket than tennis, had been persuaded to swap his bat for a racket and help out. He did his best but had lost to Holcombe Ward in straight sets on the first day and had been unable to help Wilding sufficiently to prevent Ward and Raymond Little from winning the doubles.

After he had squared the tie by beating Ward 8–6 in the fifth, Wilding found himself in an unhappy situation. His father had travelled from New Zealand to visit relatives in nearby Herefordshire, where he had been brought up, and to tour Europe with his son. A trip to Prague had all been arranged and required catching a boat that very evening. That meant two long train journeys, first to London and then a dash across town to catch the boat train to Folkestone. None of this could be accomplished if the Wildings hung around to wait for the outcome of the final rubber. Which would have been all well and good had not their long term plans been intimately tied up with the final result. For if Poidevin were to spring an upset, Australasia would be required to meet the British Isles in the Challenge Round at Wimbledon the following week. That would mean cancelling the trip to Prague.

It was Wallis Myers, well versed in the possible uses of the telegraph system, who came

ABOVE: ALTHOUGH HIS SERVE WOULD NOT HAVE MATCHED THE SPEEDS GREG RUSEDSKI
GENERATES TODAY, ANTHONY WILDING, EQUALLY AT HOME ON THE TENNIS COURT OR MOTOR
CYCLE, BROUGHT POWER AND ATHLETICISM TO THE GAME AND HELPED NORMAN BROOKES TAKE
THE CUP DOWN UNDER FOR THE FIRST TIME.

up with the answer. The resourceful newspaperman, who was accompanying the
Wildings to London, arranged for a telegram to be waiting for them, indicating the
result, when the train stopped at Swindon. One can just envisage Myers dashing into the
stationmaster's office as the steam billowed over the platform to grab the message and
tell from the result – Little having beaten Poidevin 6–2 in the fourth – that it was all go
for Prague. A little more breathlessly romantic, somehow, than receiving an e-mail.

On the first leg of the journey, Wilding, according to Myers, had been torn by con-
flicting emotions; wanting his team to win yet eagerly anticipating the pleasure of
piloting his father across the continent. As it turned out they had to wait another day
for the 20-minute run from Paddington to Charing Cross proved too much for the
handsome cab, even though baggage and Wilding's overcoat – draped over a porter's
arm – had both been left behind in the unseemly scramble. Alone, on his motorcycle,
Tony would probably have made the entire journey with time to spare.

As we have seen, the Americans proved no match for S.H. Smith and the Dohertys in the Challenge Round at Wimbledon and the following year, 1907, they were out of luck again when a depleted team went down 3–2 to Australasia on those same courts at Worple Road. Larned, Ward, Clothier and Little had all been unable to find the time for another transatlantic crossing so the ever-persistent Beals Wright found himself with a twenty-two-year-old sprinter from Yale, Karl H. Behr, as his lone partner. Even though they outlasted Brookes and Wilding in the doubles and grabbed another rubber when Wright cornered Wilding 7–5 in the fourth on the final day, the left-handed Brookes was the dominant force.

The talented left hander came through in four sets but not before Behr had given a still perspiring Wright some faint hope that his effort had not been in vain by winning the first 6–4. Wallis Myers, in his *The Story of the Davis Cup*, describes the occasion with all the verve of a Boys' Own drama:

> *'With startling nerve the American won the first set, once more giving an electrical exhibition of close quarter volleying. From the dressing room window Wright, in a fever of suppressed excitement, was watching the movements of the scoreboard in the Centre Court. Before he had dressed, the men were three all in the second bout. Was it possible the Cup might…? Wait! There was a set to the Australian. He had got abreast. The Yale boys, crowded together in a corner of one of the stands, had ceased to yell. Old George Wright of Boston had stopped clapping. Now Brookes was gaining rapidly. His jaw was set like a vice. He served and volleyed as he had never served and volleyed before. Behr was passing his hand nervously through his black hair as he walked back to retrieve. His ordeal was too great. Hold! His powder was not quite exhausted. He would steady himself to fire his last shots. He would show those Yale fellows, whom he lately captained, that the Americans went down with their colours flying. But all the while the grim, iron-nerved Australian, conscious of victory, was advancing to his goal.'*

Rudyard Kipling and John Buchan would have had difficulty making more of a tennis match than that. It was the age of rugged heroes with firm jaws pulling off daring deeds and Myers certainly did his best to capture the drama. In this instance Brookes, who had won the Wimbledon title just a couple of weeks before, was the hero, not just for beating the relatively inexperienced Behr but, more so, for the way he had dismissed Wright in straight sets on the opening day. In a letter to Wallis Merrihew, George Wright left little doubt that it had been Brookes's southpaw serve which had caused his son's downfall. 'It was a nasty serve,' he wrote. 'Fast, twisting, beautifully placed, always coming where his opponent wasn't expecting it. You couldn't do much with it. In fact you were lucky to get it back at all.'

Seventy years later we were saying the same thing about John McEnroe. From all accounts, Brookes had comparable skills. Certainly, like the formidable Lottie Dod a decade before, Brookes could turn his hand to just about any sporting endeavour. Alan Trengove, the Australian tennis historian, tells of Brookes inviting the Australian croquet champion to his house in Melbourne and, having converted the tennis court into a croquet lawn, picked up a mallet for the first time and beat his guest. Brookes was a brilliant cricketer, adept at billiards and went on to win national golf titles. In an age given to offering sporting heroes nicknames with a comic-book tone, he was known as 'The Wizard'.

With a tennis racket in his hand, Brookes had tantalising touch and a top spin forehand that, with his Eastern grip, enabled him to take the ball early with little backswing and get into the net. And then there was the serve. And yet, unlike Wilding, Brookes did not look like an athlete. He was slight and pale and frequently ill with stomach ulcers. As if expecting to catch a chill even in the hottest temperatures, he wore his shirts buttoned at throat and wrist and nearly always played in a peaked, grey tweed cap.

In the Challenge Round at Wimbledon which was played a week after the defeat of the United States, the deceptive image and abundant talent proved too much for a British team stripped of the Dohertys and even of Smith who had pronounced himself 'dissatisfied' with his form and refused to play. So A.W. Gore and H. Roper Barrett stepped manfully into the breach, offering experience, if not youth, for the cause. Gore was 39 and Barrett 33.

It should have been a mismatch but Wilding was still raw and the British pair had accumulated a wealth of tactical knowledge during their long years in the game. Despite being swept aside in the opening singles, the latter promptly recovered from two sets down in the doubles to pull off one of the most memorable victories of that era. Wilding's tendency to double-fault and Brookes's weakness on the smash enabled Gore and Barrett to steal a dramatic victory 13–11 in the fifth. Gore then won a baseline battle against Wilding in the first of the reverse singles but Roper Barrett was no match for Brookes and his lethal serve and so the Cup departed on the longest voyage of its existence – Down Under.

It cost Norman Brookes seven pounds ten shillings to get it back to Melbourne but the pride of possession had no monetary evaluation and, for a time, the trophy that was to grow in stature and fame as the years wore on became part of the Brookes household. It took pride of place on a dining room sideboard and, on occasion, Mabel Brookes would use it to hold flowers for a dinner party. There was no tray or plinth yet, for the names inscribed on the bowl were not numerous enough to require extra space and Dame Mabel, as she was to become, thought it looked 'very decorative when, filled with loose-petalled red peonies, it reflected the light of the candles'. The great Cup has had many homes over the years but this, I suspect, was one of its most gracious and becoming. After a few years, as Australasia held on to it tenaciously, it was removed to a Melbourne bank vault. Dame Mabel sounded relieved, not because of any fear that it might be spirited away in the night but because 'it dwarfed all the other trophies.'

It would be comforting to think that trophies were all that occupied the minds of amateur tennis officials in the Edwardian age but, although financial remuneration was unthinkable, the financial aspects of sending teams around the world and staging matches started to create tensions between the various national associations. All manner of offers and counter-offers were cabled around the world once it became clear that the 1908 Challenge Round would have to be staged in Australia. To visit that far-flung outpost of civilisation was not a journey that any working man could take lightly. If one included a reasonable time for acclimatisation and the actual playing of the tie, more than three months of one's life was required to complete the undertaking. Travelling from the Eastern Seaboard of the United States via the Suez Canal the sea voyage required six weeks there and six weeks back. In his report to the USNLTA, the Chairman, James Dwight reported that tickets for the team that was eventually sent, comprising Beals Wright and Fred Alexander had cost $2,400 including expenses, a huge sum of money in an era when a three bedroomed house cost precisely the same amount and the average income was $509 a year.

Prior to that, however, eyebrows had been raised over arrangements for the tie that would decide which nation would travel to meet Australasia. As Britain and the United States were the only challengers, it made sense to try and organise a tie in America in September to allow time for the winning team to re-organise and be in Australia by the end of November. The LTA's response to the suggestion that they should send a team across the Atlantic was to ask for a guarantee against gate money. Dwight replied, saying that 'such a thing in international matches was very unusual.' That did not prevent him, however, approaching the Germantown Cricket Club which initially offered a guarantee to the USNLTA of $2,500. Dwight was then prepared to offer $1,500 to the British. However the Philadelphia club was forced to withdraw the offer because its President was away and a smaller offer of $1,500 from the Longwood Cricket Club was eventually accepted and the whole sum passed on to the visitors.

Meanwhile the LTA had been trying to negotiate with the Australians, presumably with a view to playing the Americans 'Down Under' prior to the Challenge Round. The practicality of such an idea is not immediately clear but it was given short shrift by the Victorian LTA who would be hosting the Challenge Round. Their secretary, John Koch, was, in fact, incensed at the British request for a guarantee. Pointing out that the Australasian teams had never asked for a penny while sending teams to Britain, he went on to suggest that 'such a proposal, coming as it did from a country which had held four contests for the Cup, and received a large profit therefrom, considerably lowered the prestige which English lawn tennis players and the Association which controls the sport on the European Continent had always enjoyed in Australasia.'

According to the accounts published in the issue of *Lawn Tennis & Badminton* dated 29th February 1908, the 'large profit' amounted to one hundred and seventy pounds sixteen shillings and four pence. Hardly 'large' even in those days. Even so it was probably just as well that, with Larned available to play singles for the US in Boston, the British team of M.J.G. Ritchie and the Irishman J.C. Parke proved no match for the Americans and therefore were not required to trouble the LTA's exchequer for any more far-flung travels that year. And, it must be added, they were not missed for the Challenge Round of 1908 proved to be one of the most exciting contests yet held under the Davis Cup banner.

1908

Both teams prepared assiduously and, once the matches got under way, their dedication to the cause shone through. With Bill Larned unable to take so much time off, three supporters – presumably gentlemen of independent means – accompanied Beals Wright and Fred Alexander on the long voyage and the pair arrived a month ahead of time, determined to give themselves every opportunity to acclimatise to the heat and unfamiliar conditions.

Meanwhile Tony Wilding was doing his best to get his partner into shape. Billeted at the Brookes mansion on the edge of Melbourne, the New Zealander set the less sturdy Brookes a tough schedule. Allowing for the fact that 'Norman had to be very carefully handled' because of his weak stomach, the pair rose at 7.00am and, after just a cup of tea, went for a walk or short run. By 8.30 they were on the practice court and, at 11.00, played three to five sets flat out against each other. After lunch, team-mates would join them for doubles and some stroke practice. Then, Wilding told Wallis Myers: 'Skipping or running or a little game with the wall ended the athletic day. Two baths and a good deal of massage and to bed by 10.15pm. We ate anything within reason and, as a rule drank barley water but in this respect we were not rigidly particular and sometimes a very little light beer was consumed. The difficulty, of course, was to practise for one hour and a half in the broiling sun, with the thermometer over 95°F and then confine oneself to one glass of fluid in the middle of the day.'

Why they thought this was necessary is unclear unless it had something to do with Brookes's ulcers but such poor fluid replacement would certainly not be allowed today. Meanwhile preparations were being completed at the Wharehouseman's Ground (later called the Albert Ground) for one of the young nation's greatest sporting adventures. Founded as a nation only seven years before with a population still under four million, Australia was ready to flex its muscles on the international sporting stage and the Challenge Round provided the perfect opportunity. People who had never heard of the competition nor had ever played tennis were drawn to the occasion where temporary stands had been built over adjacent footpaths to accommodate the sell-out crowds. In a very real sense the Davis Cup was helping Australia create its identity as a nation even though the team also encompassed its Kiwi neighbours.

The thousands who turned out on a day of 102°F temperatures boosted by a hot wind from the interior were given a show to fit the occasion. Brookes and Alexander, the latter a tall, spare New Yorker who had refined his game at Princeton, walked out arm-in-arm in long overcoats with scarves knotted around their necks. Heaven knows what possessed them to dress like this on such a searingly hot day but Trengove quotes an observer as describing the extraordinary scene thus:

'The picture as they shed their coats and threw down the towels at the foot of the umpire's chair was suggestive of a prize fight rather than a tennis bout, for there was a bucket of sawdust, a pail of ice water, a pair of jugs of barley water, spare towels, and a small boy in white to wait on each.'

If they looked like a couple of swells, Alexander was certainly a very nervous one for he lost the opening four games of the of the match. Only then did he start to make full

RIGHT: NORMAN BROOKES' CLOTH CAP NEVER SET A TREND BUT THE SKILL OF HIS LEFT-HANDED GAME ENSURED THAT THE CUP RESIDED ON HIS SIDEBOARD IN MELBOURNE FOR MANY YEARS.

use of his net rushing style and, amazingly, clawed his way back to deprive Brookes of the first set 7–5. The achievement was even more remarkable considering the Australian had not relinquished a set in two years. Brookes's cunning and natural flair earned him the second and third sets but, after Alexander had struck back to take the fourth, both men slumped in their chairs, dampened handkerchiefs on their heads. At this point Beals Wright walked on to offer his team-mate a drink from a little bottle. It was not unknown for players to revive themselves with a nip of brandy on such occasions – soon Suzanne Lenglen would be imbibing regularly at changeovers – but Alexander declined so Wright tossed the bottle to Brookes who, smiling his thanks, took a swig. We do not know for sure what the bottle contained but Fred must have regretted passing it up. Galvanised, Brookes swept through the fifth set 6–3. Then, in perfect harmony with the spirit in which the match had been played, they departed as they had arrived, arm-in-arm.

The second rubber was a shorter affair. Wright, whose reputation down the years does not seem to have matched his considerable talent, quickly bamboozled Wilding with deceptive drop shots and lobs and won 6–1 in the fourth. The following day Wilding found himself engaged in what he described to Myers several years later as the finest doubles in which he had ever taken part. At the outset, the vociferous gallery had little reason to expect anything other than an Australasian victory. Brookes and Wilding led by two sets to love and 5–4 in the third. But Wright and Alexander staged a courageous come back and the final drama is described by R.M. Kidston writing in Australia's *Lawn Tennis* magazine.

> 'At two sets all, two games to love, Alexander serving and Brookes seemingly done, and making frequent errors, Australasia's hopes were small indeed. Till then, Wilding's fine play almost alone had saved us; but at that moment of crisis the real Brookes reappeared, and from then onwards was again the supreme master.
>
> 'Who that saw it will forget the final game of that double? Wilding was serving at 5–4. Australasia leads, and 40–15 was called. He served a double fault, and a universal "Oh!" echoed through the arena. Wright scored with a smash. Deuce. Brookes netted. 'Vantage to America. A magnificent rally followed, and in it Wright fell. Alexander, close in, alone played his two opponents. Jumping from side to side like a cat, three times he volleyed fine volleys of his opponents, and at length netted a magnificent lift-drive by Wilding, the overspin of which made it dive for the ground. He actually held his own till Wright, unperceived by him, had recovered

his feet after his fall. Again American got the 'vantage, but Brookes scored with a fine intercep-
tion, and again Brookes intercepted, smashing hard to the corner; and now Alexander fell in a
tremendous effort to reach the ball, and slid into the side boards with a resounding bump as he
failed, and then Wright tossed, and breathless we watched the ball hover and just go over the
base-line.'

So the Australians prevailed but one more rubber had to be won if the hosts were to retain the Cup and, on the following day, a Monday, Brookes returned to the court and began to make short work of Wright. The first two sets went to the left-hander 6–0, 6–3. The American, however, was not disheartened. He had noticed that, during the latter stages of the second set, Brookes had been slower to get to the net. The spike marks told the tale. The marks on the grass near the net were old ones. Those further back were new. Attacking the Brookes serve with renewed vigour, Wright wrested the third set 7–5 from an opponent who was starting to show signs of distress in the heat. Brookes virtually threw away the fourth set and girded himself for one last effort to secure the Cup. But Wright stayed with him and kept digging himself out of hopeless situations as the Australian's famous serve wilted. Twice Brookes served for the match at 7–6 and 10–9 but, especially on the second occasion, when he was just two points from victory, Brookes was not favoured by the bounce on what was now a badly scarred court. Finally, at ten-all, the Australian lost his serve again. According to the writer signing himself 'Austral', Brookes was 'giving away at the knees' and when Wright, holding match point a game later, hit a sharp return at the local hero's feet the 'game, set and match came almost as a relief to the overwrought spectators.'

So a Davis Cup classic had ended in a memorable victory for Beals Wright by 0–6, 3–6, 7–5, 6–2, 12–10. But it was to prove a vain, if heroic, effort. Wilding, resting on his bed at the Brookes's house within earshot of the crowd's groans and cheers now emerged to administer the coup de grace, sweeping past an outclassed Alexander in three sets. Not many times since has an Australian crowd cheered a New Zealand victory so lustily.

The following year, 1909, the British Isles and the United States were, once again, the only nations able to offer a challenge. And it was the British who travelled to America yet again. On this occasion the match was played at the Germantown Cricket Club in Philadelphia. The British had managed to rustle up three men this time, James C. Parke, Charles P. Dixon and Williams C. Crawley but they were no match for Bill

1909

LEFT: THE FRONT COVER OF *AMERICAN LAWN TENNIS,*
DATED FEBRUARY 15, 1909. THE MATCH DEPICTED IS
THAT IN WHICH BROOKES AND WILDING DEFEATED
WRIGHT AND ALEXANDER IN THE 1908 CHALLENGE
ROUND AT THE WHAREHOUSEMAN'S GROUND IN
MELBOURNE. WILDING THOUGHT IT THE FINEST
DOUBLES HE HAD PLAYED. THE INSERT SHOWS
F.B. ALEXANDER.

Larned and William Clothier who did
not drop a set in the singles. Clothier,
whose son Bill became a well known
tennis player and promoter, was playing
on his home turf. A tall, imposing figure, the senior Clothier would go on to
found the International Hall of Fame
at Newport and become one of the
dominant personalities in the
American game for several decades.

However neither he nor Larned were available to follow up their victory by travelling to Australia for the Challenge Round. Two youngsters from California, Maurice
McLoughlin, soon to become known as 'The California Comet' and Melville Long
were drafted onto the team more in hope than any real expectation of success. There
was much rumbling in the press, meantime, when it became clear that the US team
competing in Philadelphia would not be travelling on. According to Wallis Merrihew,
many people thought it unfair that the British should be beaten by America's strongest
team only for it to default to a weaker one for the Challenge Round. However, at the
dinner in the clubhouse after the tie, Parke refuted such notions. 'Such talk is
extremely silly,' he said in his speech, adding that none of the English team would have
been able to go to Australia, either, had they won.

So the reputation of American tennis was entrusted to a couple of young
Californians who set off by themselves after a plan to send a more experienced player
with them as guide and mentor had fallen through. Unsurprisingly, it was not easy finding someone to 'nip down' to Australia for a month or two. McLoughlin and Long
sailed on the *Aorangi* from Vancouver on 8th October, 1909 and arrived at Brisbane en
route to Sydney on 31st October. The Challenge Round was due to be played almost a

month later – 26–29th November – at Double Bay. By any standards it was a huge adventure and they set off well equipped. They carried a dozen rackets apiece, half made exactly to order by Wright & Ditson and the other half by A.G. Spalding who, some 90 years later, would find themselves supplying rackets to the millionaire professionals on the ATP Tour. Twelve of the rackets were strung and ready for use and the rest ready to be strung 'almost at a moment's notice' as Merrihew recounts, by a professional racket stringer in Sydney. They also carried no less than seventy tennis shirts.

On arrival in Sydney, McLoughlin and Long were put up at the Royal Sydney Yacht Club and immediately created a good impression. So much so that their hopeless inexperience, especially on grass, did not leave them without supporters amongst the 4,000 spectators who attended the matches. Thrown into the fray against Brookes and Wilding, they were allowed just one set in sixteen – that taken by McLoughlin against Wilding in a little preview of the battles that would follow. As 'Austral' noted, 'While badly beaten, the two game youngsters were far from disgraced... they treated us to an exhibition of hard, free hitting, purely offensive play, such as we were wholly unaccustomed to. And they were so earnest, so spontaneously enthusiastic, so spry, agile and carefree that they speedily established themselves as prime favourites with the gallery.'

Back home questions were raised about the wisdom of having sent such a young team to challenge the world's best but there was no overt criticism of the players. The one-sided nature of the 1909 Challenge ended up, after a further blizzard of letters and cables between various national associations, in playing a part in the decision not to hold any competition the following year. Everyone seems to have been keen but an Australian suggestion that the British Isles and the United States should meet in New Zealand with the winners playing Australasia in the Challenge Round was met with a cool response. It seems clear, too, that the Americans tended to take the high ground on the matter of guarantees against expenses. The British, anxious to stage a tie on their own soil after two trips to the States, offered £400 or its then equivalent, $2,000, and Dr Dwight tentatively accepted. However this was rescinded just a few weeks later on 20th May and when renewed efforts were made to play Britain Down Under, Dr Dwight cabled on 7th July, 'Shall send team if possible Davis Cup matches only. No guarantees asked nor approval possible.' But in the end it all came to nought. Even though the ever eager Beals Wright and the improving Maurice McLoughlin were available, the USNLTA were wary of sending anything but their strongest team and refused to go. More humiliatingly, perhaps, the British offering of Charles Dixon,

Arthur Lowe and Theodore Mavrogordato, was considered a 'disappointment' to the Australians and, seizing the chance to take advantage of a clause in the agreement which allowed them to reject a team they considered too weak, they did so. For Davis Cup, 1910 was a barren year.

1911

Nor did 1911 get off to an auspicious start. South Africa had wanted to enter the fray and put in a challenge only to admit, shortly afterwards, that it could not get a team together. So it was left to the British Isles and the USA to sort out which country would make the long journey south to meet Australasia. Once again, the Americans prevailed on the British to make the Atlantic voyage but the team of Charles Dixon, Arthur Lowe and Alfred Beamish nearly didn't make it. The Liverpool dock strike delayed the departure of the SS *Adriatic* for two days. Frantic cables were sent to New York asking for a postponement of the tie which had been scheduled to start on Thursday 7th September at the original site of the West Side Tennis Club at Broadway and 238th Street in Manhattan. It was clear by then that the ship would not dock until late Sunday night, 3rd September at the earliest and this, the British felt, would not give them sufficient time to prepare. With tickets sold and all the arrangements made the West Side chairman Calhoun Cragin was reluctant to accede to this request but eventually agreed that the matches could be put back two days to start on the Sunday.

Five thousand people packed the club grounds and the tennis was worth waiting for. Dixon, who had lost to Roper Barrett one match before the All England Challenge Round at Wimbledon that year, led Bill Larned 5–2 in the fifth before the American staged a brilliant come back to snatch it 7–5 while Lowe, a Wimbledon semi-finalist, also went the distance with Maurice McLoughlin before losing 6–3 in the fifth.

Any thought of an American whitewash was swiftly eradicated by the manner in which Dixon and Beamish tackled the doubles against Thomas Bundy and Raymond Little. After their 6–3, 7–5, 6–4 victory, *American Lawn Tennis* wrote, 'It was, on the part of Dixon and Beamish, a superb exhibition of scientific doubles play, an exhibition the like of which was seen only when such teams as the Dohertys, Ward and Wright, and Hackett and Alexander were in their prime. It was at once a revelation and an inspiration.'

It was, however, not enough. Larned and McLoughlin won their reverse singles in four sets apiece and the USA, with a 4–1 victory to boost their confidence, were set to challenge Australasia once more although this time the match would be played in New Zealand, ironically without the native son, Tony Wilding. Having settled permanently in England, where he had taken a job with a wood pulp company, Wilding felt that

ABOVE: THE AMERICAN TEAM THAT LOST THE CHALLENGE ROUND TO AUSTRALASIA IN CHRISTCHURCH, NEW ZEALAND IN 1911 – LEFT TO RIGHT: BEALS WRIGHT, BILL LARNED AND MAURICE MCLOUGHLIN, ALREADY DUBBED THE CALIFORNIA COMET.

Brookes could handle the defence of the Cup without him and he was right. Ironically Larned, seven times the American national champion in the first 11 years of the century, was able to make the long journey on this occasion yet should probably not have played. He suffered from rheumatism and was badly affected by the cold, damp weather that descended on Christchurch in the final days of the year. The 1911 Challenge Round was, in fact, played over the first three days of the following year as a result of the start being delayed because of heavy rain. After much soul-searching Larned, an introspective man, decided that he should play. He felt that American tennis supporters were counting on him to bring the Cup home but F.M.B. Fisher, the referee, was not the only one with misgivings. Later Fisher wrote: 'It is my opinion that Larned's physical condition produced a mental depression that was ultimately disastrous. Larned was in an awkward position. He felt that it was largely to him that his nation looked for success. So, under pressure, he elected at the eleventh hour to play.'

Walking on court after Brookes had gained revenge over Beals Wright for the 1908 defeat in Melbourne, Larned won the first set against Wilding's replacement, Rodney

Heath, but soon slumped to a four-set defeat that helped propel Australasia to a 5–0 whitewash. Fisher's talk of depression was unhappily prescient. Although his tennis career ended amidst the mists of New Zealand, so far from his home-spun triumphs, Larned went on to become a fighter pilot in those pioneering days of the First World War and rose to the rank of lieutenant-colonel. In 1921 he invented the first steel framed racket, which was soon to catch the eye of the more marketing orientated René Lacoste, but none of this success seemed to make Larned a happy man. Dogged by illness during his years on the New York Stock Exchange, he committed suicide in 1926.

The following year Folkestone flickered briefly in the annals of tennis history. The channel port hard by the white cliffs of Dover was the setting for the 4–1 victory the British Isles inflicted on France in what turned out to be the only preliminary tie before another antipodean-based Challenge Round. The Americans had been bitterly disappointed by the failure of their Challenge in Christchurch, not least because of the wearisome chore of having to send a team on such a daunting journey. One USNLTA official even suggested that the United States should withdraw from participation in the Cup unless Australasia agreed to defend on American soil. Brookes's response was curt. He was getting used to the famous trophy residing in Melbourne and, not unnaturally, his attitude was unbending. If anyone wanted the Davis Cup, they would jolly well have to come and get it. Sadly, the Americans didn't seem to want it quite enough in 1912 and failed to enter a team.

That left the British as the sole challengers but, before they left Folkestone, talks with their French counterparts led, a year later, to the formation of the International Lawn Tennis Federation, an organisation that the Americans were initially loathe to join because the British had insisted on labelling Wimbledon as the World Championships on Grass. It was only in 1923, when the ILTF dropped the term 'World Championship' and agreed to nominate the championships of Britain, France the United States and Australia as the Big Four, that the Americans joined in. It was also agreed that the Davis Cup should remain under the separate jurisdiction of the Davis Cup Nations, which is under the governance of the ITF.

Charles Dixon was captain of the British team that set sail for Melbourne. He had with him James Parke, Gordon Lowe and Arthur Beamish, a solid squad that lacked the glamour of the Doherty years. Perhaps as a result of this, the names of Dixon's men have not rung down the years like their forebears which is hardly fair because they were given no chance of success and yet returned home victorious. In large part this

ABOVE: NORMAN BROOKES AND ALF DUNLOP (BACKS TO CAMERA) WON THIS DOUBLES AGAINST
JAMES PARKE AND ARTHUR BEAMISH IN THE 1912 CHALLENGE ROUND BUT BRITAIN, INSPIRED
BY PARKES' SINGLES PLAY, SHOCKED THE MELBOURNE CROWD BY ENDING AUSTRALASIA'S
SIX-YEAR HOLD ON THE CUP.

was due to the contribution of Parke. Perhaps Norman Brookes should have taken
greater note of the fact that the Irishman was, if anything, an even more versatile
games player than the talented Australian. Before concentrating on tennis, he had
played 20 times for Ireland at rugby union; was a first class cricketer and later played
golf for Ireland, too. Irish to the core, he nursed his own luck by pinning two sprigs of
shamrock to his tennis shirt before his matches.

Luck, however, did not play too big a part in the proceedings when Parke faced
Brookes in the opening rubber of the 1912 Challenge Round at the Albert Ground in
Melbourne in front of a crowd reduced in size by the anticipated ease with which The

1912

61

Wizard was expected to lead his team to victory. Everyone was in for a shock and the reasons for it were clearly laid out in a letter that Arthur Beamish sent home:

'Brookes got to 4–1 in the first set before Parke could gauge the speed of his service or get used to its bound, Brookes at this point and, in fact, up to the third set, using his straight, fast service without the American twist and hang. When Parke became accustomed to this he hit his returns very fast and firmly all over the court. On the backhand he played a fairly high, slow shot at Brookes's body, waited for the return which was not punched (Brookes does not punch his slow volleys at all well) and then drove joyously and with the most extraordinary accuracy all over the court, passing Brookes clean at times with the finest cross court drives.'

Brookes had elected not to play in the Victorian Championships which had preceded the Challenge Round, preferring to keep Heath (deputising for the absent Wilding again) and himself away from the Britishers' gaze. In hindsight, it was a mistake. The Australasian captain was not match tight and with Parke inspired he could not prevent the visitors from taking a 1–0 lead with a 8–6, 6–3, 5–7, 6–2 victory. Dixon then defeated Heath in four sets. But the doubles went to the holders and when Brookes overcame Dixon on the final day with a capacity 7,000 now riveted by the drama, it was left to Parke to play the deciding rubber. By then it came as no surprise when his heavy ground strokes proved too much for Heath and the Cup was wrested from Australasia's grasp after six long years by an emphatic margin 6–2, 6–4, 6–4.

Parke, like many who would follow him, proved to be a competitor who played better for a team than for himself. His tournament record never matched his exploits at the Albert Ground and, referring to his decisive opening rubber victory over Brookes, he told the black tie gathering at the official dinner, 'I know that I have never played such a game in my life.' And he never played one like it again.

Back in the northern hemisphere there was a collective sigh of relief when news filtered in of the British triumph. No longer would challenging nations have to travel to the far side of the earth in search of Dwight's little pot. It would be back within reach and immediately the 1913 competition grew in size with a record seven nations challenging the new holders – Australasia, the United States, France, Germany, Belgium, South Africa and Canada.

The new campaign was significant in that the tie between Germany and France which took place at Wiesbaden – later to be the birthplace of one of the Cup's greatest stal-

1913

62

warts John McEnroe – was the first ever to be played on a surface other than grass. The red clay suited both teams but the French were handicapped by an injury to that country's first great player, Max Decugis, who had levelled the opening day's score by beating R.W. Rahe. Decugis had to default the reverse singles and the Germans won 4–1.

Neither Brookes nor Wilding were available to travel to New York for Australasia's match against the United States but the tie did not lack for interesting personalities. Apart from Maurice McLoughlin who would play one of the great Challenge Rounds at Wimbledon that year against Wilding, the Americans fielded Dick Williams, a fine player and dashing personality who had been born in Geneva of wealthy parents. Not the least of his claims to fame was that he survived the sinking of the *Titanic,* being picked up after an hour in the water after his father had drowned. Williams won both his singles to ensure an American victory, first against Stanley Doust and on the third day against Horrie Rice who was also unusual. A small figure attired in knickerbockers and long black socks, Rice was 40 years old and had once played the violin in a theatre orchestra.

So the Americans travelled to Britain to play the next round against Germany which was scheduled at Nottingham. In the meantime Canada had beaten South Africa 4–1 at the Queen's Club and then journeyed down to Folkestone to meet Belgium whom they beat 5–0. Williams and his colleagues also proved to be unsinkable against the Germans, so for the first time a proper series of preliminary rounds had produced two genuine, battle hardened finalists. The Canadians, however, were no match for their southerly neighbours and did not win a set in the three rubbers that were played against the United States at Wimbledon.

So, on the 25th July 1913 at Worple Road, Wimbledon, the British heroes who had plucked the Cup from Brookes's grasp eight months before, prepared to meet a new challenge. The holders had experience on their side but not youth. Parke and Dixon in the singles and Roper Barrett, partnering Dixon in the doubles, were ageing veterans compared with the zestful American pair. However Parke was back in his favourite environment, playing Davis Cup for the British Isles and he was not about to be cowed by the California Comet. After losing to McLoughlin the Championships, Parke had studied the way Wilding had dealt with the American's power serving in the Wimbledon Challenge Round just a few weeks before. He noted how the champion had held on to his title by standing in on the McLoughlin serve thus giving him less time to set himself for the volley. In a riveting encounter Parke battled away from the back court, passing

ABOVE: IN 1913 AT WORPLE ROAD, WIMBLEDON MAURICE MCLOUGHLIN AND H. H. HACKETT (LEFT) WON THIS DOUBLES OVER THE VETERAN BRITISH PAIR OF H. ROPER BARRETT AND CHARLES DIXON TO TAKE THE CUP BACK TO THE STATES FOR THE FIRST TIME IN TEN YEARS.

LEFT: IN COATS DESIGNED TO WARD OFF THE CHILL OF AN ENGLISH SUMMER, THE TEAMS POSE BEFORE THE MATCH – LEFT TO RIGHT: ROPER BARRETT, DIXON, HACKETT AND MCLOUGHLIN.

with studied care as McLoughlin launched himself at the net and Parke through to give the British an early lead with a magnificent 8–10, 7–5, 6–4, 1–6, 7–5 victory.

The second rubber was just as close but this time it went to the States with Williams finally overcoming Dixon, a man 18 years his senior, 7–5 in the fifth. Like most American players Williams was wearing spikes which the British thought was not quite the done thing as they tended to rough up the court, a factor which worried the serve and volleyer a good deal less than the ground-stroker. As the Americans were the net rushers, it was not difficult to understand the hosts' frustration but, possibly having learned a bit of diplomacy after Roper Barrett's criticism of Longwood 13 years before, they decided to make no official protest.

In hindsight it could certainly have made the difference because the doubles in this thrilling encounter was just as close as the first day's singles. However with H.H. Hackett's steadiness providing the anchor for the American team while McLoughlin flung himself about at the net, Dixon and Roper Barrett could not cling to their two set to one lead and went down 6–4 in the fifth. Had Parke been playing the fourth rubber, the American challenge might have been kept at arms length but by the time this great Davis Cup competitor defeated Williams in yet another five-setter, McLoughlin had reclaimed the trophy with a decisive victory over Dixon. So, for the first time in ten years, the Cup was going home to the United States.

It was something of a miracle that the competition of 1914 got played at all. Even by the time Brookes, who had wintered on the Riviera to get himself fit for another crack at the title, had deprived Wilding of his crown at Wimbledon, the lengthening shadow of war was falling across Europe.

The 1914 Davis Cup actually started on the understanding that Germany had withdrawn but after Otto Froitzheim had played well in reaching the All-Comers Final at Wimbledon where he lost to Brookes, the German No 1 changed his mind and decided that Germany would like to enter a team after all. It was a fateful decision for him and his partner Oscar Kreuzer; one that was aided and abetted by Brookes's generosity in agreeing to an American proposal that the German's earlier withdrawal be overlooked. Had Brookes refused, Froitzheim and Kreuser would doubtless have been in the Fatherland when war broke out instead of Pittsburgh. And who knows how differently their lives might have turned out.

1914

As it was Australasia, having disposed of Canada in Chicago 5–0, travelled over to the Allegheny Country Club near Pittsburgh to play Germany in the second round while the British Isles defeated the French at Wimbledon 4–1. It was the last days of July and the German war machine was preparing to engulf Belgium. The Great War was about to begin. Yet when the English writer Wallis Myers arrived in Pittsburgh he did not feel any great hostility between the players.

'Anthony Wilding had discovered an American motor that took his fancy,' Wallis wrote some time later, 'and, between his bouts of training, was sandwiching in some hill-climbing experiments. Brookes and Dunlop were enjoying recreative golf. The members of the German team, Froitzheim and Kreuzer were, when the hot day was over, in popular demand as dancing partners. Germany might be launching ultimata in Europe but there was no sign that her two lawn tennis envoys desired to fight anybody – except with a racket.'

Nevertheless the happenings in Europe were inescapable. Both Germans were in the Kaiser's army reserve and both announced that they would leave for home immediately if war was declared. And the Australasian team could not help noticing that the crowd, made up mostly of Americans with German heritage, was extremely partisan. When Brookes opened the tie against Froitzheim, German winners were greeted with wild applause while Australasian success was met with deafening silence. It was not what sport was supposed to be about in the Edwardian age and, under a poker-faced exterior, Brookes was furious. He took special satisfaction, therefore, in dispatching his opponent 10–8, 6–1, 6–2 and just as much pleasure in watching Wilding trounce Kruezer for the loss of just eight games. The doubles was even more of a rout for Australasia but, although the tie was won, etiquette demanded that the dead rubbers be played. Overnight, in the early hours of 1st August, East Coast Time, Germany declared war on Russia. Fearing disruption of his well-laid plans for a splendid final day's tennis, the Allegheny Club president took the somewhat drastic action of cutting off all telephone lines and barring reporters from the premises. Brookes and Wilding duly won the final two matches and departed with as much speed as they could muster for Boston where they were due to meet the British Isles on 6th August. Yet within three days Britain and Germany were at war and Froitzheim and Kreuzer were already halfway across the Atlantic. They never made it. Their ship was intercepted and both were interned in a prisoner of war camp in Britain for the duration. Ironically, it could easily have saved their lives.

Meanwhile Australasia and the British Isles faced off at the Longwood Cricket Club and chivalry prevailed. Parke, the indefatigable Irishman, was leading Brookes 5–4, 30–15 and serving in the fifth set of the opening rubber when Parke's racket brushed the net as he put away a volley. The winner would have given him match point. Neither Brookes nor the umpire noticed the infringement. But Parke held up his hand and the score was thirty-all instead of match point. Parke did not win another game and when Wilding survived an enervating third set in the steamy heat to beat Arthur Lowe 6–3, 6–1, 16–14 British hopes were fading. Brookes and Wilding killed them off with a ruthless display in the doubles and with the British players keen to set sail for home, the reverse singles were abandoned.

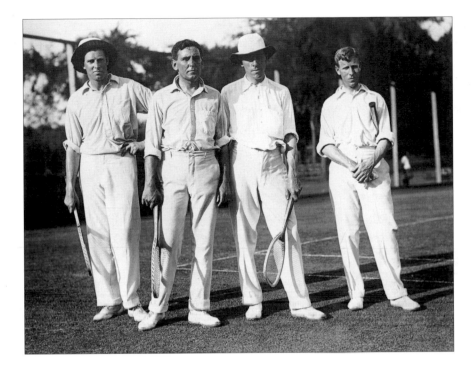

ABOVE: A TOUGH-LOOKING BUNCH, THIS QUARTET OF WILDING, DUNLOP, BROOKES AND
DOUST PICTURED AT LONGWOOD, WOULD GO TO THE FOREST HILLS A WEEK LATER AND RE-
CLAIM THE CUP FROM THE UNITED STATES IN THE AUTUMN OF 1914 AS WAR CLOUDS
GATHERED IN EUROPE.

The West Side Tennis Club had moved into its splendid new home at Forest Hills by
the time Brookes and Wilding arrived for the Challenge Round that was played
13th–15th August. The great bowl that would house so many famous matches in the
years to come was yet to be built. Stands were erected in front of the Tudor style clubhouse and 12,000 people turned up – the largest crowd ever to watch a tennis match
up to that time. The opening rubber was relatively brief, Wilding disposing of Richard
Williams in straight sets. So it was around 4pm when Brookes and Maurice
McLoughlin walked out to begin what would be remembered as one of the finest battles the Davis Cup had yet produced.

It certainly remained vividly in the mind of a young boy who was in the audience
and who would grow up to become one of the game's finest writers. In his book
Covering the Court, Al Laney would remember what effect McLoughlin's 17–15, 6–3,
6–3 triumph had on him.

'My confidence was shaken many times before that terribly long first set was over. Brookes gave the impression that he would never yield no matter how many thunderbolts our man might hurl at him, blows one never could have imagined possible with a tennis racket.

About halfway through, after what seemed an eternity, Brookes, who had served first and thus was forcing McLoughlin to battle for his life every time the American served, was love-forty against service. You would have to be a teenager again, I suppose, to suffer as I suffered then. But at this crisis, McLoughlin served three balls that Brookes could not even touch with his queer-shaped racket.

Other crises came later, near the end we could not know what was near. Brookes was again within a point of winning the set, and each time the answer was the same, an unreturnable service. Was ever a boyhood hero more worthy of worship?'

It was the longest set the Davis Cup had ever known and it finished Brookes. His strength sapped by the humidity and the effort required to stay with a younger, faster opponent proved too much. But he had recovered by the time he and Wilding faced McLoughlin and his friend Tom Bundy the following day. Bundy had been a controversial choice, somewhat forced on the selectors by McLoughlin's insistence that he should play but, in fact, it was the Comet himself who let the side down, especially in the early stages. The Americans, cheered on by a partisan crowd ill-schooled in the etiquette of watching a tennis match, tried hard to get back into the match but were eventually beaten 6–3, 8–6, 9–7.

Brookes knew that he had to win the first reverse singles against Williams to give Australasia a proper chance at winning the Cup. Wilding was not as fit as he had been and McLoughlin, desperate to revenge his defeat at Wimbledon the year before, would start a strong favourite if it all came down to a fifth rubber. At the outset there seemed little to hinder Norman's plans. He won the first two sets off Williams 6–1, 6–2 and served for the match at 8–7. But the American fought back and grabbed the set 10–8. Instead of merely celebrating this reprieve, the crowd's abuse heightened to hysteria. Amidst verbal abuse of court officials, Brookes, seething at such unsportsmanlike behaviour, stuck fingers in both ears – a gesture that only incited the crowd to further acts of stupidity. The Australian was called a cry baby and bottles were thrown onto the court. Some people leapt the fence and were arrested by police. Williams was appalled as the pair left the arena for the ten minutes break and Mabel Brookes was fearful of what might happen to her husband when he returned if the crowd continued to

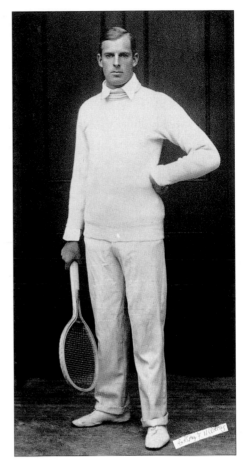

behave in such ugly fashion. In Crowded Galleries, she wrote:

'As he passed by the Davis Cup, he gave it a little reassuring pat and a twirl which was, I knew, quite unpremeditated. Once more he had regained his poise; there would have to be more than shouting and pop bottles to get him rattled. There was a moment's silence as he passed the Cup and came onto the court. Then the crowds recognised that all they had done was yet not enough, and he was returning, unbeaten, for more; and they started to applaud and the noise rose in volume until the cheering voices became a roar... A ballboy handed Norman his discarded racquet and the sound from the gallery lifted almost to hysteria. It was an ovation, a recognition of pure fighting guts. It was also hard on Dick Williams. He played well and doggedly, but the end was in sight.'

The end was in sight for many things. The lights, as Britain's Foreign Secretary Edward Grey would remark so memorably, were going out all over Europe. He suggested they would not be lit again in his lifetime. Brookes duly completed his victory; Wilding, his mind elsewhere, duly lost the fifth rubber, meaningless in every way except for the fact that it was the last match this magnificent sportsman would ever play. On returning to England, Wilding, eager to put his great passion for machines to best use, sought the help of his friend Winston Churchill, then First Lord of the Admiralty, to get him assigned to a motorised division in the British army once he had enlisted. Churchill obliged but, a mere nine months after that last Davis Cup triumph at Forest Hills, Prime Minister Asquith interrupted the business of the House to rise and announce, with deep regret, that Captain Anthony Wilding had fallen in Flanders.

CHAPTER SIX

TILDEN

*Big Bill becomes a star...playing his own sweet game.... Tilden banned
and the French plead for his re-instatement.... The Four Musketeers sharpen
their swords...and finally triumph*

THE GREAT WAR WAS OVER and Tony Wilding was dead. Others fell, too, in the most devastating carnage ever visited upon the human race but, for the little world of lawn tennis, Wilding was the greatest loss.

The age of Bill Tilden and the Four Musketeers was about to dawn but, in 1919, it was impossible to shake off the past. The ugly memories, the agony of perished loved ones, the bitterness towards the enemy – all these were emotions that lingered as the world community struggled to get itself back on track. It was not surprising, perhaps that people reached quickly for happier pastimes that had been laid aside during the height of the conflict and the Davis Cup was one of those. Its very nationalism fitted the mood of the age for there was a need to wave flags and play anthems in peaceful settings while still demonstrating partisan fervour for one's nation. People were coming to terms with the idea of having a national tennis team and Mabel Brookes, wife of the man who would later become Sir Norman, noted in her fascinating autobiography *Crowded Galleries* the change of perception that wrought.

> *'There is something that brings savour to life as nothing else when, reading his international sport news, the man in the street puts down his paper and says, "WE won the tennis" – the little "WE" automatically lifts the player involved into a sort of hierarchy. He belongs to his country... he has fought a battle, done a job for the people who now see themselves with him as one and indivisible.'*

Given the fierceness of sporting competition that has existed between the two countries over the years, it is difficult to envisage Australia and New Zealand being united as one on the tennis court but there seems little doubt that both Brookes and Wilding, the Aussie and the Kiwi, were acclaimed equally in Melbourne and Christchurch. Strangely the first hint that this partnership of nations might not last came at the official dinner for the first post war Challenge Round played between Australasia and the British Isles at Double Bay, Sydney. Brookes was the captain of the winning team and this somewhat austere man revealed the unsentimental side of his nature when he suggested in his speech that, the following year, the Cup should be defended in Australia rather than New Zealand, as was planned, as the latter country had produced no true successor to Wilding and would not, therefore, be represented on the team.

Brookes had spent much of the war as a Red Cross commissioner in Cairo and it is possible that the death of his friend four years before felt like a distant tragedy. They had embraced silently at Boulogne before Wilding rode off to the front on his motorcycle a few weeks before he was killed. On their last evening together Wilding had urged his friend not to enlist, citing his responsibility to his family, his age and, only half jokingly, suggested he would be a nuisance in the army because of his stomach ulcer. It must have come as a shock, therefore, to those who knew them both when Brookes suggested that the idea of honouring Wilding's memory by playing the 1920 Challenge Round in Auckland should not be carried through. Perhaps Brookes, knowing his old partner so well, felt that Wilding would have understood for, as his biographer Wallis Myers has written, the New Zealander 'was too practical to be sentimental, too honest to be suave.'

But sentimentality won the day. Brookes was overruled by his colleagues on the Australian LTA and the Challenge Round, introducing Tilden and his American team to the southern hemisphere, was duly played at the Domain Cricket Ground in Auckland; a white flag fluttering at the net in remembrance of the fallen hero. Observing a minute's silence before play began, Brookes doffed his cap.

But we are ahead of the story. Perhaps the gesture most indicative of the way sporting contests were viewed in the days before television ratings and huge prize money distorted sport's essential values was the decision of the USLTA not to compete in 1919. The United States had not entered the war until 1917 and had, therefore, suffered less than other nations. This was considered sufficient reason for the Americans to stand aside and allow others to regain their playing strength before offering another Challenge. This sense of chivalry mirrored the type of thinking that was only just beginning to die out, namely that practising too much was not the right thing to do as your opponent might not have had the chance to avail himself of such opportunities. Truly, it was a different age.

So, with the Americans sitting out, the British Isles seized the opportunity of making another appearance in the Challenge by beating France at Deauville. After making the long journey to Sydney, Algernon Kingscote, Arthur Lowe and Alfred Beamish found a much changed Australasian team. Brookes had been nursing a powerfully-built young man called Gerald Patterson since childhood when the boy used to pick up balls for his father Tom and himself when the two men played on Norman's own court in the Melbourne suburb of Kew. Now a strapping athlete with much of Brookes's fighting spirit but less of his skill, Patterson would become the first man to win Wimbledon at its new home on Church Road. He also righted the Australasian ship at Double Bay, beating Lowe after Kingscote had preyed on the nerves of the other player Brookes had brought onto the team, James O. Anderson, a hard hitting, hard living man with a typically long, lean Aussie face who was to become a Davis Cup stalwart for many years. Brookes took the court himself with Patterson to cut Kingscote and Beamish to pieces in the doubles 6–0, 6–0, 6–2 and set up what finished as a 4–1 victory.

The problems of sea travel cropped up again in 1920 when the departure of the ship that the US Team had planned to sail on was delayed so long that the players were in danger of missing Wimbledon. Happily the Secretary of War, Newton D. Blake, was a tennis fan and agreed to allow Dick Williams, Bill Tilden, Bill Johnston and Charles Garland to sail on the US Army transport vessel, *Northern Pacific,* which got them there in time. The list of challengers for the Cup had grown to six. Apart from the United States, the British Isles, Canada, France, Holland and South Africa were all entering teams. But first there was Wimbledon to play and Tilden's chances of making his Davis Cup début were thrown into doubt when he injured his knee chasing a lob against Zenzo Shimizu in the All-comer's final. The American Davis Cup captain, Sam Hardy, was nervous about Tilden suffering further injury with matches to be played right after the Championships but the thought of Patterson retaining the title with a walkover in the Challenge Round was dispiriting to everybody, especially the American camp who realised that Big Bill had a great opportunity of becoming the first American to win the men's singles crown. So, with the knee heavily taped, he played and, aiming his attack at Patterson's weak backhand, wrested the title from the Australian in four sets.

A week later, Tilden, showing no signs of discomfort, helped the States beat France at Eastbourne and then, back at Wimbledon, led the States to a 5–0 victory over the

ABOVE: BILL TILDEN. HE BESTRODE THE TENNIS WORLD LIKE A COLOSSUS UNTIL, DAGGERS DRAWN, THE USLTA CONSPIRED TO BRING HIM DOWN. YET, FOR THE GAME IN THE 1920s, HE WAS ALWAYS CAESAR.

ABOVE: ZENZO SHIMIZU AND ICHIYA KUMAGAE PUT JAPANESE TENNIS ON THE MAP BY REACHING THE CHALLENGE ROUND OF 1920.

LEFT: MANUEL ALONSO, SPAIN'S TOP DAVIS CUP PLAYER BETWEEN THE WARS.

British which was closer than the score indicates. Three of the rubbers went to five sets with the redoubtable James Parke, happily recovered after twice being wounded in the war, only succumbing to Johnston 6–2 in the fifth after a great struggle. The doubles, in which Parke and Kingscote initially led Tilden and Johnston by two sets to love, took place largely in the rain with the Americans playing in spikes for much of the time. 'Thanks are due to all four players for their disregard of rain,' wrote *Lawn Tennis & Badminton*. 'At times it literally pelted down and yet except for a brief halt prior to the final set there was no cessation in play. It was certainly very sportsmanlike on the part of our visitors to continue with their opponents leading them by two sets to one.' What the groundsman had to say about this state of affairs is not recorded.

The Dutch defaulted the final round, so the Americans set sail again at the end of the year for New Zealand, departing from Vancouver on the SS *Niagara* in the first week of December, a full month before the Challenge Round was due to be played. After the remembrance for Wilding, Brookes, having selected himself for the singles despite his age – he was 43 – threw himself into a memorable battle with Tilden in the opening rubber. The veteran left-hander held set point at 5–3 only to lose the first 10–8. Tilden also took the second but Brookes continued to worry the tall American with his kicking service and suddenly reeled off nine games in a row to take the third 6–1 and lead 3–0 in the fourth. Tilden hauled himself back to parity at 3–3 and then Brookes, visibly tiring, made life even harder for himself through his innate sense of fair play. He signalled to the umpire that his opponent had been wrongly double-faulted. The umpire refused to change the call, however, so Brookes hit the next serve out of court and Tilden held. Showing the instinct for the kill that would win him so many matches in the years that followed, Big Bill slammed the Australian's weakening serve back at his feet and closed it out 6–4.

Patterson, unable to protect his backhand from Johnston's assault, was beaten 6–3, 6–1, 6–1 and there was no way back for Australasia. The Americans regained the Cup with a 5–0 victory and the Auckland crowd were left to ponder how different it might have been had Tony Wilding been alive.

By 1921, the world was trying very hard to enjoy itself again. Smart young men were haring around in Bugattis with amazing young ladies in the passenger seat while in all the swish night clubs from Monaco to Manhattan the flappers kicked their heels and danced the Charleston. Lawn tennis fitted snugly alongside this socialite revelry but the Davis Cup offered something more. Stretching boundaries beyond the normal confines of the Eastern Seabord, the South of France and Wimbledon, the international team competition drew more and more interest from countries around the world.

Suddenly Davis Cup ties were being played all over the place. Belgium, for whom Jean Washer was starting a long family association with Belgian tennis, defeated Czechoslovakia in Prague; Spain came to London only to get beaten 4–1 by the British Isles in a tie played at the London Country Club in Hendon while in the second round India sprang a surprise by beating France in Paris. The Indians, in turn, went down to Japan in Chicago but Zenzo Shimizu and Ichiya Kumagae were far from finished. They travelled on to Newport, Rhode Island and astonished an Australasian team missing Norman Brookes and Gerald Patterson by winning 4–1. In the preceding weeks, the Australasians had been good enough to defeat Canada 5–0 when that nation, led by a gentleman rejoicing in the name of Henri Laframboise, had staged its first home tie at the Toronto Lawn Tennis Club and then, a week later, the British Isles 3–2 at the Allegheny Country Club near Pittsburgh. Their work still not done, Norman Peach, the Australasian captain, then helped James O. Anderson to dispatch Denmark 5–0 at Cleveland. But neither Anderson, nor John Hawkes, who was re-instated as the second singles player to face the Japanese, had been asked to deal with a player as wily as Shimizu. Taking the sting out of Anderson's powerful strokes, he returned everything with genteel accuracy and won in straight sets. The modest crowd at the famous Newport Casino were almost as mesmerised as the Australians. They never recovered their composure and secured their only victory in the doubles.

At Forest Hills in the Challenge Round, a crowd of 14,000 turned out to see what kind of a fight the Japanese could put up against Big Bill Tilden and Little Bill Johnston, the duo who would dominate American tennis throughout the twenties. Johnston wasted little time with the left handed Kumagae but Shimizu, whom Tilden described as having one of the most brilliant, subtle brains in tennis history, caused his opponent all manner of trouble on a hot, humid September afternoon.

Tilden had been ill at Wimbledon that year and was suffering from a boil on his foot. Shimizu made the most of this by drop-shotting and lobbing his way though the first two sets 7–5, 6–4 and was leading 5–3 in the third before Tilden started to hit out desperately and turned it around 7–5.

On a hot day, those steps leading up to the locker room at the West Side Tennis Club have never been an inviting prospect and they seemed like a mountainside to Tilden now. Having made the climb, Bill staggered straight into a cold shower. When his captain Sam Hardy asked what he could do for him, Tilden commanded, 'Undress me!'

Hardy knew better than to hesitate with Tilden. Sacrificing his suit, he reached into the shower and helped to pull Tilden's clothes off. Then a doctor was summoned to lance the boil and remove the pus. When the players returned to court, Tilden was a new man while Shimizu, who had neither changed nor showered, felt stiff and soon seized up with cramps. Tilden won the last two sets for the loss of only three games.

Japan eventually lost 5–0 but the very act of getting to the Challenge Round had put the game on the map back home and turned the Davis Cup into a competition

ABOVE: AT FOREST HILLS IN THE 1921 CHALLENGE ROUND, BILL TILDEN NEEDED A SHOWER
AT THE BREAK BEFORE HE COULD RECOVER AND BEAT THE TALENTED ZENZO SHIMIZU.

that encouraged every nation to join in. For some, however, the spirit was willing but
the wherewithal weak. In 1922 a record 14 countries issued a challenge but Canada,
the Philippines, Hawaii (then a separate nation) and even Japan for whom Kumagae
had retired, were unable to come up with suitable teams.

But a significant double début occurred in Copenhagen when Jean Borotra and

1922

ABOVE: AUSTRALIA'S NEW STAR GERALD PATTERSON, LEFT, ON HIS WAY TO BEATING THE
FRENCHMAN ANDRÉ GOBERT IN THE THIRD ROUND OF THE 1922 COMPETITION AT LONGWOOD.

Henri Cochet helped France beat Denmark 4–1 in the second round. Although
Jacques Brugnon had been part of the team that had lost to India the year before, this
was the first time the nucleus of the Four Musketeers appeared in Davis Cup colours.
French tennis was on the eve of an 'epoch glorieuse'.

With Gerald Patterson, the first post-war Wimbledon champion, now leading
Australasia under the captaincy of his mentor, Norman Brookes, France found themselves outplayed later in the year in Boston despite a five set victory for the 20-year-old
Cochet against Patrick O'Hara Wood. Spain were Australasia's last opponents before
Challenge Round showdown against the United States in New York and only the mercurial Manuel Alonso, with a five set victory over O'Hara Wood after the Australian had
been footfaulted on match point in the fourth, prevented a clean sweep.

The 1922 Challenge Round showed Tilden at his most petty and vindictive. Against his wishes, the USTA nominated Vincent Richards to partner Tilden in the doubles. Vinnie Richards had been hailed as a wonder boy when he won the US Doubles championship with Tilden at the age of fifteen. He was one of Bill's boys; one of the protégés he liked to nurse through adolescence, not necessarily for sexual gratification but often for companionship and fulfilment as a coach. But he expected a degree of subservience. When Richards started to get cocky and talk about closing the gap between himself and the maestro, Tilden started poaching shots in outrageous fashion when playing in their third National Doubles final, so that Vinnie was completely upstaged and made to look a fool.

Tilden was still unamused by Richards's attitude and, unforgivably, carried the dispute on court with him in the doubles against Australasia. The fact that the United States were already 2–0 up and very unlikely to lose either of the reverse singles, did not excuse Tilden's blatant decision to throw the match. Apparently determined to prove the selectors wrong, Tilden won just seven points off his own racket in three appalling sets while committing 25 unforced errors. According to Tilden's biographer, Frank Deford, 'There was name-calling in the USLTA for months thereafter about the selection of Richards. He was not allowed to play doubles again for the United States for three more years.'

So what kind of man was this colossus who was suddenly bestriding American tennis with his long, angular looks, biting wit, imperious manner and late blooming talent? A strange man, for sure, a man as unique in his way as the other extraordinary personalities this game has attracted over the years – Suzanne Lenglen, Martina Navratilova, Ilie Nastase, John McEnroe, Boris Becker, to name but a few. Not the least extraordinary aspect of Tilden's career was that he didn't start winning anything of significance until the age of 27. He then went on to dominate the game like few before or since winning three titles at Wimbledon, seven at Forest Hills, including a six-year sweep from 1920 to 1925, and leading an American team that won the Davis Cup seven consecutive years through the twenties. Tilden raised the game's profile, often notoriously, to a level it had never known before.

Deford captures the man brilliantly in his book *Big Bill Tilden* and tells the story of Bill as a schoolboy playing at Germantown Academy in Philadelphia when one of his friends, Frank Deacon, came by and saw him hitting balls wildly out of court. Using the nickname he hated, Deacon called out, 'Hey, June, take it easy!'

'Tilden stopped dead,' writes Deford, 'and with what became a characteristic gesture, he swirled to face the boy, placing his hands on hips and glaring at him. "Deacon", he snapped, "I'll play my own sweet game."

'And so he did, every day of his life. He was the proudest of men and the saddest, pitifully alone and shy, but never so happy as when he brought his armful of rackets into the limelight or walked into a crowded room and contentiously took it over. George Lott, a Davis Cup colleague and a man who actively disliked Tilden, was nonetheless mesmerised by him. "When he came into a room it was like a bolt of electricity hit the place," said Lott. "Immediately, there was a feeling of awe, as though you were in the presence of royalty. The atmosphere became charged and there was almost a sensation of lightness when he left."

'Tilden himself said, "I can only stand crowds when I am working in front of them, but then I love them." Obviously the crowds and the game were his sex. For a large part of life, the glory years, all the evidence suggests that he was primarily asexual. It was not until he began to fade as a player and there were not enough crowds to play to that his homosexual proclivities really took over.'

Deford goes on to point out, however, that for all the excesses of drama and melodrama, his passion for competition was itself even superseded by another higher sense – that of sportsmanship. This despite his spiteful treatment of Richards which, in any case, had nothing to do with the honour of the game, merely the petty part of his own insecure nature.

'Tilden was utterly scrupulous, obsessed with honour, and he would throw points (albeit with grandeur, Pharisee more than Samaritan) if he felt the linesman had cheated his opponent. Bill was the magistrate of every match he played, and the critic as well. "Peach!" he would cry in delight, lauding any opponent who beat him with a good shot.'

That Bill Tilden was a peach of a player was never in doubt. As Deford points out, those who think of him simply as a guy with a cannonball serve don't know the half of it. The only thing he didn't do well on a tennis court was volley. To him, serve and volley types were dullards. He was far more interested in the more testing mechanics of the game. He wrote some of the best 'How to Play' manuals ever known. What he wanted from his own game was variety and everyone who opposed him will talk of the vast repertoire he carried in his arsenal. He did have a cannonball serve but used it sparingly, mixing it with a high kicker to the backhand and the heavy slice which pulled the ball the other way. But the serve was only part of it. Fred Perry, who played him more than a hundred times on the professional tour in the thirties, got a longer, closer look than most. 'Sometimes he would play slow, sometimes fast,' wrote Perry in his autobiography. 'He would mix top spin with slice. He was always trying something different. When Tilden walked on court he was the king. He dominated the scene.'

With Perry on the other side of the net that was not an easy thing to achieve. But Tilden was also ready to learn even after he had passed his peak. He asked Perry to practise with him one day and, after asking for a series of shots low and wide to the forehand, told Fred, 'After playing so many matches with you and studying your style, I realised that the continental grip, not my own Eastern grip, is the only one for that sort of shot. I felt I wouldn't be the complete tennis player unless I mastered it.' Tilden was in his early 40s at the time.

Manuel Alonso, the best Spanish player of Tilden's era, noted the amount of time Tilden had taken to perfect his footwork. 'It was like seeing Nijinsky dance across the net,' Alonso said. 'I saw Nijinsky once and he went across a whole stage in three jumps. Tilden was that way. He played a game that made you feel so uncomfortable. Even if you had played very well, you came off court feeling that you had not done well at all.'

Tilden did so well that the United States went on winning the Davis Cup. Mostly with Bill Johnston, the only man capable of offering him more than token resistance in championship play during this period, playing second singles, the Americans held the Cup for seven years before the power was transferred back across the Atlantic with France holding it for the next six.

In 1923 and 1924, the Australians, playing for the last time as a combined entity with New Zealand and then, finally, in '24, simply as Australia, made two more stabs at wrenching the Cup out of American hands. In '23, having beaten Hawaii in a tie played in Orange, New Jersey; then Japan in Chicago and the French, with the 19-year-old René Lacoste playing singles, at Boston, the Australians knew they would be in for a far more difficult time at the West Side in New York and so it proved. Anderson managed to level the tie on the first day by beating Johnston in five sets but he could not repeat that success in the reverse singles against Tilden, losing 7–5 in the fourth. The States retained the Cup by a 4–1 margin.

1923

In 1924, the Australians gained some measure of revenge over Shimizu and his colleagues by beating Japan 5–0 at Providence, Rhode Island and then moved onto Boston for the Inter-Zone final against a French team that proved somewhat more

1924

difficult to subdue than 12 months previously. This time Lacoste won both his singles over Patterson and O'Hara Wood but Jean Borotra could not win either of his and the Australians ensured a passage to the Challenge Round – to be played this time at the Germantown Cricket Club in Philadelphia – by beating Lacoste and Jacques Brugnon in the doubles.

Although Tilden and Johnston assumed the doubles duties in the Challenge Round, Vinnie Richards, still only 21, had been forgiven sufficiently to be entrusted with a singles berth and he did not let the side down. Beating O'Hara Wood in straight sets on the opening day, he completed

LEFT: JEAN BOROTRA, THE BOUNDING BASQUE, AND HIS EXTRAVAGANT BACKHAND.

BELOW: RENÉ LACOSTE AND A BACKHAND OF GREATER PRECISION.

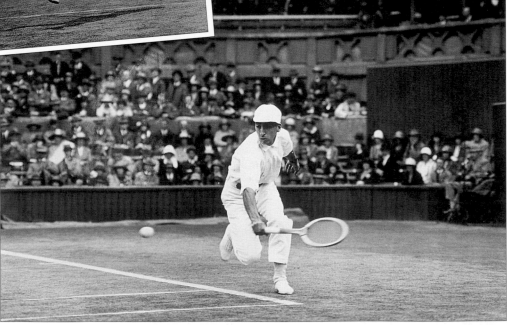

ABOVE: RENÉ LACOSTE – DRIVING FORCE IN FRENCH TENNIS THROUGH THE 1920S.

a 5–0 rout by disposing of Patterson by the same margin in the second of the dead rubbers. But it was Tilden who set the tone of the tie in his own inimitable way. His 6–4, 6–2, 6–2 victory over Patterson, one of the strongest players of the era, was described thus by American Lawn Tennis: 'Throughout the match Tilden looked as if he were merely practising his strokes, or experimenting with them. He paid comparatively little attention to Patterson's shots. If they were good, as they not infrequently were, he let them go. It was his own shots that he was thinking of most of the time, studying them as if he were in a laboratory and they specimens.'

For the next two years, the Four Musketeers spent their time sharpening their blades in the preliminary ties as, with the certainty of Douglas Fairbanks advancing through the hordes with his trusty rapier on the silver screen, they fought their way through to the Challenge Round, never losing more than one live rubber in any tie

ABOVE: THE CROCODILE – NO INSIGNIA YET ON THE SWEATER OF RENÉ LACOSTE, THE
YOUNGEST AND MOST INVENTIVE OF THE FOUR MUSKETEERS.

1925 they played. But, for those two years, 1925 and '26 in Philadelphia, their skills were still insufficiently honed to handle the two Bills. The 5–0 margin of the first encounter was, however, misleading. Jean Borotra took Tilden to five sets in the opening rubber and then, in a match that no longer had any bearing on the result, Tilden and René Lacoste put themselves through one of the most thrilling and exhausting duels in the history of the Cup. National honour and personal pride were what drove the American to extract a 3–6, 10–12, 8–6, 7–5, 6–2 victory over the much younger Frenchman who, according to Wallis Myers 'had been dreaming of his first meeting with Tilden since he first put shoe to court.'

As the dream became reality Tilden looked stunned. In his certain and unhurried fashion, Lacoste led the man who had not lost an important match for six years by two sets and 4–0 in the third. The American appeared to be on the point of collapse. Still not in the best of health, he frequently staggered about court and, at changeovers, poured water over his head. It mattered little for he was already soaked in sweat. Calling for a bottle of aromatic ammonia, he swigged great gulps of it before his captain, Sam Hardy, could restrain him. But it seemed to work. Fighting back to take the third set and benefiting from the seven-minute break, he slowly started to take control with his bold placements. Even then he had to save four match points at 5–6 in the fourth before the man who was already known as the Crocodile was forced to succumb.

Lacoste, the youngest and most introverted of the four men who would lead French tennis to its greatest glories, simply went back to the drawing board. He knew he did not have Tilden's power or flair but he became determined to overcome these shortcomings through meticulous preparation. Even so, he might never have beaten the man he admired so much, had Tilden not re-injured a chronically damaged knee when their meeting in the 1926 Challenge Round stood at one set all and six-all in the third. The score was already 4–0 to the States and Tilden should have stopped. But a combination of vanity and bravery forced him to continue until, finally, Lacoste nailed him 8–6 in the fourth.

A year later, still in Philadelphia, Lacoste repeated that victory and this time it mattered a good deal. Under the shrewd and meticulous guidance of their captain, Pierre Gillou, the Musketeers had proved their versatility en route to the Challenge Round by defeating Romania 4–1 in Paris; Italy 3–2 in Rome; South Africa 5–0 at Eastbourne and Japan 5–0 at Boston. Now finally, they were ready for the Americans. While the USLTA squabbled amongst themselves as to who should replace the successful doubles team of Richards and Williams now that Richards had turned professional, the French team, according to Wallis Merrihew, was 'a homogenous one, keyed up to concert pitch and sanguine of success. Everything had been planned, all was ready.'

Borotra and Brugnon would play doubles so as to leave Cochet and Lacoste fresh for the singles. Tilden, at the age of 34, was being asked to carry a heavier burden. After Bill Johnston, who was 33 himself, had fallen in three sets to Lacoste after a summer in which he had played little tennis, Tilden carried that burden against Cochet with his customary élan, buoyed no doubt by the warmth of the support he received from his home-town crowd. It has not always been that way. With his flam-

ABOVE: THE US TEAM OF 1925 – LEFT TO RIGHT: DICK WILLIAMS WHO SURVIVED THE *TITANIC*,
VINNIE RICHARDS WHO WAS TILDEN'S PROTEGE, 'LITTLE BILL' JOHNSTON WHO WAS 'BIG
BILL'S' BIGGEST RIVAL AND THE MAN HIMSELF, WILLIAM J. TILDEN 2ND.

boyant arrogance and queer mannerisms, sections of Philadelphia society had not
taken well to their native son. But now, the nobility of his achievements and his unwavering dedication to his country's cause touched a chord of sympathy amongst the
12,000 well-heeled spectators crammed into the Germantown Cricket Club and they
helped him survive a spirited fight back from Cochet to win in four sets.

Just when he needed to husband his energy, Tilden had expended much emotional
energy in arguing with the selectors over the choice of his partner in the doubles.
Johnston had been nominated but he was a spent force and, indeed, retired after the
tie. Tilden wanted his friend Frank Hunter to play and the USLTA only bowed to Bill's
wishes one hour before the doubles was due to start on the Friday afternoon. A 6–0
scoreline in the fifth set to the Americans suggests that Tilden was vindicated in his

choice of partner as, in a sense, he was. But Borotra and Brugnon were well satisfied. One of their main aims had been to keep Tilden out there for as long as possible and five sets, sprinkled with lobs and enervating rallies, had done the job. Against Lacoste the following day, Tilden found himself ground into the turf by the relentless accuracy of the Frenchman's stroke play. Often driving down the middle of the court and varying his length with looped returns off the backhand, the Crocodile got Tilden between his jaws and never let go, winning in four sets to draw France level at 2–2. It was spitting with rain when Little Bill took the court against Cochet to play his last Davis Cup match and no one knew whether the specks of wet on the cheeks of some spectators were from the rain or tears that had been shed at Big Bill's demise. He had looked startled as he left the arena, arms aloft to acknowledge applause of a kind he had never heard before at this club where a great career had been born. Now he had to rely on his old partner and rival to prevent the Cup going to France.

Johnston gave it all he knew but he seemed a small, almost pathetic figure as he struggled for breath; advance warning of the tuberculosis which would strike him shortly afterwards. Nevertheless, having managed to win the second set, Johnston fought back again in the fourth, offering the emotional crowd one last moment of hope. At 2–5 down, he broke Cochet's service to love and suddenly it was the Frenchman who looked bewildered. 'I suddenly felt empty and uncoordinated,' he remarked afterwards. 'Almost as if I was unable to connect with the ball.'

He was saved, not by his captain Gillou, but by the soothing voice of Lacoste. Gillou had become too nervous to remain in the captain's chair and Lacoste, both the baby and the intellectual leader of the team, had taken his place. Reassured by René, Cochet went back out there under the glowering clouds and, at the end of a tumultuous rally worthy of the historic prize it earned, won the first match point to close out the fourth set 6–4 and so enable France to become the first non-English speaking nation to hold the Cup. The moment was vividly recalled by Lacoste in his autobiography:

> *'Madame Cochet fainted; Pierre Gillou sprang up like a child; I took off my overcoat and sweaters; Brugnon dropped his pipe and Borotra – well, you can imagine him justifying his reputation as 'The Bounding Basque'. Everything after that seemed like a dream. The Davis Cup delivered to our team, a thousand photographs, uniting the players with the French Ambassador and the American Minister for War, Dwight Davis, the giver of the Cup. The memories of it all seem like a fantasy.'*

ABOVE: FRENCH CAPTAIN PIERRE GILLOU RACES UP TO EMBRACE HIS MAN AS A TRIUMPHANT HENRI COCHET SHAKES HANDS WITH BILL TILDEN AFTER THE AMERICAN HAD BEEN RE- INSTATED AMIDST THE DRAMA FOR THE 1928 CHALLENGE ROUND AT THE NEW STADE ROLAND GARROS.

But it was real enough and for Davis, surely, a moment of mixed emotions. He would have felt for his compatriots in their defeat but he was delighted, too, that his vision of the competition he had created becoming a truly international affair had now taken hold. Other European nations would be inspired by the Cup's presence in Paris as, indeed, they were. But another World War would be fought before any of them would emulate the success of the Four Musketeers.

1928

The following year brought about one of the most bizarre situations Davis's great competition has ever created and, inevitably, Bill Tilden was at the centre of it. The extent of Tilden's fame, in an age when sport received nothing like the space or promi- nence in the news media that it does today, can be gauged by the furore that erupted when the USLTA attempted to have Big Bill removed from the Davis Cup team that was due to play Italy in Paris and, assuming a widely anticipated victory, France in the 1928 Challenge Round at the spanking new Stade Roland Garros. The tumult relegated the assassination of Mexico's President-elect and lost aviators in the Arctic to secondary leads on the front pages of American newspapers. The US Ambassador in France became embroiled in the controversy which also reached the desk of President Coolidge at the White House. And the cause of it? Newspaper columns that Tilden had been writing most of his life but which, in the eyes of some officials, had contained comments that were 'too current', thereby infringing those well-known rules sporting bodies erect to protect themselves from criticism, aimed at them by people who know more than they do. Players, for instance.

The problem the USLTA had with their No 1 player over this particular issue was that Tilden had been a journalist long before he became a tennis champion. He had been writing ever since leaving college and, when he joined the long list of top athletes who had their names above columns appearing in all the popular papers, he, as usual, was different. For the words below were written by Tilden himself. His gaunt, willowy frame may have resembled a ghost on occasion but he never employed one to write his articles and that put the USLTA in a very difficult position. How could they stop a man following his career? Heaven knows but they tried. In 1924, after a hearing on the subject, the USLTA issued a ruling that all players must stop writing about tennis for remuneration on 1st January 1925. Tilden's response, to the Association's utter astonishment, was to sign a contract to write a syndicated column worth $20,000 a year. Mike Myrick, who virtually ran American tennis through the twenties whether he was actually President of the USLTA or not, was apoplectic. Even Holcombe Ward, a member of that original Davis Cup team, was pressured into admitting that, while Tilden was a great tennis player and interesting writer, he was also a 'bad influence.'

Climbing onto his highest horse, Tilden had a field day with that. Righteous indignation poured forth and the public bought it. A Bill Tilden Fair Play Society was formed and eventually another meeting was convened, sensibly bringing in non-tennis people like the polo star Devereaux Milburn and Senator George Wharton Pepper. They finally decided that a player could write about the game as long as he did not cover the event he was participating in. Thus it was that, when Tilden's articles from London in 1928, were trailed as 'Tilden Reviews First Week's Play at Wimbledon', Dr Sumner Hardy, a USLTA official living in San Francisco and reading his Chronicle over breakfast, decided that this was too current. It was then that grown men, as Frank

Deford observes wryly, prepared to assemble and ponder that possibility.

In fact, certain members of the USLTA saw this as another opportunity to clip the wings of the only bird in their aviary who not only flew about in his own sweet time but frequently pelted them with droppings from a great height. The objection to the articles was merely a means to an end, just as the row over whether Niki Pilic should have played Davis Cup for Yugoslavia in 1973, which led to the Association of Tennis Professionals boycotting Wimbledon, was merely a ruse by the amateur International Lawn Tennis Federation to curb the growth of professional player power.

So, while men in frock coats were pondering his fate across the Atlantic, Tilden took the *Golden Arrow* from Victoria Station to the Gare du Nord and on 19th July, was lurking somewhere in the Carlton Hotel when Joseph Wear, a Davis Cup committeeman officiating at the draw of the tie between the United States and Italy, announced that the man who was supposed be captaining the American team had been removed from the post. Although it was not spelt out there and then, a USLTA meeting in New York had decided to ban Tilden for violating Paragraph 4, Section B of the 'Amateur Writer Rule.' Wear's statement was greeted with near-hysteria. Journalists were scrambling for phones when Tilden made a dramatic entrance and many stopped to cheer him. A member of the Italian team Baron Umberto de Morpurgo, embraced him and said, 'I'm sorry, Bill, this has taken all the fun out of it.'

The French Federation were thinking much the same thing but for rather more practical reasons. They had just spent a fortune on building this magnificent new tennis stadium on the edge of the Bois de Boulogne and had been selling tickets by the sack load. The attraction of the Four Musketeers against an American team led by Bill Tilden was irresistible. Take out Tilden and with him went the bubble from the champagne. Within hours of the news getting out, people were asking for their money back. It was a mixture of French arrogance and good business sense that led the French Federation to complain over the fact that the opposition was actually making itself weaker. They thought the Musketeers could win whether Big Bill played or not – and they were right – but they also knew just how much money they would lose if he didn't.

Happily for the French, Tilden was not the sort of man to go quietly. His melodramatic entrance was made with the timing of a man who had worked in the theatre and he had the lines to go with it. 'I refute all charges!' he cried out. 'We will win the Davis Cup!' The scene was surreal. The press were cheering and his would-be opponents, the Four Musketeers, were crowding around him in commiseration. 'Ah! Mon pauvre

Beel. Quel dommage!' And they meant it. The Musketeers had striven so hard over so many years to bring the Cup to Paris and now they wanted the honour of defending it against the only foe who mattered. Even members of his own team, like George Lott who personally couldn't stand him, rose up in indignation at the absurdity of the ruling. In fact it was Lott who suggested that the whole American team should go on strike. Tilden talked them out of it but Wear, who had taken Tilden's place as captain on orders from New York, did resign from the USLTA in protest. And even the Association President, Samuel H. Collom, who had been at sea when the suspension order came through, was so appalled at the reaction on his arrival in Paris that he immediately got on the phone to Mike Myrick in New York and argued for so long that his phone bill came to $1,950. But even at that expense, Collom obviously had little clout. Myrick and a group of cronies ran the USLTA and they were not going to relent. Not, at least, until they discovered to their horror that the American public were siding with Tilden. In their hearts, they were hoping that their team would lose to Italy but Frank Hunter, John Hennessy and Lott deprived them of that easy escape route by winning 4–1.

By this time diplomatic telegrams were zinging across the Atlantic. The French Federation had contacted the Quai d'Orsay over the issue and the French Foreign Office, in turn, were leaning on the American Ambassador, Myron Herrick. Urged on by Washington with the tacit understanding that President Coolidge was in favour, Herrick virtually took over the selection of the team for the Challenge Round. Agreeing to let the USLTA discipline Tilden after it was all over, the Ambassador allowed the association to announce that, 'in the interest of international good feeling', Tilden would be permitted to play in Paris.

All this took place barely 24 hours before the tie was due to begin and, having heard of his reprieve at the draw, Tilden rushed off to Roland Garros to practise, something he hadn't done for days. 'He was practically hysterical,' said Junior Coen, another of Bill's boys who had been brought onto the team. 'He couldn't hit a damn thing so finally he just stormed off.'

A wind storm was blowing when the Challenge Round finally got underway. The red clay was swirling around the Centre Court, then surrounded by wooden stands and a fire started in one corner. By the time it had been put out, an emotional and disorientated Tilden had lost the first set to Lacoste 6–1. There should have been no way back from that for a 35-year-old playing the reigning Wimbledon and US champion. Tilden had lost to the Frenchman in their four previous meetings and surely this was going to be a fifth. But, ever the improviser, ever the artist, Tilden changed his make-up. If the role doesn't work one way, try another. So he started slicing every shot and, ignoring whatever power was left in his strokes, began outsteadying the steadiest of opponents. 'If Tilden could not beat Lacoste as Tilden,' wrote Deford, 'then he would beat Lacoste as Lacoste.'

And he did: 1–6, 6–4, 6–4, 2–6, 6–3. His team mates watched in growing disbelief and Lott described it as a 'display of versatility that has never been equalled.' (And it probably never was until Arthur Ashe slow-balled Jimmy Connors to defeat in the 1975 Wimbledon final).

For Lacoste, the shock was profound. Slumped in the dressing room afterwards, he asked of his team-mates, 'Two years ago I knew at last how to beat him. Now, on my own court, he beats me. I never knew how the ball would come off the court, he concealed it so well. I had to wait to see how much it was spinning – and sometimes it didn't spin at all. Is he not the greatest player of all time?'

There are those, even today, who will answer Lacoste in the affirmative. But even the greatest player could not save his team that memorable weekend in Paris. Cochet defeated Hennessy 6–0 in the fourth and after Cochet and Borotra had kept Tilden and Hunter on court for five sets before giving France a 2–1 lead, Big Bill had little left to offer against Cochet and went down, fighting as best he could, 9–7, 8–6, 6–4.

So the Cup stayed in Paris, as it did the following year when the Americans returned. Tilden, suspended for the remainder of 1928 on his return to New York, was back on the team for a Last Hurrah that seemed in danger of becoming a sad farewell when Cochet toyed with him in the opening rubber of the 1929 Challenge Round. A score of 6–3, 6–1, 6–2 was humiliating but the new doubles team of Wilmer Allison and John Van Ryn kept the United States in the tie by beating Cochet and Borotra and then Tilden restored his reputation by beating Borotra who seldom gave him much trouble. Cochet, on whom great responsibility had fallen with the permanent withdrawal through illness of Lacoste, won a nervous decider over Lott 6–3 in the fourth.

———

That was supposed to have been Tilden's swansong but, after Allison, Lott and Van Ryn had taken the States past Canada, Mexico and Italy in the previous rounds, Joseph Wear, re-instated as chairman of the US Davis Cup committee, announced that Tilden would be returning to the team. The man who had won Wimbledon the year before had been called in as coach for the Inter-Zone tie against Italy that had been played in Paris just a few days before – a tie that had been more of a struggle for the Americans than the 4–1 score suggested. Allison, in fact, had staged one of the great recoveries against the ambidextrous Giorgio de Stefani after falling behind by two sets to love. Having levelled at two sets all, Allison seemed doomed again when the Italian led 5–1 in the fifth but he refused to give in and, fighting for every ball on the slow clay, battled all the way back to clinch it 10–8. After Lott had beaten de Morpurgo, Allison and Van Ryn won the doubles in five sets. Allison, with good reason, looked weary in the dead rubber while losing to de Morpurgo and Wear offered this reason for replacing the young Texan with Tilden for the Challenge Round. The French Federation, having just spent even more money building the Centre Court as we know it today, were

BELOW: THE TEAM THAT WOULD DEFEAT THE UNITED STATES FOR THE THIRD STRAIGHT YEAR LINE UP AT ROLAND GARROS IN 1929 – JACQUES BRUGNON, HENRI COCHET, PIERRE GILLOU, RENÉ LACOSTE AND JEAN BOROTRA.

delighted to welcome back their biggest box office attraction but the man himself was not so sure. Tilden accepted the offer to play 'against my wishes and despite my better judgement'. None of this, of course, stopped him going out and producing another mesmerising performance against the hapless Borotra despite the fact that he had turned an ankle in practice the day before. The man with the trademark beret, who would still be playing tennis in his nineties must have thought he was finally in with a chance against Big Bill but, not for the first time he was wrong. At 6–2, 5–2 down Tilden stopped limping and promptly won five straight games. Suddenly Borotra didn't know where his next point was coming from and Tilden re-affirmed the hold he had on the Bounding Basque by winning 7–5 in the fourth. It was America's only victory in the tie. Cochet brought down the curtain on Tilden as the Davis Cup player – surely the greatest of his roles – by beating him in four sets in the second of the reverse singles on a day that saw people try to storm the gates of Roland Garros after thousands had been turned away. Big Bill was big business but now it was all over. Tilden had played in 11 successive Challenge Rounds and only two men had beaten him – Lacoste twice and Cochet three times. It required the emergence of the great Don Budge seven years later for the United States to get near the Challenge Round again. Within two months of that 1930 meeting in Paris, Tilden had signed a movie contract and turned pro. He still had roles to play. But none as glamorous as the Davis Cup.

CHAPTER SEVEN

PERRY

Bamboozled in Berlin, Fred finally leads Britain to glory in Paris.... Fainting and fighting, the English hero dominates the world game.... Bands play 'God Save the King' as Perry, Cochet and the Cup tour the Paris night spots

THE WORLD MIGHT HAVE BEEN IN THE THROES OF THE GREAT DEPRESSION but the Davis Cup continued to thrive. Twenty nations entered the European Zone in 1930 and new stars were emerging to challenge the dominance of the Four Musketeers. Some were giants in every sense like the 6-foot 3-inch Czech, Roderick Menzel, who wrote poetry when he was not unleashing high kicking serves at opponents on the tennis court. Or Frank X. Shields, grandfather of Brooke, whose good looks led him into all manner of escapades with the opposite sex, not the least of which was the night he drove a girl from Paris to Le Havre so that she could catch the ship for New York and then sailed with her, attired in his dinner jacket. For the whole voyage, he could only emerge from her cabin at night for he had nothing else to wear. Presumably they shared toothbrushes.

And then there was Baron Gottfried von Cramm, possibly one of the best players never to have won Wimbledon. Universally admired as one of the great sportsmen of the age, von Cramm fell foul of Hitler and was imprisoned on homosexual charges. Later he was actively involved in the plot to assassinate the Fuehrer and, unlike some of his co-conspirators, survived to help rebuild German tennis after the war.

But none of these could match the personality or achievements of the man who single-handedly revived British interest in the Davis Cup and went on to become the greatest English player of all time. Frederick J. Perry was the son of a Labour Party MP who did not fit into the middle class fabric with which lawn tennis, in the 1930s, was inextricably entwined. Unlike his friend and Davis Cup coach Dan Maskell, who came from an equally modest background, Perry did not help his cause by giving full reign to his cocky, caustic wit and ruthless ambition. As an opponent, Fred would have been a handful today. He must have appeared totally insufferable in that era when cries of

ABOVE: SLEEK AND GRACEFUL, FRED PERRY IN ACTION AT WIMBLEDON IN 1933 – THE YEAR HE
HELPED BRITAIN WIN THE DAVIS CUP FOR THE FIRST TIME IN 21 YEARS.

'Oh! Jolly good shot, old chap!' echoed round country club lawns. Above all he was a
winner. He led Britain to four consecutive Davis Cup triumphs and won Wimbledon in
three successive years. He also won the other three Grand Slams at least once, something only Don Budge and Rod Laver, who both did it in a single calendar year, and
Roy Emerson have subsequently achieved.

For Perry, the Davis Cup experience began in an unlikely setting against an unlikely opponent – Plymouth where Britain had decided to play Monaco in the first round of the 1931 competition. He beat R. Gallepe 6–0, 6–1, 6–2 and never looked back. Under the captaincy of the durable H. Roper Barrett and supported by Bunny Austin, Pat Hughes and Charles Kingsley, Perry helped Britain get all the way to the Challenge Round for the first time since 1919. Having overcome Menzel and his huge serve in Prague, the British fired a warning salvo across the bows of all the leading Davis Cup

1931

BELOW: EVEN WITH DIRTY KNEES AND BLACK LEATHER SHOES, FRANK SHIELDS SEEMS TO HAVE HAD A CERTAIN STYLE – CERTAINLY A VERY DIFFERENT ONE FROM ANDRE AGASSI WHO MARRIED HIS GRANDDAUGHTER, BROOKE.

nations by coming from behind to defeat the United States on clay in Paris in the Inter-Zone final. The tie was played only a couple of weeks after the American Davis Cup captain had put the importance of the Cup above that of Wimbledon by refusing to allow Shields to play the final against his compatriot Sidney Wood. Shields had twisted an ankle while beating Borotra in the semi-final and it was decided not to risk further damage with the Inter-Zone final so close – thus creating the only walkover ever known in a Wimbledon final. It is not difficult to imagine what kind of reaction Tom Gullikson, the current US captain, would receive from Pete Sampras if something similar was suggested today.

But, in 1931, the Davis Cup was the priority in American minds. Unfortunately it did them no good. Even though the States established a 2–1 lead with Shields, obviously fit as he charged the net for lunging volleys, beating Perry in straight sets and Lott and Van Ryn winning the doubles, the British came back powerfully. Perry avenged the defeat he had suffered at the hands of Wood at Wimbledon that year with a four-set victory. Austin, with what Fred described, as that 'neat, copy book, flawless style of his' did exactly the same thing, reversing the victory Shields had scored over him at Wimbledon to win in four.

The Challenge Round, played a week later as summer storms deepened the red of the clay at Roland Garros, was to act as a sparring contest between the Four Musketeers and the brash young Englishman who would throw down the kind of challenge that d'Artagnan would have understood. The four Frenchmen had developed a close bond over the years, adopting the same code as Alexander Dumas had written for his heroes, 'One for all and all for one.' But they had retained their individuality, none more so than Borotra whose flamboyant personality so infuriated opponents. Like Tilden, Perry was determined to match any hint of gamesmanship with more of his own. It had been one of Borotra's party pieces to race for a wide-angled shot and end up in the lap of any pretty girl sitting close to the court. In his autobiography, Perry describes how he retaliated:

> 'We knew the owner of an haute-couture place on the Rue Royale just round the corner from the Crillon where we were staying so I dropped by and asked him if one of the models could come to the tennis that afternoon.
>
> The girl's name was Hélène Raillaire, and I remember her well, not just because of this little story, but because, sadly, she was later shot by the Germans during the Second World War as a

member of the French Resistance. She was a stunning looking girl. We decked her out in a big hat and sat her right next to the court, opposite the baseline. In the very first game, I put up an easy lob which Borotra smashed into the corner. As he hit it, I took off in the opposite direction, over the wall and onto Hélène's lap. She gave me a big red lipstick kiss and the place was in uproar.'

Borotra was less amused and lost to Perry 6–4 in the fifth. The LTA didn't think it funny, either and gave Perry a rocket afterwards. His response was typical. 'I told them I didn't believe in going out on court to come second, even in the gamesmanship stakes.'

On the final day, with rain frequently interrupting play, Austin trimmed Borotra's sails still further to level the tie at 2–2 but, against Cochet, Perry was powerless. The weather had turned the court into a red marsh and everything that Perry did, Cochet did better. The Frenchman had been the player Fred had modelled his game on and now all he saw across the net was a smaller mirror image of himself, inspired throughout by an ecstatic, applauding crowd. Cochet, ensuring France would hold the Cup for the fifth consecutive year by winning 6–3 in the fourth, was carried from the court shoulder high by his supporters.

Not that the British were too downhearted. The LTA, having recovered from Hélène's kiss, gave the players a big dinner at the Savoy and a spirit of optimism prevailed. So much so that Trevor Wignall, a sports columnist on the *Daily Express,* invited Perry, Dan Maskell and Henry Cotton to lunch at the RAC Club in Pall Mall one day in 1932 and told them he was going to write a piece predicting that, within two or three years, Perry would win Wimbledon; Maskell would coach a winning British Davis Cup team and Cotton would win the British Open golf. By 1934 Wignall looked like a genius.

First, however, Roper Barrett's team

RIGHT: THE BERET STAYS IN PLACE AS BOROTRA RISES FOR A SMASH.

had to suffer the indignity of being beaten in Berlin.[1] The defeat was made all the more unpleasant because it took place under the complacent smirk of Adolf Hitler. The players were introduced to the little corporal who was just tightening his iron fist over the German people and Daniel Prenn must have felt particular distaste as he shook his hand. The German No 1 was Jewish.

But, in the end, the decisive moment on the sunken bowl of a Centre Court at the famous Rot-Weiss Club came when Perry, lumbered with having to play the deciding rubber again, led Prenn 5–2 in the fifth having roared through the fourth 6–0. On match point, with Prenn serving, Perry hit a clean forehand winner down the line and moved forward to shake hands. But a late call from the foot fault judge indicated that Prenn had strayed over the line. It had been a first serve so the German had one more serve to come. He won it. And he won the next point, too. And the next five games to take the set and the match 7–5 and give Germany a 3–2 victory. Years later, Fred still had no explanation as to why or how he completely lost the plot but he remembered how he and Austin, who had been beaten by von Cramm in the first reverse singles, were both roasted in the press for throwing the tie away.

The Germans went on to score a shock 5–0 win over Italy in Milan but came unstuck in the Inter-Zone Final in Paris where the United States unveiled the man who would probably have rivalled Tilden's Davis Cup exploits had he not turned pro two years later. Ellsworth Vines was considered by many – Jack Kramer amongst them – to have been one of the finest players of all time. The tall Californian had the fastest serve of his era and hit his returns with tremendous force off the ground. In 1932 he had not only helped the States defeat Australia 5–0 in Philadelphia by defeating Jack Crawford, the best of the new generation of Australians, but had blasted his way through Wimbledon for the loss of only 19 games, crushing Bunny Austin the final 6–4, 6–2, 6–0.

Against Germany, Vines faced von Cramm in the first reverse singles after Allison and Van Ryn had given the Americans a 2–1 lead. Despite clay not being his natural surface, he outplayed the Baron in four sets. The French – and Borotra in particular – were, however, a different *plat du jour*. In the opening match of the Challenge Round, Borotra kept leaping forward to take an early ball and rush the net. Vines's backhand collapsed under the onslaught and, to everyone's surprise, he lost in four quick sets. Cochet had a harder time subduing Allison who then kept America in the tie by team-

[1] Germany had only been re-admitted to Davis Cup play in 1927, having served a nine-year suspension following World War I.

ABOVE: AMERICA'S MOST CONSISTENTLY SUCCESSFUL DOUBLES TEAM OF THE 1930s – JOHN VAN RYN AND WILMER ALLISON.

ing with Van Ryn to beat Cochet and Brugnon. The following day Allison should have levelled the scores when he reached match point for the fourth time against Borotra in an exhausting duel that had seen the Bounding Basque wear out three pairs of plimsolls. Borotra hit a second serve that landed a good four inches out. Relieved, Allison whacked the ball into the stands and started walking to the net. But there was no call. Even some French fans booed the decision and the American, emotionally and physically spent, won only one more point to go down 7–5 in the fifth. The French had retained the Cup with a 3–1 lead but, as Vines got the better of Cochet in the dead rubber, the phrase 'what if' was to be heard as people debated the fairness of the line-calling over their late night cognacs.

ABOVE: THE SHORTS THAT BUNNY AUSTIN PIONEERED WHILE PARTNERING FRED PERRY IN THE
DAVIS CUP SOON BECAME DE RIGUEUR FOR EVERY PLAYER. FEW HOWEVER OPTED FOR THE
THREE-PRONGED SUPPORT FOR HIS RACKET HEAD.

1933

The year of 1933 proved to be triumphant for Britain but left a dark stain on the history of the Davis Cup. Apparently impervious to the global threat that Hitler presented, the Davis Cup nations blithely acquiesced when the Nazi regime ordered the removal of Dr Daniel Prenn from the Davis Cup team. Prenn, although a naturalised German, came originally from Poland – a race Hitler detested almost as much as Jews. A Polish Jew was obviously more than he could stomach. Clicking their heels, the German LTA passed a rule stating that non-Aryans would, in future, be barred both from representing Germany and from sitting on tennis committees.

To their credit, Bunny Austin, who was already actively engaged in public debate over the growing threat of war, joined Fred Perry in writing a letter to *The Times* on

15th April, 1933, decrying the German action over Prenn, who, incidentally, soon emigrated to England. They wrote: 'We have always valued our participation in international sport … because it was a human activity that contained no distinction of race, class or creed. For this reason, if for no other, we view with great misgivings any action which may well undermine all that is most valuable in international competition.'

If the International Federation were not even inclined to write letters, let alone sus-

BELOW: BARON GOTTFRIED VON CRAMM PLOTTED AGAINST HITLER DURING THE WAR. BUT HERE, BEFORE THE FUHRER HAD HIM IMPRISONED, GERMANY'S GREATEST PLAYER PRIOR TO BORIS BECKER IS FORCED INTO HUMILIATING SUPPLICATION.

pend Germany from Davis Cup competition, they were hardly alone in their *laissez-faire* approach. Governments were doing nothing to curb the excesses of Nazism and only Wilding's friend, that largely marginalised and disparaged member of Parliament called Winston Churchill, was speaking out in a council of influence. But they called him a warmonger.

After beating Egypt and Holland, the Prenn-less Germans came a cropper in Berlin against Japan, now led by one of the most skilful players of the period, Jiro Satoh. A baseliner who could dart into the net to kill the point with well placed volleys, Satoh set the Japanese on the road to a 4–1 triumph by beating von Cramm in four sets in the opening rubber. However, appearing in their fourth consecutive semi-final, Japan again found this round to be the limit of their capabilities. On this occasion, they were confounded by the unveiling of a new stroke unleashed by a new player – the 16-year-old Australian Vivian McGrath and his double-handed backhand. Long before Cliff Drysdale and Jimmy Connors introduced it to the modern game, McGrath discovered the greater power that two hands bring for some players and used it to out-hit the orthodox Satoh 7–5 in the fifth of what turned out to be a vital reverse singles. The match was played on clay in Paris while, on grass at Eastbourne, Britain were crunching the Czechs en route to the All England Club where they would face Australia in the final of the European Zone.

McGrath might have been the surprise package on the Australian team but Jack Crawford was the linchpin. A quiet country boy who had learned the game on his parents' home-made court near Albury, Crawford, parted his hair down the middle and liked to play with sleeves buttoned to the wrist. He was as neat as his strokes which came naturally because he rarely exerted himself on the practice court. That, however, did not stop him becoming the first foreigner to win the French Championships when he defeated Cochet in the 1933 final and then going on to deprive Vines of his Wimbledon crown – a notable double that very few players have achieved. Exuding all the confidence of a new champion, Crawford defeated Austin in the opening rubber then Perry, not bothered by young McGrath's strange strokes, beat him in straight sets. Because Perry had injured a shoulder while winning the doubles with Pat Hughes, he stayed behind for treatment with his favourite osteopath Hugh Dempster, while Roper Barrett took the team to Paris to prepare for the Inter-Zone Final against the United States.

It was agreed that he should catch the boat train over to Paris the following Wednesday and it was almost dusk by the time Perry arrived at Roland Garros for a gentle hit with Dan Maskell, the All England Club professional who, for the first time, had been invited to accompany the team as coach on an overseas trip. Maskell kept Perry on court long enough for him to get the feel of the clay and, by the time the pair had changed, the rest of the team had already left for dinner back at the five star Crillon where they were ensconced in some comfort. Realising it was too late to join them, Perry suggested that they find something nearby. Their choice of the Café Royale, situated by the lake in the Bois de Boulogne was, Perry realised, going to cost the LTA more than they might have expected but Fred waved aside Maskell's hesitation. 'Those LTA officials don't do too badly every evening. Come on, let's have a good dinner but keep me away from the shellfish!'

As soon as they stepped inside, the *maître d'hotel* greeted them by name and, in mid tune, the dance band switched to 'God Save the King.'

Out of the side of his mouth, Maskell murmured, 'Do you know these people, Fred?' Perry swore he had never been in the place in his life before and the evening's unexpected welcome was compounded when the owner insisted that their sumptuous meal was on the house. The pair had a tough time convincing their team mates of what had happened when they returned to the Crillon. But there was no longer any doubt that Davis Cup tennis had caught the imagination of the French public and there was a good crowd on hand at Roland Garros to see Perry and his colleagues take on the Americans.

Although Perry was the star attraction, it was the fine form of Bunny Austin, already wearing the shorts that he had pioneered, finding that sweat soaked long flannels weighed him down towards the end of a long match, who carried the British to victory against the United States. He completely outplayed Vines 6–1, 6–1, 6–4 on the opening day and, after Lott and Van Ryn had kept their team in the match by winning the doubles, Austin then proceeded to clinch another appearance in the Challenge Round by defeating Allison in four sets.

If Austin dressed for practicality, Perry, ever the deep-thinking mischievous schemer, dressed to gain psychological advantage. With an attention to detail that would leave today's stars with their baggy, shapeless, black and white outfits speechless, Perry used to deliberately wear off white slacks and shirt at the start of a match. Then, if it went beyond three sets, he used the ten minute break to change into the kind of dazzling white trousers and cotton shirt that could have graced a Persil advert. Having brushed his hair neatly, Perry used to stride back on court looking twice as fresh as his opponent. As Fred admitted, it was just window dressing but it did nothing to raise his opponent's spirits which was exactly the intention.

From their headquarters at the Crillon, the British spent a relaxed time in Paris waiting for the Challenge Round to begin. In the care of Maskell and their trainer, Tom Whittaker, already at Arsenal Football Club, a team he would later manage with distinction, the players practised, played golf and ate the best French food. They were celebrities wherever they went. The enormity of the occasion was brought home to them when the draw ceremony was held amidst the ornate splendour of the Hotel de Ville with the gleaming silver bowl standing on a table draped with the Tricolour and the Union Jack. While the Mayor of Paris prepared for the ceremony, Maskell sidled up to the Cup and found himself surprised by its size and thrilled by the great names he saw engraved on it – Larned, the Dohertys, Gore, Brookes, Wilding, Tilden, Johnston and those four Frenchman who would soon be facing his colleagues across the net. Except...

Maskell had literally bumped into an astounding piece of news at the end of the British practice session the previous day. Just as he got to the top of the little staircase that leads to the dressing room, he ran into Borotra who was on his way to the courts. Immediately Maskell thought Jean did not look quite his usual ebullient self.

As Maskell recalls in *From Where I Sit,* Borotra offered the information that they had just picked their team.

> *'You and Henri for the singles?' ventured Maskell.*
> *'No, I'm not playing.'*
> *'Not playing? That's extraordinary. Surely, though, you are playing doubles?'*
> *'Well, yes, with Brugnon.'*
> *'So I suppose Christian Boussus is the second singles player.'*
> *'No – André Merlin. They had the greatest difficulty deciding between Boussus and*
> *   Merlin but that's the decision.'*

Maskell was incredulous. Merlin, a 19-year-old, had never played a live Davis Cup singles before and now he was being asked to face Perry and Austin in the Challenge Round. When Roper Barrett was told of Maskell's conversation, the canny captain was suspicious. 'Let's wait for the draw,' he cautioned. 'This could be a French plot to make us overconfident.'

But it wasn't. When the two captains handed the French Federation secretary the envelopes containing the names of their chosen players in a ritual that continues to this day, Merlin's name was read out after that of Cochet.[2] There was a buoyant mood in the British camp when the players returned to Roland Garros that afternoon for a final practice session. And their confidence seemed justified when, on a stiflingly hot summer's afternoon, with the sun's heat reflected off the unprotected concrete stands, Austin gave Britain a 1–0 lead by overwhelming the nervous young débutant 6–3, 6–4, 6–0. Despite losing the first set 10–8 and trailing Cochet 5–3 in the third, Perry, hitting his classic running forehand with ever increasing confidence, increased that lead by winning 6–3 in the fifth. If the tall Englishman looked his usual cool self as he walked off court, it was a *façade*. As soon as he was in the privacy of the British dressing room, he passed out cold. When he came round to find Roper Barrett and Maskell fanning him, he couldn't remember who won. Everyone was sworn to secrecy and the captain immediately took the wise precaution of replacing Perry in the doubles with Harry Lee.

Perry always maintained that it was mental, rather than physical exhaustion, that caused his blackout. 'It is hard for anyone who wasn't there at the time to understand the strain of playing the Challenge Round of the Davis Cup in Paris. We were trying to take the Cup away from the French on their own territory and Paris was like a seething cauldron. You never knew what was going to happen and everything you did was like another step along a tightrope. There were 15,000 people jammed into that stadium and every time there was a bad call, it took four or five minutes to silence the eruption. Everyone was whistling and jeering. It's very nerve-racking to play tennis in that kind of charged atmosphere. And to try to beat Cochet, who, let's face it, was my idol, in such a decisive match was a staggering responsibility. I think, when I beat him, the bottom dropped out of my act. I think it was the sheer joy and relief of thinking, "My God, we made it!".'

But it was not over, not for Britain and not for Perry. Brugnon and Borotra kept French fingertips on the Cup, which sat gleaming in the sunlight at the front of the President's box, by beating Hughes and Lee in straight sets. Then Cochet, making his last appearance for France, outfoxed Austin in a fascinating duel that relied on all the greatest clay court skills – guile, deception, placement and control. It went all the way

[2] Forty-nine years later, writing in the programme for the 1982 Davis Cup final against the United States in Grenoble, Cochet suggested that Borotra had decided he was not fit enough to play but, obviously, this was the not the impression he gave Maskell.

to 6–4 in the fifth after Cochet had twice been a set behind and the crowd were almost as drained as the players by the time Henri levelled the tie for France at 2–2.

So, once again, Fred Perry, the guy from the wrong side of the tracks, was called upon to shunt Britain into the station. He had not always been successful in the past and this time, despite the inexperience of the opposition, he was barely in a fit state to walk on court. Roper Barrett had packed him off to bed midway through a practice session the previous day and the man who admitted to feeling 'like a wet sock that had been put through a wringer' after beating Cochet was now feeling better but 'far from one hundred per cent.'

André Merlin, *au contraire*, seemed completely at ease as he began a match in front of Albert Lebrun, President of the Republic, and a cheering crowd of 15,000 that would decide the destiny of the Davis Cup. Passing Perry whenever the Englishman advanced behind his early-hit forehand, Merlin took the first set 6–4 and continued to dominate the match with his speed and superb racket control. Lobbing and passing, Merlin reached set point twice in the second set – set points which, in all probability were match points, because few in the English camp felt Fred was in good enough shape to fight back from two sets to love down.

But it was then that an honest Frenchman came to Britain's rescue. On one of the set points, Perry hit a shot down Merlin's backhand side and the ball hit the line, leaving a clear mark. Correctly, the ball was called good but that did not stop pandemonium from breaking out. Boos, whistles and catcalls rent the air but the call stood even though the next time Perry turned around the honest linesman was no longer there! But it was a turning point and English experience started to take its toll on youthful French flair. Perry eventually got himself in a winning position, breaking Merlin to lead 5–4 in the fourth at two sets to one up.

'I remember some pompous idea I had in mind of showing the French nation how to finish off a tennis match,' Perry recalled, 'but I promptly lost the game and needed to work very hard to break Merlin again for a 6–5 lead.'

It is interesting that Perry, whose ego was a match for anyone's, takes pains in his autobiography to share his moment of pending triumph with someone who obviously played an important part in making it happen. The art of captaincy in most sports revolves around knowing your men and knowing, not merely how to deal with them, but when. This is especially so in Davis Cup tennis and it was now, in this cockpit of sweat, noise and desperate nervous tension that Roper Barrett decided to intervene. As

Perry changed ends, waiting to serve for the match, the tie and the Cup for a second time, the veteran of the first Davis Cup tie ever played 33 years before, took his player by the elbow and said in those matter of fact tones that Englishmen of a certain station are so good at: 'Nice day... big crowd... Look over there in that corner: now there's a good-looking girl. I'll tell you what, win this game and I'll get you a date with her.'

Perry knew he was just talking to take his mind off the enormity of the moment but, as he admitted, 'It certainly did the trick. It changed the whole picture for me. I wasn't straining any more. I held serve and won the match that brought the Cup back to Britain for the first time since 1912. After standing motionless for the national anthems, I managed to get myself back to the dressing room and passed out for the second time in three days, drained as before.'

Prior to that Perry had been swamped by fans and his team-mates who rushed onto the court while the crowd, so partisan before, stood to cheer the British victory in the most sporting fashion. For six years the Four Musketeers had jealously guarded that silver bowl but now it was gone. The Cup, however, had not quite finished with its Parisian experience. After the official dinner at the Crillon, Cochet turned to Perry and suggested they go out and hit the town – and take the Cup with them.

'We can't do that!,' said Perry, for once upstaged by someone else's audacity.

'Oh, yes we can,' said Cochet. Enlisting the help of a few friends of Henri's, the pair spirited the Cup off into the night, carrying it from one *boite de nuit* to the next, up the hill to Montmartre and back to the Champs Elysées; bands striking up with the Marseillaise and God Save the King every time Cochet and Perry appeared. Champagne sloshed around in the big bowl and everyone slurped from it although Fred, recovered somewhat by this time but always a very limited drinker, did little more than sip. It was, however, a memorable evening and the Cup found itself being admired in places that were very far removed in decor and decorum from Mabel Brookes's sideboard. At 7.00am, with a pink dawn breaking over the Louvre, a very happy and slightly tipsy little party of revellers were to be found weaving their way back across the Place de la Concorde, followed by a band they had picked up along the way. Oblivious, the LTA officials found Dwight's little pot resting happily back on its plinth a couple of hours later, ready for its journey to London. The team barely had time to recover from a rough Channel crossing before they were presented with a telegram of congratulations at Dover from King George V. Then, as the *Golden Arrow* chuffed its way through Kent, Perry and Austin stood by the window, holding the Cup aloft for the

ABOVE: THE HATS HAVE IT! BACK IN DOVER AFTER A ROUGH CROSSING AND A NIGHT OF MUCH
CELEBRATION IN PARIS, THE BRITISH TEAM DISPLAY THEIR TROPHY AFTER BEATING FRANCE AT
ROLAND GARROS IN 1933 – LEFT TO RIGHT: FRED PERRY, BUNNY AUSTIN, PAT HUGHES,
HERBERT ROPER BARRETT AND HARRY LEE.

little groups of people gathered in their back gardens to wave them on their way.
Victoria Station was a mob scene as Perry and Austin were lifted onto the shoulders of
supporters from Ealing, where Fred still lived. For a nation struggling through the
Depression, the achievement of a tennis team had offered a little moment of pure joy.

With Perry in his pomp, Britain retained the Cup for another three years. Tennis
became one of the most widely followed sports in the land as the young man from
Ealing rose in prominence, if not yet in popularity. The class distinctions were still too
pronounced and Wimbledon crowds were slow to warm to him – even when he
became the first Englishman to win the Championship for 25 years. Yet such was his

celebrity that the *Evening Standard* placards around the West End on the afternoon he beat Jack Crawford carried just one word: 'Fred'. For tennis fans, 1934 was a vintage year at Wimbledon. After the Championships, they had the opportunity of watching the United States, for whom Shields had to defeat McGrath in the deciding rubber, beat Australia in the Inter-Zone Final on No 1 Court before welcoming their victorious team back to Centre Court for the first Challenge Round played in Britain since 1913. Fresh from a stay at the Grand Hotel in Eastbourne where the bracing sea air and beautiful grass courts at Devonshire Park offered perfect preparation, Roper Barrett's team should have been in top shape to deal with the American challenge. However, during the course of his five-set victory over Sidney Wood, Perry ricked a muscle in his back.

RIGHT: FRED PERRY CAN'T TAKE HIS EYES OFF THE CUP AS CAPTAIN ROPER BARRETT CARRIES IT OFF THE CENTRE COURT AT WIMBLEDON AFTER DEFEATING THE UNITED STATES IN THE 1934 CHALLENGE ROUND.

BELOW: FRED PERRY TAKES FLIGHT AGAINST FRANK SHIELDS ON THE CENTRE COURT.

Apart from the fact that he had trouble getting up from the dinner table that evening, the situation became more critical when Hughes and Lee lost to Lott and the new-comer Lester Stoefen in the doubles. Perry was due to play first reverse singles against Shields and, from a British point of view it was essential that he win because Woods was considered favourite to beat Austin in the fifth rubber. So Perry was packed off to Hugh Dempster's surgery near Marble Arch and, after some manipulation, Fred heard a couple of twangs 'like banjo strings snapping.' Dempster told Tom Whittaker to keep him warm right up to the start of the match so Perry was bundled up and driven straight to the All England Club where he spent the next two hours muffled in a couple of sweaters despite it being a hot July day.

Dempster had done his work well. Perry's back stood up to one of the longest Davis Cup matches played to that time and enabled the British star to squeeze past Shields 6–4, 4–6, 6–2, 15–13 – squeeze being the operative word. Having saved two match points in that fourth set, Shields came in behind an approach and feinted right. Perry pushed the ball to the giant American's backhand side and although Shields dived for it, he was too late. On the third match point, Shields came in again and seemed convinced that, this time, Perry would go cross court. But Fred outguessed him and, with a packed Centre Court screaming in delight, nudged the ball once again to the exact same spot on the backhand side. As the players met to shake hands at the net, Shields grinned and said, 'You son of a gun. Right in the same goddam place!'

Perry realised the crowd must have wondered what they were laughing about but, as Fred noted, the man who would be Andre Agassi's grandfather-in-law were he alive today, was always a happy-go-lucky sort of fellow and, above all, a good sport.

The following year, a rather more dedicated champion emerged from Oakland, California. Don Budge, was tall, red-haired and blessed with a backhand that is still called one of the best the game has known. He would, before the war clouds gathered again, become the pre-eminent player in the world, achieving what Allison Danzig of the *New York Times* called 'The Grand Slam' by winning all four of the world's premier championships in the same calendar year of 1938. But, in 1935, Budge took his first tentative steps up the ladder of fame, beginning his Davis Cup career in about the same kind of inauspicious circumstances as Perry had done – beating Kho Sin Kie of China in four sets in an American Zone tie played in Mexico City. Two rounds later, the scene and the circumstances were rather different. In the Inter-Zone Final at the All England Club, Budge introduced himself to Wimbledon audiences by beating

Gottfried von Cramm's new colleague Henner Henkel as Germany, who had scored a fine win over the Czechs in Prague in the previous round, were swept away 4–1. Budge and von Cramm only met in the fifth rubber when all had been decided but the interesting scoreline of 0–6, 9–7, 8–6, 6–3 in favour of the young American foretold something of the battles that lay ahead.

In the Challenge Round, the 5–0 whitewash for Britain was a little misleading. Austin had been two sets to one down before beating Allison 7–5 in the fifth while Hughes and his new partner Raymond Tuckey also needed five to overcome the experienced team of Allison and Van Ryn. That victory ensured Britain would retain the Cup because Perry, in their first meeting of note, had proved too at ease on the Centre Court for Budge who lost in four sets.

The year of 1936 brought about some housekeeping changes in the Davis Cup. The idea of running a qualifying competition in the crowded European Zone had proved unpopular, mostly because the ties were played at the end of the previous year in a similar format to that which is followed today for the Soccer World Cup. It was thought to be generally too confusing for Davis Cup and, in 1936, 19 nations, most of them afforded first round byes, were entered directly into the European Zone. Australia, however, was not one of them. They had decided it would be a briefer and, hopefully, more profitable exercise to enter the American Zone and they were proved right. After receiving a walkover from Cuba, they took on the Americans in Philadelphia and emerged victorious despite Budge winning both his singles against Jack Crawford and Adrian Quist. The doubles proved pivotal but the new partnership of Budge and Gene Mako could not hold on to its two set to love lead and were eventually beaten 6–4 in the fifth by Crawford and Quist.

1936

ABOVE: GOTTFRIED VON CRAMM CLASPS THE HAND OF JACK CRAWFORD AFTER THE TWO GREAT
RIVALS OF THE 1930S COME OFF COURT IN BERLIN IN THE THIRD ROUND OF THE EUROPEAN
ZONE IN 1935.

In the Inter-Zone Final played on Wimbledon's No 1 Court, von Cramm gave
Germany a 1–0 lead in after a heart-stopping fifth set against Quist who doggedly
refused to lie down after injuring his ankle on a day of gusty winds and high drama.
The Australian, playing with his ankle heavily strapped, was 3–5 down in the fifth when
he broke back, saving a total of five match points in two games. Serving ahead, Quist
then missed three match points himself when von Cramm battled out of a 0–40 situation in the sixteenth game, riding his luck when one of his drives caught the tape and
dropped dead into Quist's court. Finally, at 10–9, the Baron used up the last remnants
of German fortune by closing it out after missing four more match points. The
Australians drew level when Henkel felt too flu-ridden to continue against Crawford
after losing the first two sets and, the following day, McGrath stepped in for the injured
Quist to help Crawford beat von Cramm and a revived Henkel in the doubles.
McGrath then proved a capable singles deputy for Quist as well by clinching a place in

the Challenge Round with a four set win over Henkel.

Years later during the long hours Fred Perry and I sat next to each other in BBC Radio's Centre Court commentary box at Wimbledon, the former champion did not reminisce unless urged to do so but the affection he had for that fabled arena laid out in front us was always made very clear. No matter how the crowds had treated him early in his career, he had formed a bond with the place that remained unbroken to the day he died. And occasionally, he alluded to the way he felt at the end of this 1936 Challenge Round when, once again, he had been called upon to win the whole thing in the fifth rubber. Britain's 2–0 first day lead and been wiped away by Crawford and Quist who defeated Hughes and Tuckey in the doubles before Quist outplayed Austin in four sets. The match had take longer than the score suggests and Perry was bombarded with all sorts of needless advice from LTA officials on how important it was to get a good start and ensure that he was ahead of Crawford if the match had to be suspended for the night. Not for the first time, Fred got fed up with officialdom.

'What time is it now?' he snapped. '5.45pm? Right, we'll be off court, finished, by 7.15pm!'

Then Perry strode out and, coming in behind every shot, no matter how hard or deep Crawford hit his returns, rushed the Australian to a 6–2, 6–3, 6–3 defeat. As a Last Hurrah it took some beating. Only Perry himself knew that he would never play at Wimbledon again because the LTA were making precious little effort to persuade him to stay amateur. But, soon, there was someone else who realised that this was Fred's farewell. Finding Dan Maskell waiting for him behind the green tarpaulin that shields the entrance to the players' waiting room from the eyes of the crowd, Perry handed the coach his rackets and retraced his steps to stand on the edge of that lawn he had graced with so much verve and skill and, for the last time, surveyed his kingdom. 'I knew then that he was saying goodbye,' Maskell told me years later. 'It was an emotional moment for Fred and, as you might imagine, for me, too.'

Perry won the US Championship for the third straight year at Forest Hills, completing his victory over Budge by keeping a new ball in his pocket throughout the final game so that it was 'a bit hot' by the time he blasted it for a match point ace – a Perry ploy if ever there was one. Then, after losing in the final of the Pacific Southwest in Los Angeles, he turned pro. It would be two years before Don joined him and by then he had rivalled Fred for honours in the amateur ranks.

Apart from the uniqueness of the Grand Slam, Budge's greatness could be mea-

1937

115

ABOVE: DON BUDGE GIVING FULL REIN TO ONE OF THE GREATEST BACKHANDS THE GAME
HAS EVER SEEN AS HE TRIES TO GET THE BETTER OF FRED PERRY AT WIMBLEDON IN
THE CHAMPIONSHIPS. THE PAIR WERE TO BECOME LONG-TERM RIVALS ON THE
PROFESSIONAL CIRCUIT.

sured by the manner in which he returned the United States to pre-eminence in the
Davis Cup. Seizing on Perry's absence to wrest the Cup from the British in 1937, Budge
and his team-mates, most notably Frank Parker, Bobby Riggs and Don's doubles partner Gene Mako, retained it against the challenge of Australia in 1938. Although still
an amateur, Budge was, in attitude and preparation, a thorough professional. Maskell,
a clinical judge of champions on a tennis court, wrote of him: 'Totally devoid of histrionics, Don Budge set about the business of winning tennis matches with a directness
of purpose that was never blurred by doubt. Never once did I see him quit on a shot,
no matter what the pressure.'

Although supremely confident in his own ability, Budge was not so arrogant as to
believe he could not improve. The backhand was God-given but Maskell was not the
only one to notice a weakness when drawn wide on the forehand side. It was a weakness Budge recognised and, by the time he swept the board in 1938, he had worked so

hard on the shot that no one could expect to profit from it any longer.

In 1937, Budge set out in the Davis Cup as if he meant business and never broke stride although, in one of the greatest of all Davis Cup duels, von Cramm did his best to trip him. But that was after Budge had taken the United States through two rounds of the American Zone against Japan and Australia for the loss of just one set – to Australia's John Bromwich – in six rubbers of singles and doubles. In the meantime Germany had fought its way through a European Zone of 20 nations, eliminating Austria, Italy, Belgium and Czechoslovakia along the way, to arrive at Wimbledon for an Inter-Zone showdown with the Americans that would linger in the annals of Davis Cup history.

The Americans had been billeted in a flat overlooking the Thames, just down the road from the Hurlingham Club, for most of the summer. They had been welded into a tight-knit unit by their captain Walter Pate who believed a team should act and play and live as a team. Outside distractions were forbidden. No one was allowed to go to a theatre or a movie. Apart from practice, Budge, Mako, Parker and Bitsy Grant, who would be a controversial choice for a singles berth in preference to Parker against Germany, were allowed to indulge in the thrills offered by the putting green at Hurlingham on their way home to dinner. The only guest allowed to join them there was the actor Paul Lukas, a tennis fan who was friends with Budge and Mako. If this was amateur tennis, it was very professional in outlook.

As a sophisticate and socialite who was at home in London as he was in Berlin, the Baron, who usually stayed at the Savoy, would not have countenanced such strictures but he was, nonetheless, forced to tug the forelock when the Fuehrer called just before he was due to go on court on the deciding rubber against Budge. Ted Tinling, the famous couturier who was working for the All England Club at the time, was in the dressing room when the call came through. It was Tinling's job to get the players out on court in time and he was exasperated when Ellis, the dressing room attendant, turned to von Cramm and said, 'Long distance for you, sir.'

Tinling watched as the Baron's body stiffened as he listened to the voice on the other end of the line. 'Ja, mein Fuehrer!' he repeated almost a dozen times. The previous year Hitler had been infuriated as the great black American Jesse Owens had refuted claims of Aryan superiority by winning four gold medals under the Nazi leader's nose at the Berlin Olympics. Now Hitler wanted to show the world how Germany could rule at the Mecca of tennis. Von Cramm had done his best on the opening day by beating Grant in straight sets. Budge quickly evened the score with a crushing win over Henkel and the next day Mako, razor-sharp at the net, was the star of the doubles as he and Budge beat von Cramm and Henkel. The German No 2 then made sure of the finale everyone had been hoping for by beating Grant in four sets.

As if the deciding rubber would not be riveting enough, spice was added to the drama by the presence of Bill Tilden in a role that some people found hard to take – that of coach to the Germans. Tilden had never made any secret of his love for the German people and preferred playing in Berlin to just about anywhere else. But the sight of him cheering for von Cramm as the drama unfolded was almost too much for the nationalistic fervour of the future television star Ed Sullivan who was in the act of taking off his coat in readiness for a punch up, yelling 'Why, you dirty son of a bitch!' when Paul Lukas and Jack Benny managed to restrain him. It was a match that hardly needed a side-show. In his book *Budge on Tennis* Allison Danzig wrote: 'The brilliance of the tennis was almost unbelievable with the big preponderance of the points being earned rather than won on errors. The gallery, enraptured by the scintillating display to a degree that it forgot its allegiance to the Baron, looked on spellbound as two great players, taking their inspiration from each other, worked miracles of redemption and riposte in rallies of breakneck pace that ranged all over the court. Shots that would have stood out vividly in the average match were commonplace in the cascade of elec-trifying strokes that stemmed from the racquets of two superb fighters until the onlookers were fairly surfeited with brilliance.'

Budge had lost the first two sets as von Cramm, still either shaken or stirred by that call from the Fatherland, produced his most fluent tennis and took a two set to love lead. But Budge started to make inroads with his backhand, levelling the match at two sets all and seemed poised to take charge when he was forced back on his heels by a brilliant German counter attack in the fifth. Von Cramm raced away to a 4–1 lead but here it was the American's temperament as much as his racket ability which won the day. Captain Pate, at a loss to know what tactical suggestion to offer next, simply patted his man on the back at the next change over and said, 'Don, I still think you can win this match.' Budge looked his captain in the eye and said, 'Don't worry, Cap. I won't let you down. I'll win this one if it kills me.'

It didn't and he did. With the kind of courage that epitomises sporting heroes, Budge risked all with an aggressive strategy that required him to take everything early and crowd the net behind do-or-die approach shots. Rushed, von Cramm was forced into error and his break was soon snatched away. Budge drew level at 4–4 and then broke to lead 7–6. The German, fighting for a lot more than a tennis match, saved five match points before going down 8–6. The following year, von Cramm publicly criticised the Hitler regime while playing in the Australian Championships. On his return home, he was charged with homosexual activities involving a Geman Jew and imprisoned for a year. The hearing was heard in camera and there were rumours that Henkel had informed on him. As Alan Trengove suggests, it is inconceivable that this would have happened had the Baron won that match against Budge and led Germany in a Challenge Round against Britain. Prenn was a Pole but von Cramm was everything Hitler wished his fantasy of a master race to be – German, Aryan, aristocratic and a hero. No one, of course, came to his rescue. Once again the international authorities jumped at the sound of the little corporal stamping his foot. The All England Club, in one of its less glorious moments, let it be known that von Cramm's entry would not be accepted on his release and, as before, it was left to a player to make a stand against tyranny. Budge was furious at the treatment of his foe and cancelled an arrangement to play in Germany in 1938.

By then, the Davis Cup was safely in America's keeping. A mere four days after the completion of the Inter-Zone final against Germany, the Americans returned to Wimbledon on the 24th July to tackle a British team that, without Perry, was, as Maskell described it, 'like Hamlet without the Prince.' Bunny Austin did his best to set Britain on the winning path by beating Frank Parker, who had replaced Grant as the second singles player, but Charles Hare, asked to make his Davis Cup début in a Challenge Round, had just one good set in him when faced with the awesome presence of Budge. The American took time to get the hang of Hare's big left-handed serve and the outcome could still have been different had a call gone in the Englishman's favour when Hare was serving for the first set at 5–4, 15–30. Even Budge agreed that the serve was an ace but the linesman disagreed and Don was not disposed to make a fuss on his opponent's behalf. Hare eventually lost the set 15–13 and won only three more games.

After Hughes and Tuckey had lost their Wimbledon doubles title to Budge and Mako at the Championships two weeks before, it was decided to substitute Frank Wilde for the valiant Hughes, whose record had been blighted over the years by the need to pair him with deputies for a weary Perry. On this occasion it was a fair gamble that didn't quite work – Budge and Mako coming through 12–10 in the fourth. As usual, the doubles proved critical as Parker, passing with care as Hare rushed the net, deprived Britain of the Cup with a straight set victory. So once again, Dwight's little pot was homeward bound, nestling this time on Walter Pate's spare bed in his cabin on the aptly named SS *Manhattan*. In Manhattan itself, a ticker tape welcome awaited them.

1938

In 1938, Britain's fortunes dipped further when the excellent Yugoslav team headed by Franjo Puncec and Drago Mitic beat them in Zagreb in the second round. Puncec, in fact, went undefeated in nine Davis Cup singles that year before Germany, themselves without von Cramm, edged Yugoslavia 3–2 in the European Zone final in Berlin. Not that the Germans proved any match for Australia in the Inter-Zone final staged at the Longwood Cricket Club. Bromwich and Quist took care of them 5–0.

The Challenge Round was closer but the United States were given a wonderful start by a little player who would back himself to win all three Wimbledon titles the following year and collect. Bobby Riggs, a gambler until his last breath, was clever enough to place his winnings into a savings account in a London bank in 1939 and returned after the war to pick up some nice pocket money. Prior to that, the crowds at the Germantown Cricket Club in Philadelphia had been given a close up of Riggs's tactical ability as the little Californian played on Quist's nervousness over the foot fault rule – which then required the server to keep one foot on the ground no matter how far behind the baseline he stood – to give the United States a 2–0 lead following Budge's defeat of Bromwich. The Australians won the doubles but Budge settled it with a straight set defeat of Quist to earn the United States her twelfth Davis Cup triumph.

With the Grand Slam achieved and his duty done as far as Davis Cup was concerned, Budge decided it was time to cash in and he duly signed professional forms. Yet the United States still felt they had a reasonable chance of hanging on to the Cup even as it became obvious that the experienced Australian team would battle its way through to challenge them. The growing threat of war did not seem to harm the competition

1939

in 1939 for 26 nations entered, 20 of them in the European Zone. Czechoslovakia, however, did not feature. That ill-starred nation had been swallowed up by Hitler and Menzel, apparently of his own free will, had suddenly turned up in German colours as a more than capable replacement for von Cramm. However, having seen them through the early rounds, Menzel only played doubles in Zagreb and that was enough for Puncec and Mitic to get Yugoslavia through to the Inter-Zone final in New York where the Australians beat them 4–1.

Back at the Germantown Cricket Club in the last Challenge Round before World War II created another hiatus, the United States got away to a fast start against the

Australians with the impish Riggs completely bamboozling Bromwich in straight sets while Parker got past Quist in five. It seemed that America really could win without Budge. And, indeed, they might have done had not Walter Pate got into a terrible tangle over the selection of his doubles team. Initially he had favoured Mako and a highly promising 20-year-old midshipman from the Naval Academy called Joe Hunt. But then a couple of untried youngsters, Jack Kramer and Welby Van Horn, attached to the team as sparring partners, started whipping Mako and Hunt in practise. That led to a series of endless permutations which included Riggs and Mako getting badly beaten by Hunt and Kramer. Walter then threw the dice and came up with the Hunt-Kramer combination. Kramer was 18, and neither had ever played such an important match.

In an eerie repeat of the tie Brookes and Wilding had played in America 25 years earlier, Britain and the Commonwealth declared war on Germany a matter of hours before the doubles began. Somehow Quist and Bromwich managed to keep their minds on the tennis and exploited the rawness of their young opponents to win in four sets. Recently knighted, Sir Norman Brookes calmly predicted that Australia would achieve what no nation had ever achieved in a Challenge Round – a fight back to win from two rubbers down. He was right.

While the chatter amongst the 7,500 crowd was of the Maginot line and the sinking of the British ship *Athenia,* Quist took himself off to a secluded court with Fred Perry in tow a matter of minutes before he was due to face Riggs in the first reverse singles. There, Quist practised hitting harder for the sidelines than he had ever done before in an attempt to counter the newly-crowned Wimbledon champion's speed and guile. No longer worried by the threat of foot faults – that problem had been eradicated under the eagle eye of Brookes – Quist played one of his greatest matches, recovering from a Riggs-inspired slump in the third and fourth sets, to win 6–4 in the fifth. Bromwich, hitting furiously to Parker's forehand, then played like a man inspired to win the decider 6–0, 6–3, 6–1. For the first time playing as one nation, Australia had won the Cup; their extraordinary feat highlighted by having done so from two rubbers down, something no other team has achieved in a challenge on Final round. As it had when Australasia had triumphed at Forest Hills in 1914, the Cup itself stayed in New York for safe keeping while the world attended to other business.

CHAPTER EIGHT

POST-WAR YEARS

Dwight Davis' last words.... Kramer and Schroeder talk all night
Down Under.... Rules are changed for a crippled war hero....
Aussie sportsmanship at Forest Hills

WORLD WAR II WAS NO KINDER TO THE TENNIS WORLD than its predecessor. Joe Hunt was killed in a training flight; Henner Henkel died at Stalingrad. Jean Borotra's mixed war – appointed Minister of Sport for the Vichy Government and later imprisoned by the Nazis – resulted in Wimbledon refusing his entry in 1946. Such were the scars the conflict left in its wake.

And peace came only just in time for Dwight Davis. By November 1945, when Sir

Norman Brookes paid a final visit to his home in Washington DC, the Cup's founder was a dying man. He was, from all accounts, not an easy person to get to know. Mabel Brookes talks of his reserved exterior; his hidden strengths and long thoughts. 'But once his affection centred on a friend, it remained secure and unchanging.'

The Brookeses had visited Davis during his time as Governor of the Philippines in 1925 when he lived in the Malacanan Palace in Manila and tried to grow orchids at his country retreat at Baguio. He and Norman had

RIGHT: JACK KRAMER AND TED SCHROEDER, LIFELONG FRIENDS, ARE ACCOMPANIED BY THE AMERICAN CAPTAIN, WALTER PATE, AS THEY TAKE THE COURT FOR THE DOUBLES IN MELBOURNE.

BELOW: KOOYONG WAS PACKED IN 1946 WHEN JOHN BROMWICH, LEFT, MET TED SCHROEDER IN THE CHALLENGE ROUND.

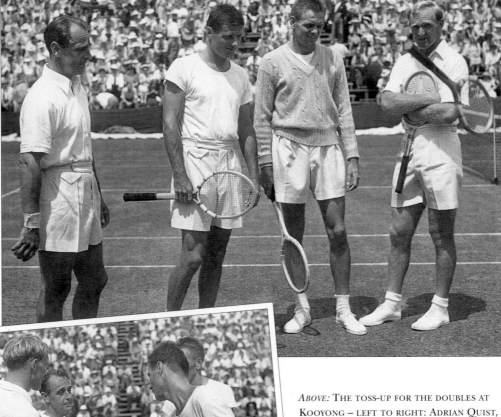

ABOVE: THE TOSS-UP FOR THE DOUBLES AT KOOYONG – LEFT TO RIGHT: ADRIAN QUIST, TED SCHROEDER, JACK KRAMER AND JOHN BROMWICH.

LEFT: AND THE HANDSHAKE AFTER AN AMERICAN VICTORY.

often played golf together, too, once enjoying a holiday at Gleneagles. Now it would be their last meeting and Davis found himself reminding his old friend of just what it all meant to him.

Dame Mabel remembers Davis telling her husband, 'Don't keep the Cup too long, Norman. It is meant to travel. Its appearance in any country brings a flock of exterior implications very beneficial to sporting unity in the tennis world and the tennis world is a big world. If I had known of its coming significance, it would have been cast in gold.'

In one respect, Sir Norman complied immediately. Australia could not prevent the

United States from winning the Cup back the very next year. But Davis's broader vision was doomed to remain unfulfilled for another 28 years. Throughout all that time only Australia and the United States held the Cup and, even when South Africa broke the mould in 1974, it was by default because India refused to play them in the final. But at least Dwight had lived to see the excitement his trophy created and, to this day, the silver gleams as brightly as gold ever would.

The war had changed many things, not least the manner in which people travelled. When Walter Pate's team won through to the Challenge Round in 1946, they became the first team to fly to Australia. Even if their propeller plane did take four days to make the journey, it made the distant continent seem so much more accessible and that, in itself, was a boost for the Davis Cup.

The early rounds provided examples of patched-up teams testing the water again, feeling their way into peaceful competition. Two of the giants, France and Britain who met in the first round in Paris, provided perfect examples. The British were unrecognisable from the glorious team of the 1930s. That, however, did not prevent them fielding an interesting doubles combination in John Oliff, who had been tennis correspondent of the London *Daily Telegraph* before the war, and Henry Billington who would have been thrilled to see how well his grandson was to play the game 50 years later. That grandson is called Tim Henman. They lost, however, to Marcel Bernard, who was to win the French title that year, and Bernard Destremau. In fact the British didn't win a rubber, largely because of Bernard's exceptional talents and the emergence, of the giant Yvon Petra who would make it a French double in 1946 by winning the first post-war Wimbledon. Petra was only able to walk because he had been operated on in prisoner-of-war camp by a sympathetic German doctor who realised his injured knee required urgent attention. In the European Zone semi-final, however, the unchanged Yugoslav team of Puncec and Mitic came to Paris and proved too strong for the French when Puncec overcame Petra 6–0 in the fifth set. But it had been close – every rubber had gone to five sets.

With Lennart Bergelin and Torsten Johansson beginning a post-war campaign that would lead Swedish tennis to ever greater things, the Yugoslavs went down 3–2 at Varberg. In the next round, the Swedes themselves were outplayed by Jack Kramer and his colleagues at Forest Hills. After serving in the Coast Guard during the war, Kramer had emerged as a large, dominating athlete with a shrewd tactical brain sitting under his close-cropped crew cut. His Davis Cup career was brief because he had other things on his mind – like turning pro and creating the legendary Kramer tour – but the impact was considerable. Kramer defeated Bergelin and Johansson in straight sets before taking that plane down to Melbourne and attacking the Australians on their own grass courts at Kooyong. At Kramer's insistence, his life long friend Ted Schroeder had joined him by this time and the pair had everything wrapped up after three rubbers. The Australians were open-mouthed. They thought the US captain had made a tactical error by preferring Schroeder, a droll, pipe-smoking graduate of Stanford University to the more reliable Frank Parker. Kramer had made an issue of Schroeder's ability to raise his game for the big occasion at a general team meeting called by Pate and won the support of other members of the squad in Bill Talbert, Tom Brown and Gardnar Mulloy. Despite losing the fourth set 6–0 to John Bromwich, Schroeder, who would play at Wimbledon for the only time in his life in 1949 and win it, justified Kramer's faith by taking the fifth 6–3 with his powerful serve and volley game. Kramer outhit Dinny Pails in straight sets and then, paired with Schroeder, disposed of that experienced combination of Bromwich and Quist in straight sets. The Cup was on its way back to America.

Names that were to resonate through the game in the coming decade started to make their mark in 1947. At Scarborough, Eric Sturgess helped South Africa defeat Britain, for whom Tony Mottram was embarking on a long association with the Davis Cup. At the same time Philippe Washer was putting Belgian tennis back on the map, helping them reach the third round of the European Zone where those Yugoslavs prevailed once again. But no one made a bigger impact than a burly Czech left-hander called Jaroslav Drobny who would develop into a legend in the game after he defected, first to Egypt, before settling in England and becoming, in 1954, one of the oldest men ever to win Wimbledon. 'Old Drob' as he is known affectionately, was a player in his prime in 1947 and, by beating Mitic in five sets in Zagreb, he helped Czechoslovakia quell the Yugoslav threat and reach the Inter-Zone Final against Australia in Montreal. There Drobny secured the Czechs' only point by beating Pails but, in partnership with Vladimir Cernik who was the instigator of their defection in 1949, Drob continued to ensure that Czechoslovakia was a force in the Davis Cup for three more years. The decision to defect, however, had serious repercussions inside Czech sport and the country withdrew from Davis Cup for five years after their two top stars fled.

1947   The 1947 Challenge Round at Forest Hills was hardly devoid of incident even though, from a purely tennis point of view it was dominated by the fine singles of

ABOVE: OFFICIALS AND PLAYERS LINE UP FOR THE 1947 CHALLENGE ROUND AT FOREST HILLS –
LEFT TO RIGHT: USTA EXECUTIVE AND POWER BROKER JULIAN MYRICK, DON MCNEILL WHOSE BEST
YEARS WERE SWALLOWED UP BY THE WAR, DAVIS CUP CAPTAIN ALRICK MAN, TOM BROWN, GARDNAR
MULLOY, BILL TALBERT WHO WAS TO CAPTAIN FUTURE TEAMS, TED SCHROEDER AND JACK KRAMER.

Kramer and Schroeder who ensured that the Americans kept the Cup by a 4–1 margin. It could, however, have been different if the Australians' strict code of
sportsmanship which sometimes necessitated overriding rule technicalities held sway.
In the fourth set of the second rubber, with Schroeder leading Bromwich by two sets
to one, the American started cramping in his right arm and a masseur was called to the
court to treat him. In the radio commentary box, Fred Perry immediately recognised
a breach of the rules and quickly informed the American captain Alrick Man. When
Man and the referee Dr Russell Davenport realised what had been allowed, they
cringed with embarrassment and went straight to Roy Cowling, the Australian captain,
and asked him to accept a default as Schroeder's treatment for cramps had clearly
breached the rules. Cowling flatly refused, stating that, as far as the Australians were
concerned, Schroeder, who had completed the fourth set 6–3, had won fairly. After
Bromwich and Colin Long had won the doubles, Schroeder still needed to beat Pails
to give the US an unassailable lead but that did not prove easy. Pails fought back from
two sets to love down and had a match point before relinquishing the final set 10–8.

Not, however, before Schroeder had tried just about every way of combating the slippery grass court; removing his shoes to play for a while in his socks; then bare feet and eventually spikes.

In 1948, two players who were to make their own very individual impact on the game in the years ahead made their Davis Cup débuts for Denmark against Egypt in Copenhagen. Kurt Nielsen, who would go on to become the only man ever to reach two Wimbledon finals unseeded, and Torben Ulrich, a bearded, jazz-playing mystic who would play his best tennis as a 40-year-old professional on the World Championships Tennis tour 20 years later, took their nation through to the third round before falling to Italy.

A more remarkable re-appearance was made by Hans Redl who had played for his native Austria in 1937 and then for Germany the following two years. From 1948 to 1955 he would represent Austria again – but without his left arm which he had lost in the war. To accommodate this resilient competitor, the rules of lawn tennis were

BELOW: IMMEDIATELY WORLD WAR II WAS OVER, SCANDINAVIA BEGAN TO PRODUCE A HOST OF GREAT DAVIS CUP PLAYERS, LED BY THE SWEDES LENNART BERGELIN AND ULF SCHMIDT. BUT THE DANES WERE ALSO TO THE FORE WITH THE ULRICH BROTHERS, JURGEN AND HIS JAZZ-PLAYING BROTHER TORBEN, AS WELL AS KURT NIELSEN (SHOWING OFF A COPYBOOK BACKHAND HERE) WHO WENT ON TO BE A RESPECTED DAVIS CUP REFEREE.

changed to allow a player with one arm to rest the ball on his racket before flipping into the air to serve.

Even without Kramer who had gone off to revive pro tennis with the inimitable Bobby Riggs, the Americans were still too powerful for Australia who were struggling to produce world-class performers. Adrian Quist, now a 35-year-old player-manager, and newcomer Bill Sidwell played singles in the Challenge Round. They were routed 5–0 by an American team sporting Frank Parker and Schroeder in the singles with Bill Talbert and Gardnar Mulloy taking care of the doubles. Little did the tennis world realise that, back home on the farm, Harry Hopman was rearing the first generation of his tennis dynasty. They were called Frank Sedgman and Ken McGregor. Two years later Australian tennis would have entered its golden age.

In 1949, the Italians, led by an ex-boxer called Gianni Cucelli, beat France in a thrilling European Zone final in Paris but could not win a match against Australia at the Westchester Country Club in New York. Sedgman, a somewhat green 20-year-old, was making his first overseas trip under the captaincy of Cliff Sproule after funds had been raised to pay his travel expenses by a campaign, led by Hopman, in the *Melbourne Herald*. But again the Australians were thwarted at the final stage, losing 4–1 in the Challenge Round to an American team that included a striking young athlete called Pancho Gonzales. Although seven months younger than Sedgman, Gonzales, born of Mexican parents in Los Angeles, was possessed of all the tough street-fighting qualities of a kid who had needed to battle discrimination and the snobbism of country club ethics to make his mark. Happily, Perry Jones, who mirrored Hopman at least as far as his strict, no-nonsense approach to discipline was concerned, took Gonzales under his wing. As Jones ran the Los Angeles Tennis Club with every inch as much power as the movie moguls were running Paramount and MGM down the road, Gonzales was protected and nurtured without ever losing the instincts of a jungle cat. His claws were too long for Sedgman at Forest Hills and he beat the Australian in straight sets to put the US on the road to victory. A year later, needing the money, Gonzales joined Kramer in the pro ranks and was lost to the Davis Cup and the world's great championships until the advent of Open Tennis in 1968.

1949

CHAPTER NINE

THE HOPMAN ERA

*Hopman re-emerges with Sedgman and McGregor.... Hoad and Rosewall
take over and set attendance record in Sydney.... The US plucks Olmedo
from Peru to thwart Hop.... Stolle makes Dad proud*

ENTION VINCE LOMBARDI, JOHN GOODEN, MATT BUSBY or ALEX FERGUSON and you
are talking about the most successful sporting coaches of all time. But none can
boast a record quite as staggering as that of a little Australian called Harry Hopman.
Over a span of 20 years, players who were coached and inspired by Hopman won thirteen Wimbledon singles titles between them while the same group appeared as losing
finalists 12 times. Inevitably individuals like that meant that Australia would do well in
the Davis Cup. But 15 victories in 18 years? That is sporting domination of a very rare,
if not unique, kind.

And so what kind of man was Hopman? 'A bastard,' says Fred Stolle before adding
in the same breath, 'but I came to respect him so much that when I wanted to send my
son Sandon to a tennis camp I sent him straight to Hop's.'

Stolle, a champion at Roland Garros and Forest Hills and three-time Wimbledon
finalist, was one of those players who needed to prove himself to Hopman before the
old fox was persuaded he could play. At one Davis Cup dinner in the early 1960s,
Hopman got up and told the Australian tennis world that he didn't think Stolle was
good enough to represent Australia in Davis Cup. 'I felt the size of a dime,' says Fred.
'I was absolutely crushed.'

But not completely crushed because Stolle, gathering his resolve and his battered
ego, showed Hopman that he was wrong, just as Roy Emerson had done a couple of
years before when Hopman had said much the same about the man who would end
up with a 34-4 Davis Cup record for Australia. It was the Hopman way. Nothing personal, just a professional evaluation. Either the victim of Hopman's assessment was
tough enough to handle it or he wasn't. And if it was the latter, Hopman didn't want
him representing Australia anyway. Some players decided they couldn't handle that

kind of regime and, for a variety of reasons, quit Australian tennis. Ken Fletcher, good enough to have been seeded No 3 at Wimbledon one year, went to England; Bob Hewitt emigrated to South Africa for whom he performed great Davis Cup deeds over the years and Martin Mulligan made his home in Rome and played for Italy. All three might have played for Australia had not Hopman had the most incredible production line of champions one sport has ever seen at his disposal – Frank Sedgman, Ken McGregor, Lew Hoad, Ken Rosewall, Mervyn Rose, Rex Hartwig, Ashley Cooper, Mal Anderson, Neale Fraser, Rod Laver, Roy Emerson, Fred Stolle, John Newcombe and Tony Roche.

Everyone who ever played for Hopman uses phrases like martinet and strict disciplinarian to describe the way he ran his teams. Yet something in Harry changed when he left Australia under something of a financial cloud in the early 1970s to set up shop in America. At the Port Washington Academy near New York, where he taught before creating his own place in Florida, Hopman was partially responsible for the development of a couple of unruly youngsters called John McEnroe and Vitas Gerulaitis.

'I don't know what happened to Hop,' says Emerson, 'but I was amazed by the way he put up with either of them. He actually went to bat for McEnroe in some appeal case later on. Had any of us behaved anything like McEnroe we would have been thrown off the team.'

Neither McEnroe nor Gerulaitis, right up to the moment of his untimely death in 1994 were the type who bowed to authority. Yet no one has ever heard either of them refer to their inspirational mentor, in public or in private, as anything other than 'Mr Hopman'. From those two, respect doesn't come any bigger than that.

It didn't take Hopman long to detect McEnroe's extraordinary potential and he had been just as accurate about another left-hander some 20 years earlier in Brisbane, where Hopman went every year to coach promising young Queenslanders under a scheme sponsored by the *Courier Mail* newspaper. Emerson, then a 17-year-old at Brisbane Grammar School, recalls the day when Hopman suggested they walk over to a certain court at the famous Milton Tennis Centre to watch a youngster he had spotted.

'It was Rod Laver,' says Emerson. 'Rod was a couple of years younger than me and we found this scrawny little kid in a bush hat with his bandy legs hitting over the ball on both sides and whacking it everywhere – in the air, into the fence. Hop watched for a few minutes and then turned to me and said, "Mark my words, this kid will win Wimbledon some day." '

Although brusque, demanding and authoritarian to a degree that present-day stars would never tolerate, Hopman's dedication to the welfare of those in his charge was never questioned. Emerson echoes the opinion of many when he cites Hopman's ability to judge people's character and the methods required to bring the best out of each individual as one of the big secrets of his success. 'Technically, he didn't teach us that much because most of us had our own coaches anyway,' says Emerson. 'But, once you were on the Davis Cup squad he taught you everything tactically and demanded peak physical condition.'

Throughout his career, Hopman was on the lookout for the talent of tomorrow and was always ready to offer a helping hand to a youngster of promise. This held true throughout his life. I have a letter he wrote, concerning a couple of boys I wanted to send out to his camp from England, welcoming them and promising to take care of their expenses. He was 79. Only a few weeks later, on 27th December 1985, he said to his wife, Lucy, 'Well, must get back to the court', got up out of his chair, took two steps and fell dead.

Hopman had been 44 when he was recalled to the post of Australia's Davis Cup captain. Almost unobtrusively compared with the high profile he enjoyed in his halcyon years, Hopman had been captain of the team that had won that memorable Challenge Round against the United States in 1939. But after the war this fine doubles player and former Australian squash champion devoted most of his time to journalism. Soon, however, he would divide his day, finishing at the *Melbourne Herald* by lunch time and then, aided by his first wife Nell who was a top-class player herself, take to the courts to coach the small group of youngsters he had earmarked for stardom. The best of them was Frank Sedgman, a fleet-footed, pigeon-toed son of a carpenter who looked very suave in a white dinner jacket at the Wimbledon Ball on the night he became champion a few years later. Hopman would soon reach out of state to bring in a strapping young Australian Rules footballer from Adelaide called Ken McGregor as well as Mervyn Rose and George Worthington who would go on to become coach at the All England Club before dying from cancer at a tragically young age.

1950

With a group like this, Hopman had the ammunition to challenge for his old job and, supported by a public who were getting tired of annual tennis lessons from the Americans, he was appointed Davis Cup captain in 1950 and took the players mentioned above off on tour with the addition of an old hand, John Bromwich.

In the European Zone where 22 nations had entered, 1950 was one of the best years for Danish tennis with Kurt Nielsen and Torben Ulrich scoring notable victories over France and Italy before succumbing to Sweden and its new star Sven Davidson in the Zone Final at Bastad. By the time Torben's Davis Cup career ended in 1977, the father of rock star Sven Ulrich had played 40 ties, placing him thirteenth on the all-time list of Cup stalwarts. But for the Ulrich family as a whole the record is still more remarkable. Torben's brother Jorgen played Davis Cup between 1955 and 1971 while their father, Einer, had represented Denmark from 1924 to 1938. In all the Ulrichs played in 80 ties and 226 rubbers, making them, as far as participation is concerned, the first family of Davis Cup competition.

Lennart Bergelin did his best to keep Sweden in the Inter Zone Final against Hopman's Australians at Rye, New York by beating both Bromwich and Sedgman. A natural ball player, Bergelin's rise had been helped during the latter period of the war by practice sessions at the famous Kunglihallen with Gottfried von Cramm whose visits from Berlin were cloaked in his friendship with King Gustav, an avid tennis player. There might, however, have been ulterior motives because, according to Missie Vassiltchikov in *Berlin Diaries* in an entry dated 16th April, 1944, 'We found Gottfried very low as he has been asked by Sweden not to return… Could this be a British intrigue?' As Vassiltchikov, a White Russian aristocrat who helped those plotting against Hitler, knew a lot more than she let on, it can be assumed that Bergelin benefited from top class practice through visits brought about by higher designs.

At any rate, Bergelin, later to become even better known as Bjorn Borg's coach, could not prevent Bromwich and Sedgman beating Davidson and himself in the doubles which, as so often is the case, proved decisive.

For the 1950 Challenge Round at Forest Hills, Hopman sprang a surprise by naming Ken McGregor for the singles in place of Bromwich and it proved to be his first master stroke. McGregor had suddenly found his best form in practice and carried it onto the big bowl at the West Side where he shocked Ted Schroeder by winning in straight sets with a performance that Hopman described as 'simply terrific.' As Sedgman had already disposed of Tom Brown, the Americans' hold on the Cup was already slipping by the time Sedgman and Bromwich edged past Schroeder and Gardnar Mulloy 6–4 in the fifth. The final margin was 4–1 and suddenly Australia was a force in world tennis once again. Back home the game became more popular than ever. In Australia, an outdoor country that was already enjoying a relatively high standard of living compared with war-ravaged Europe, tennis was far from being a sport

ABOVE: HARRY HOPMAN WAS BACK IN CHARGE AND 1950 WAS THE BIRTH OF THE NEW ERA FOR
AUSTRALIAN TENNIS. HERE HE IS WITH HIS EARLIEST CUP WINNING TEAM –
KEN MACGREGOR, MERVYN ROSE, HOPMAN, FRANK SEDGMAN, JOHN BROMWICH AND
GEORGE WORTHINGTON WHO BECAME A COACH TO BRITAIN'S DAVIS CUP TEAM IN THE 1960s.

confined to exclusive country clubs. There were courts in every public park and local
neighbourhood clubs were affordable to everyone. They were the breeding grounds
for the generation of champions who would play a significant part in shaping
Australia's image throughout the world. To Americans, especially, who had a very hazy
idea of what Australia was all about, the success of Hoad, Rosewall, Laver and their colleagues, all exuding a spirit of sportsmanship and camaraderie, became the Australian
way. In American eyes, the 'Aussies' were good guys and it is hard to imagine a nation
being blessed with a better group of travelling diplomats.

1951   In 1951 both Germany and Japan were allowed back into the competition and that
meant an amazing revival in the fortunes of the Baron. Although 42 years old, von
Cramm demonstrated why had been rightly regarded as second only to Perry and

Budge amongst world stars in the 1930s by outplaying opponents half his age. Beating Mitic in the first round against Yugoslavia, von Cramm went on to score two amazingly decisive victories over the young Danes, Nielsen and Torben Ulrich in Berlin although what mental state the visitors were in, playing in the old German capital with the Nazi occupation of Denmark still a clear and painful memory, can only be imagined. Nevertheless von Cramm was one of those Germans who could truly be said to have opposed Hitler and it was good to welcome him back into the tennis world as a valued friend. Germany went all the way through to the Zone Final at Bastad before Bergelin and Davidson proved far too strong, winning 5–0.

Bergelin, however, could not translate that form onto the grass courts of Australia later in the year when Sweden travelled Down Under to play the Inter-Zone Final against the United States in Melbourne. Schroeder, who had only been added to the American squad at the last minute after a spell of poor form, returned to his combat-

BELOW: THEIR DAVIS CUP DAYS DONE, JOHN NEWCOMBE SALUTES LEW HOAD IN TRADITIONAL AUSSIE STYLE. NEITHER MAN ALLOWED A LATE NIGHT TO INTERFERE WITH HIS ABILITY TO OVERWHELM AN OPPONENT THE NEXT DAY.

ive best and destroyed the big Swede in straight sets. With a muscular youngster called Tony Trabert making an early impact with an equally emphatic victory over Davidson, Sweden was outclassed.

The Challenge Round, the first to be played in Sydney since the first World War, became front page news and hundreds of people poured into the grounds at White City to watch the practice sessions. It soon became clear that Hopman still did not have complete control of his team when he found himself losing an argument with the four Australian selectors, of whom Sir Norman Brookes was one, over the second singles spot. Hopman wanted McGregor but Brookes, as a left-hander himself, tended to favour southpaws and so it was that the name of Mervyn Rose came out of the hat when the draw was made at the old Australia Hotel on Christmas Day.

All Hopman's fears about the weakness of Rose's backhand were realised when he lost in straight sets to Vic Seixas, a wartime pilot in the US Air Force who did not embark on an illustrious Davis Cup career until his late 20s, Sedgman levelled the tie by beating Schroeder in straight sets and then teamed with McGregor to win the doubles over Schroeder and Trabert. Although too upset to practise when he heard he had

been passed over for the singles, McGregor showed what he was made of by bouncing back brilliantly to play a full part in the victory that Australia desperately needed to keep their hands on the Cup. Schroeder, who realised this would probably be his last Davis Cup singles, prepared in a way that is not so surprising to anyone who knows this off-beat character. He chewed the cud, as they might have said at the time, with his best pal, Jack Kramer, who had turned pro but was coaching the team. They played gin rummy till 4am in Jack's hotel room before strolling around Sydney until sunrise.

Movingly Kramer described that night in his autobiography. 'If you break down both our careers and our whole friendship, the friendship and memories go on, but what more is there really than this night at the end of a career and that other night in 1939

LEFT: TONY TRABERT'S RACKET BENDS WITH THE FORCE OF HIS PENDING SMASH AS HE TOWERS OVER DAVIS CUP PARTNER VIC SEIXAS.

ABOVE: TEENAGERS KEN ROSEWALL AND LEW HOAD TEAM UP FOR AUSTRALIA AGAINST
THE UNITED STATES IN FRONT OF THE WORLD-RECORD CROWD OF 25,578 AT SYDNEY'S
WHITE STADIUM.

12 years before? That was the time when he came and stayed in my room just before I played my first Davis Cup match. He slept on the floor and we talked almost till dawn. We were so excited, teenagers, almost babies. And now here we were, so many years later, thousands of miles away in Sydney. There had been so much and we found ourselves talking about it all. We had both won our Wimbledon, both won Forest Hills. Together we had won a Davis Cup and defended it. And God, there had been a whole war, too, and wives and children. And here it was at the other end, another hotel room, another very long night…'

The lack of sleep should have affected Schroeder but it didn't. After dawn had broken, they had breakfast and a hit and Ted was ready to take on Rose whom he beat in three long sets to keep America in the tie. Sedgman, however, was all over Seixas in the decider to ensure that the pattern of Davis Cup Challenge Rounds in the Christmas sunshine would become something of a tradition in the following decade.

But before Adelaide could take its turn to stage the Challenge Round 12 months later, the Australian LTA had to deal with the predatory advances being made by American promoters to Sedgman, the nation's new sporting hero. The association found itself squirming in the hopeless position that so many amateur organisations were forced to face in the years before Open Tennis – that of having to raise money to persuade a player to stay amateur. Such was Frank's popularity that the first ingenious idea was to open a public subscription fund which raised the not inconsiderable sum of £5,473. It was marked down as a 'wedding gift' for Frank and his wife. Businessmen got into the deal and helped Sedgman acquire a petrol station and an interest in a business that made straws. But, in reality, everyone was simply clutching at them. Sedgman came from a working-class family and needed the security that money brings and the Americans were waving it at him. Bobby Riggs was involved originally but backed out when Pancho Gonzales started pushing him for a greater cut on the deal Riggs had set up to tour with Gonzales, Pancho Segura, Sedgman and himself. With Sedgman enjoying his greatest year – in 1952 he won Wimbledon and Forest Hills and lost to Drobny in the final at Roland Garros – Kramer, who had been playing on Riggs's tour but didn't rate him as a promoter, felt the opportunity was too good to pass up. 'So for a lousy 10 per cent, I got into promoting,' Kramer joked. Not that he regretted starting with Sedgman whom he describes as the quickest man he ever played and one of the straightest he ever dealt with. Meeting the Australian at the Athenaeum Court Hotel in London during Wimbledon, the negotiations were brief.

Kramer asked Sedgman how much he wanted. Sedgman said $75,000. 'You got it,' said Kramer and a handshake followed. Nothing would be formalised until the Australian star had finished his year and fulfilled his commitment to his country.

With Seixas and Trabert far too strong on grass for the Italians, Cucelli and the long armed newcomer Fausto Gardini in the Inter-Zone Final in Sydney, the Americans moved on to the courts behind the lovely cricket ground at Memorial Drive, Adelaide for the 1952 Challenge Round. Hopman had his way this time and replaced Rose with McGregor who gave his fellow South Australians plenty to cheer by demolishing Trabert who was on leave from the US Navy and clearly lacking match fitness. Sedgman had already outvolleyed Seixas and when the famous Sedgman-McGregor combination, which had cleaned up the Grand Slam of doubles titles the year before, beat Seixas and Trabert in four sets, the Cup was once again secured for Australia. Despite a large hue and cry in the press and a personal plea from Sir Norman Brookes both Sedgman and McGregor signed for Kramer immediately afterwards and the nation gulped its beer a little more anxiously as sports fans or, in other words, the majority of the population contemplated the early demise of Australia's tennis fortunes. But they couldn't see the end of Hopman's rainbow.

———

On Glenferrie Road, which passes the famous tennis club at Kooyong, a tram stopped one afternoon just after Christmas in 1953. Nothing extraordinary in that. They have been stopping there ever since. But never again has a driver climbed out of his cab and, putting himself in imminent danger of electrocution from the live pole, clambered onto the roof. From that vantage point he was able to relay to his passengers the precise score of the fourth rubber of an extraordinary Davis Cup final between Lew Hoad and Tony Trabert.

The passengers in the tram were not the only interested parties. The whole nation, far beyond the confines of a Melbourne suburb, had virtually come to a standstill. Radios blared in work places and on the edge of cricket fields. Beating England at cricket had always been the Australians favourite pastime. Now beating the Americans at tennis was becoming a passion of equal proportions. But how were they going to achieve it? Pray that Rose could rise to the challenge and wheel out someone like Bromwich? Not Hopman. The old fox had a couple of new cubs ready to go.

Lew Hoad and Ken Rosewall were both only 18 years old when they were asked to perform heroics for their nation and such was the anticipation that surrounded the

ABOVE: IN STYLE, LOOKS AND TEMPERAMENT THEY WERE OPPOSITES. BUT KEN ROSEWALL
AND LEW HOAD BECAME KNOWN AS THE TERRIBLE TWINS BECAUSE THEY WERE SO GOOD AND
EPITOMISED SO COMPLETELY EVERYTHING AUSTRALIANS WANTED FROM THEIR YOUNG
SPORTING HEROES.

Challenge Round that extra stands had to be built at Kooyong, boosting the attendance to 17,500 – a world record crowd for a tennis match until it was beaten at White
City, Sydney the following year.

Hoad, a muscular athlete with the looks of a blond Adonis who is still reckoned to
be one of the strongest men ever to play the game, would open up against Vic Seixas,
already something of a veteran, while Rosewall, small, dark and introspective, would
play the second singles against the powerful Tony Trabert.

If Hoad was supposed to be nervous, he never showed it. Powering his groundstrokes so low over the net that Seixas was forever lunging for a return, Hoad blasted his way into Davis Cup history with a 6–4, 6–2, 6–3 victory. The crowd were in ecstasies but Hopman knew that it was unlikely to remain so clear cut. As usual he was right. Trabert, built along similar lines to Hoad, who would become a lifelong friend, ruthlessly exposed the weakness of Rosewall's serve and quickly levelled the tie, winning 6–3, 6–4, 6–4.

In later years, many an opponent came to realise that the sight of a dejected Rosewall hanging his head was no cause for optimism. But the Australian selectors thought little Kenny had had the stuffing knocked out of him by Trabert and overruled Hopman by replacing him in the doubles with a talented country boy called Rex Hartwig. Hopman had felt it was far more injurious to Rosewall's state of mind to cast him aside than to play him alongside the supremely confident Hoad, the partner with whom he had already won the French title on the pair's first European tour the year before.

In this instance, Hopman was both right and wrong. He was right about Hoad and Hartwig as a team for, although they were to win Wimbledon together two years later, they were too raw to overcome the fact that, basically, both were right court players. They were also unsettled by the unnerving tactics Trabert and Seixas employed. The crossover system required the net man to turn round and signal his intentions to his partner – to cross or not to cross. It may have been the question but Hopman did not like it. He felt it was unsportsmanlike conduct because it interrupted the flow of the match and broke his players' rhythm. Not that Hoad and Hartwig had much rhythm in any case because the Americans dominated the entire match, winning 6–2, 6–4, 6–4. But Hopman, as we shall see, was wrong in thinking a day on the bench would undermine Rosewall's confidence.

So the tie went into the third day with the United States holding a 2–1 lead. Could the teenagers work a miracle and win both their matches? The selectors, to name but one group, were desperately hoping they could because they had taken a terrible shellacking in the press for dropping Rosewall from the doubles. The little guy with his carefully parted hair and schoolboy grin suddenly found himself in the national spotlight. Telegrams flowed in. 'Australian mothers are behind you,' one read. More importantly, perhaps, Kenny's own mother was flown down from Sydney after Gerald Patterson, who knew a bit about Davis Cup pressure, persuaded the International Lawn Tennis Club of Australia to pay her airfare.

On Rosewall would fall the burden of winning the fifth and deciding rubber if Hoad beat Trabert. Such an achievement would buck the trend of history. Only twice before in a Challenge Round had a country fought back from 1–2 down – Lacoste and Cochet had done it against the United States in Philadelphia in 1927 and Quist and Bromwich, also against the States, in Haverford in 1939. But all those players had been experienced campaigners. Australia was now asking a couple of boys to do a man-sized job.

Not that Hoad looked too much like a boy as he traded his own heavy artillery with that of the equally explosive Trabert. The first set turned into a titanic struggle with Hoad saving no less than eleven break points against his serve before, finally at 11–12, he got Trabert 30–40 down; chipped a short return and just changed the direction of his follow up volley in time to direct it away from the backhand side that Trabert had anticipated.

Light rain soon started to fall, making the grass slick and Trabert, the heavier of the two, was most affected. He asked permission from the referee, Cliff Sproule, to put on spikes but even then he could not prevent Hoad claiming the second set 6–3.

However as the court became wetter, so the footing started affecting Hoad, too, and, trailing 1–4, he reluctantly came to the conclusion that he should also wear spikes. But he had never even practised in them and this beautifully balanced mover suddenly started to look clumsy. The set went to Trabert 6–2. After the interval Hoad continued to struggle for timing as Trabert cleverly fed him low skidding balls. 'Don't worry,' Hopman urged him at changeovers. 'It'll come to you. Just keep going.'

It was not easy. Alan Trengove, the doyen of the Australian tennis writers who was not much older than Hoad at the time, remembers his notebook becoming sodden as the rain continued. But no one seemed inclined to stop. Certainly the Americans did not want to because Trabert grabbed the fourth set 6–3 and clearly had the momentum. Even through the early stages of the fifth set, the crew cut American seemed the likely winner. He held serve more easily than Hoad and then sent his opponent sprawling in a vain attempt to reach a short ball. A strangled hush fell over the crowd as Lew lay there, face down, inert. Hopman rushed on court with a towel in his hand and, sensing that his man was unhurt, threw the towel over the blond head and said, 'Come on, Musclebound. You can't lie there forever.' Lew looked up with that crinkly-eyed grin and clambered to his feet. A light-hearted moment, handled expertly by Hopman, had eased the tension. Even when Hoad broke a string a few games later, his captain ensured that Hoad would turn it to his advantage by telling him, 'The dry and tighter strings will give you an advantage on a wet court.'

ABOVE: ONE OF THE GREAT DAVIS CUP DUELS OF THE CENTURY – LEW HOAD SERVES TO TONY
TRABERT IN THE 1953 CHALLENGE ROUND AT KOOYONG.

Hoad soon found it to be true and immediately started to get more pace on his
shots. The set went to 5–5 and then Hoad, crucially serving first, moved ahead 6–5. A
fierce top spin return helped put Trabert in trouble at 0–30. Then came a disastrous
double fault and, after three hours that had held a nation spellbound and a gallery in
various stages of emotional exhaustion, Hoad had three match points. Moving in on
the first, the Australian chipped a ball low to the advancing Trabert who could only
half-volley it into the net. Two rubbers each! The crowd went wild and as Hoad walked
off, a man in the crowd yelled to Prime Minister Robert Menzies, who was in the
stands, 'Give him a knighthood, Bob!'

By then everyone agreed that the court was too wet for further play so it was the following day that the ultimate burden fell on Rosewall's young shoulders. Typically, he
carried it lightly and went about his work with less fanfare and drama. Seixas managed
to win the second set but he was upset by some dubious line calls in the third and

ABOVE: HARRY HOPMAN WITH HIS SECOND GENERATION OF CUP WINNERS – REX HARTWIG,
LEW HOAD, HOPMAN, KEN ROSEWALL AND MERVYN ROSE.

could never overcome the deadly accuracy of the little youngster's glorious backhand
or the neatness of his volleys. When Rosewall almost nonchalantly completed his 6–2,
2–6, 6–3, 6–4 victory, a thousand cushions were thrown in the air as Harry Hopman
stood by his chair, grinning knowingly.

Trabert summed it up best. 'I've been playing tennis since I was six,' he said. 'But
this is the first time I have been beaten by two babies and an old fox.'

———

1954

By 1954 Adrian Quist, writing in the *Sydney Morning Herald,* was not the only observer
to bemoan the fact that the Davis Cup was turning into an annual battle between
Australia and the United States with no other nation capable of mounting a serious
challenge. This was not what Dwight Davis would have wanted but if one word could

have summed up the problem it would have been 'grass.' Even though three of the four Grand Slam Championships of that era were played on grass, it was still not the natural surface for the European nations who made up over two-thirds of the Davis Cup entries in the 1950s. And it was more than just a question of numbers. Jackie Brichant and Philippe Washer from Belgium; Fausto Gardini, soon to be joined by a more classical Italian stroke maker in Nicola Pietrangeli and the young Frenchman Pierre Darmon were all highly talented performers who might have been expected to give anyone a close fight on their own European clay. But with the Cup bobbing back and forth between two grass-court playing nations and locked into its Challenge Round format, they never got the chance. Worse still was the fact that, while Australia were the holders, geography dictated the logic of playing the Inter-Zone Final Down Under – on grass. That meant a head start for the United States who beat Italy in 1952, Belgium in '53 and Sweden in '54, all on grass, for the loss of just one rubber – Brichant beating Seixas in the match at Brisbane.

The Swedes had less excuse because they were brought up during the long winter months on fast boards – as, indeed, were the Danes. However, faced with a bunch of bronzed, well-fed Americans they seemed to blink in the glare of the Australian sun and, in 1954, only Bergelin, in taking Seixas to five sets, gave the spectators at Milton anything to get excited about.

Down in Sydney, excitement was an inadequate way to describe the public mood on the eve of the Challenge Round. This was a rematch of the epic 12 months before – a tie that Alan Trengove, who has seen more than most, calls 'probably the best ever played in Australia.' In anticipation of what was to come, Sydneysiders responded with unprecedented enthusiasm. Thousands poured into White City just to watch the teams practise as 16,000 temporary seats were being erected to increase the capacity to 25,578, a Davis Cup record that has never come close to being equalled. Even then £90,000 had to be returned to unlucky ticket applicants. From all accounts, the authorities were lucky to get away with it. Today's safety regulations would probably have balked at allowing the huge bleachers that rose high above the skyline of the surrounding rows of typical two or three storey houses. 'It was pretty scary,' Trabert recalls. 'We climbed up to the top and the whole thing was swaying three or four feet.'

Happily no one was so depressed by what they saw that they threw themselves off the top although the tie did turn out to be a major disappointment for Australia. It had been a year when everything started to catch up with the Sydney 'twins'. Like so many teenage prodigies, they suffered a letdown and were affected by outside distractions. Hoad was called into the army for national service and got bitten by a spider. More importantly – as the spider was not poisonous – both Lew and Ken were bitten by love. It was the lasting sort because Hoad was to marry Jenny and Rosewall Wilma but, during the year only Rosewall's appearance in the Wimbledon final where he lost to Drobny, offered the kind of performance everyone had been expecting. And now that loss of form and concentration was to come home to roost as Hoad, beginning against Trabert on a warm day of full winds that must have made the higher perched spectators sea sick, blew hot and cold. At his best, Gordon Forbes would describe Hoad as 'a majestic player, with a superb and flawless selection of strokes, and a court presence as arresting and fearless as that of a handsome god.'

Trabert himself has been just as fulsome in his praise. 'If I had my best day and Lew did, too, there was no way I could beat him,' Tony said. 'He just had more ability.'

But the crew cut young man from Cincinnati with a smile as wide as the Mississippi was a roll-up-the-sleeves fighter blessed with a good tennis brain and, in a variety of conditions, he was a match for anyone. Certainly Trabert was a big match player and this was as big as it got. The crowd was fair but it was noisy and, as we have noted, huge. Trabert grabbed the first set 6–4, but lost the second 6–2 as Hoad tried to cut down on the errors while staying true to his attacking instincts. Hoad fought back from 3–5 down in the third and broke the American serve again to lead 7–6. Two aces took him to set point. The momentum, fuelled by the atmosphere, would surely have been enough to propel him to victory had he been able to grab a two sets to one lead. But, on a point that Trabert remembers well, both men found themselves at the net after Hoad had come in behind his serve and Trabert had advanced behind a backhand approach. 'Lew hit a volley which flew straight at my chest,' Trabert recalls. 'All I had time to do was stab at it and it dropped back over the net. It surprised Hoady and he put his shot just outside the line.'

It was the turning point of the match. Trabert went on to take the set 12–10 and won the fourth 6–3. With some of the pressure removed, Seixas went on court determined to attack Rosewall's forehand and cut out errors of his own. With the little Australian struggling to find his first serve, Ken's game began to fall apart after the pair had split two long sets and Seixas won in four. The selectors resisted the temptation to switch to the reigning Wimbledon champions Rose and Hartwig for the doubles and stuck with the 'twins'. But neither Hoad nor Rosewall were able to show their home

ABOVE: POWER AND GRACE – WHAT WOULD LEW HOAD HAVE DONE WITH A GRAPHITE RACKET?

town crowd what they were truly made of, Seixas and Trabert, completing one of the finest Davis Cup displays in American tennis history, seized the Cup with a four set win and it was 10-8 in the fourth.

In 1955 the disparity between the best of Europe, on their own courts, and the power of the two leading nations when allowed to perform on grass was stark. Italy had a great year right up to the moment they flew to the States to meet Australia in the Inter-Zone final in Philadelphia. Fausto Gardini, soon to be dubbed The Spider of Milan because of his spindly frame and the way his left arm seemed to imitate the right as he hit the ball, now had a little baseliner called Beppe Merlo to help him lift Italian tennis. A 5–0 thrashing of a German team finally bereft of von Cramm in Munich was

1955

one thing but when they defeated Nielsen and the Ulrich brothers by the same score in Copenhagen, they demanded to be taken seriously. Pietrangeli was brought in for Merlo when Britain put the Italians on grass at the Priory Club at Edgbaston and proceeded to beat Roger Becker and Billy Knight. Gardini had already beaten Knight, who was actually happier on clay, in the opening rubber so when Pietrangeli and his towering partner, Orlando Sirola, defeated Mike Davies and Bobby Wilson in the doubles it was all over and Italy were on their way to a third consecutive whitewash, all achieved away from home. Finally against Sweden at home in Milan, where incredibly, Gardini would never lose a match throughout his Davis Cup career, The Spider and his little side-kick Beppe ensured Italy would win again, this time by 4–1, when Gardini beat Davidson and Merlo wore down Bergelin, both in five sets.

But in Philadelphia, Italy faced Hoad and Rosewall and it was no contest. Hoad crushed Gardini 6–3, 6–2, 6–0 and Rosewall, in a match that displayed two of the sweetest backhands you ever saw, proved too good for Pietrangeli, winning 6–4 in the fourth. Hopman had decided to break up the Hoad-Rosewall doubles partnership on the grounds that Ken's serve was a liability and that the pair lacked variety. So Hartwig was brought in to partner Lew and placed in his proper position in the deuce court. The combination proved good enough to win Wimbledon that year and it was certainly good enough to handle Pietrangeli and Sirola who were beaten in straight sets. In Europe, the Italians had played twenty rubbers and lost one. In America, the matches were about as tight as Merlo's floppy strings. Australia strolled it 5–0.

To everyone's astonishment, they strolled the Challenge Round, too. After making the draw, US Secretary of State John Foster Dulles, a long time fan of the game, told Harry Hopman that, unfortunately, he could only stay for the first two days. Hopman cheekily told him not to worry because he wouldn't miss much. Nor did he. Seixas's powers were declining and he proved no match for Rosewall in the opening rubber as the Australian unveiled his new, crisp volley. Never one to give up, Seixas fought back bravely to win the

LEFT: ON GRASS NICOLA PIETRANGELI WAS FORCED TO PLAY HURRIED VOLLEYS BUT ON CLAY THE ITALIAN IDOL WAS THE SUPREME ARTIST.

third set after losing a big battle for the second 10–8 but, at 32 he no longer had the stamina for a protracted struggle and went down 6–2 in the fourth. Although Trabert made no excuses, a blistered racket hand did him no favours against Hoad who ripped too many winners past the American to allow much argument and also won in four. Hartwig was the outstanding player on court in a riveting doubles that he and Hoad clinched 7–5 in the fifth over Seixas and Trabert. The Cup belonged to Australia again.

In a result that would be reversed many years later in Nantes, Italy recovered from the shock of going 2–0 down against France in the semi-final of the 1956 European Zone to win 3–2. In one of the most exciting ties ever played at Roland Garros, Darmon defeated Pietrangeli 6–3 in the fifth before Paul Remy refused to be undone by Merlo's pitter-pat tactics and won in four. Remy had the veteran Marcel Bernard as a doubles partner and neither was strong enough to withstand the Pietrangeli-Sirola combination who thereby kept Italy afloat. Merlo then levelled the tie by confounding Darmon and Pietrangeli disposed of Remy to complete an amazing comeback. The Swedes were then humbled 5–0 in Bastad only for Italy to fly off to the States to face another humiliation of their own. In the first Inter-Zone Final, the United States beat them 4–1 at Forest Hills. Ham Richardson, who, like his captain Bill Talbert, had proved that diabetics could play top class sport, had replaced Trabert – inevitably, a new recruit for Kramer – and quickly made his mark by beating Pietrangeli in straight sets. When the ever dependable Seixas defeated Sirola and then joined with Richardson to overcome the formidable Italian duo in four sets, it was all over – the full- bodied wine of Europe again seeming like a very modest vintage on the other side of the Atlantic.

Talbert had to find another singles player when his team travelled to Australia to face India in the second Inter-Zone Final. Richardson, unhappy at the expenses being offered to his wife and himself, had decided to return to his studies at Oxford University and so it was that a very different character called Herbie Flam, a wiry Californian with a weak serve but a strong heart, who found himself confronting the silky skills of Ramanathan Krishnan in the Western Australian city of Perth. The heart won. Flam came through in five sets and Seixas came up trumps yet again, beating Naresh Kumar before he and Sammy Giammalva won the doubles.

1956

Melbourne was hosting the Olympic Games in 1956 and Australia were considered a shoo-in to retain the Cup against this American team stripped of its most potent performer. Yet there were still 16,000 people cramming Memorial Drive in Adelaide for the Challenge Round to see Rosewall play his last match as an amateur. It was accepted that Ken would join the Kramer tour immediately after the tie and it was a mild surprise that Hoad, electing to play the big tournaments one more year in an eventually fruitless pursuit of the Grand Slam, didn't join him. But at least the 'twins' got a last chance to play for Australia as a doubles team, wrapping up a routine victory by beating Seixas and Giammalva in four sets after Hoad had beaten Flam and Rosewall had scored another victory over Seixas on the opening day.

1957

After retaining his Wimbledon crown in 1957, Hoad accepted the $100,000 that Kramer was offering and joined Sedgman and Rosewall in the professional ranks. So Hopman had to turn to his production line again and it did not fail him. But before that a great deal of thrilling Davis Cup tennis had been going on around the world with Britain back in the limelight. In Mike Davies, Bobby Wilson, Billy Knight and Roger Becker, the British had produced worthy successors to Tony Mottram who had soldiered on gamely in the immediate post-war years in a vain attempt to bring his nation the kind of glory Fred Perry had produced in the 1930s. Ultimately the new generation would not be much more successful but they got themselves involved in some amazing duels, not the least of which came about at Roland Garros in the third round of the European Zone.

Davies, a fiery young Welshman who would go on to master mind Lamar Hunt's World Championship Tennis tour as Executive Director ten years later, gave Britain an unexpected lead by beating Darmon. Then Wilson, who could be brilliant on his day, extended it with an equally fine victory over Robert Haillet. The French began a counter-offensive with the unlikely duo of Paul Remy, now 34, and Jean Claude

Molinari taking the doubles. Wilson then lost a cliff hanger to Darmon 7–5 in the fifth which left Davies to retrieve what had been a handsome lead and turn it into victory.

His chances of doing so seemed remote when Haillet, who was to become Davies's colleague on the Kramer tour a few years later, won the first two sets. But Davies fought his way back into the match winning the third, and sensing that the Frenchman was tiring in front of 15,000 supporters on a gloomy summer's evening with storm clouds building over the Bois de Boulogne, he swept through the fourth 6–1. But Haillet refused to be humiliated and fought back from 2–4 to 4–4 in he fifth. Then Davies broke again and takes up the story: 'Storming the net, I reached 40–0 only to see him hit a beautiful forehand cross-court to the far corner. Racing madly, I missed it and took a bone-crunching dive into the red dust. Badly shaken, I lost the next point as well. It was almost dark by now and I knew that if he could win this game, the match would be suspended at 5–5. On my third match point, I served but he returned majestically and came to the net. I lobbed; back it came. My only chance, I decided, was to keep on lobbing, deeply and accurately over his head. Four times he smashed it back. Then came the vital one too many. Darkness beat him and he slammed it yards beyond the baseline.'

By any standards it was a memorable battle but another was to follow in damp, blustery conditions at the Royal Leopold Club in Brussels. Philippe Washer, so talented and so temperamental, had lost to Davies in the opening rubber and then, banging balls out of court and kicking his racket around, had done little to help Jackie Brichant in the doubles which Davies and Wilson won in four sets to give their team a 2–1 lead. The British captain, Herman David and their Australian coach, George Worthington, were hoping that Washer's brittle mood would enable the far from stoic Wilson to close it out in the fourth rubber. But, with tennis being the game it is, the gods decreed otherwise. Wilson took the first set only to collapse under the strain as 6,000 Belgians bayed for his blood and Washer, looking positively serene, won it 6–0 in the fourth. So once again Davies was called upon to play the decider. The Welshman began well, taking the first two sets but the crowd roared Brichant back into the match as the Belgian began to worry Davies with clever changes of length and pace. Soon it was two sets all and Davies felt the first twinges of cramp in his tiring legs.

'The final set remains a kind of nightmare haze,' he wrote later. 'I think I was almost punch drunk. In my exhaustion I could hear the crowd chanting and applauding thunderously each time I made an error. I played out the set on my reflexes and when

Brichant won it 6–2, I collapsed on the bench, crushed physically and mentally.'

Such are the vicissitudes of Davis Cup tennis, the mental pressure and the burden of playing alone out there for one's country often underestimated by those who have never experienced it.

Belgium, one of the earliest participants in the Davis Cup, ensured that 1957 would be their most successful year by scoring an equally creditable victory over Italy in the Zone Final with Washer proving his big match pedigree by coming back from two sets to one down to beat Pietrangeli. As was the custom during this period, two Inter-Zone Finals were scheduled to be played in Australia during the run up to the Challenge Round. First the United States had to beat the Philippines, a force in Asian tennis during this period thanks to the tenacity of Felicisimo Ampon, a tiny master of his craft who stood little over five foot tall and weighed no more than a bamboo shoot – apparent handicaps that did not prevent him from amassing a 40–35 record in 36 ties. The Americans, however, were far too strong on grass and didn't lose a set. It was different, however at Brisbane where the United States then had to play Belgium for a place in the Challenge Round. Washer, refusing to be daunted by the grass at Milton, kept Belgium in the tie by beating Herbie Flam in the fourth rubber. So Seixas, still serving his country at the highest level, was required to beat Brichant to ensure victory which the 34-year-old Philadelphian did in straight sets.

Down at Kooyong it was a different story. Hopman had two new boys in the Queenslanders Ashley Cooper and Mal Anderson who had been waiting in the wings for their turn in the sun and although both opening rubbers went to five sets neither failed their captain. Both grabbed their opportunity with the kind of aplomb one had come to expect from those schooled in the Hopman ethic. Having served their apprenticeship, none of the players who actually made it onto one of Hop's teams was ever found to be lacking in what it takes to win big matches. With Australia in the Challenge Round so often, it meant that there were rarely any nice warm-up ties against inferior opposition, matches that might allow a newcomer to test the water. The Challenge Round was the deep end – the only end in which Hopman's players were allowed to wallow.

Cooper, who worked hard to thin out a muscular pair of legs that had the girls swooning at Wimbledon when he won the title the following year, maintained a relentless serve and volley attack against Seixas in the opening rubber to win 6–3 in the fifth and then Anderson won in five against Barry MacKay who had been chosen in preference to Flam. A giant of a man, nicknamed 'Bear' by his friends, MacKay came from Cincinnati, the same city as his captain, Bill Talbert. Like so many of his contemporaries, he went on to become a pillar of Kramer's professional tour before becoming Mr Tennis in San Francisco where he ran tournaments for many years. A booming serve might have given him the edge on grass but 20 double faults allowed Anderson to prevail and when Mal was teamed with the left handed Mervyn Rose in the doubles, Seixas and MacKay found it all too much and the American challenge fizzled out.

Patience amongst supporters of American tennis was wearing thin and, inevitably, a change of captaincy was considered to be the answer. This was hard on Billy Talbert, one of the game's great figures who went on to direct the US Open, but drastic measures were required. Few, however, were prepared for one quite as drastic as appointing as captain a 70-year-old who had never even seen a Challenge Round, let alone played in one. But then Perry T. Jones was special. As we have noted, he was the czar of tennis in southern California, a stickler for discipline and detail like Hopman and, after his first year in charge, few were still suggesting his appointment was a mistake although there were some who still questioned his methods.

The Jones method in this instance centred around a cat-like young athlete from the University of Southern California. He was fast, aggressive and talented. He was also not an American. The fact that Alex Olmedo was, and remains to this day, a Peruvian did not worry Jones one iota. He knew the rules and the rules stated that anyone who had not played for the country of his birth in Davis Cup could play for another country providing he had been resident there for three years. People thought the young man would be brought in for one or two doubles at most. People didn't know.

For two years Olmedo was the hottest thing in the amateur game. He not only won the Davis Cup for the United States just about on his own but whipped a youngster named Rod Laver in the final of a Wimbledon he dominated from start to finish. The Chief, they called him, because he looked like some Inca warrior and no one relished taking him on. Nor did anyone want to tangle with Perry Jones so, for once, even Basil Reay, the little bureaucrat who ran the ILTF with a dictatorial air from Barons Court in London, decided to keep his mouth shut over the eligibility question. Reay, however, was less amenable when it came to issuing edicts about where ties should be played. The festering resentment that clay court nations harboured towards their grass dominated – and therefore Cup dominating – counterparts was growing year by year and all pleas to redress the balance fell on deaf ears. Enrique Morea, the Argentine player who would play another role as referee in an infamous tie in Bucharest several years later, was just one of many who found the system unfair. 'We are not allowed any say in where we play and have to take long trips with little consideration of what that costs us,' said Morea when Argentina was forced to play the US at Rye, New York in the Zone Final. Nor did the Italians like being told to fly from one coast of Australia to another to play the US in Perth after defeating the Philippines in Sydney in the Inter-Zone Finals. But Reay's word was law. Some years later he would deny Kenya access to the Davis Cup on the basis that they were not good enough. Reay had never been to Kenya and had never watched a Kenyan play. The game, at this period of its history, was not well managed.

It was in Perth that Perry Jones unleashed Olmedo on the unsuspecting tennis world for the first time. On a grass court, the elegant and increasingly successful Italians found themselves overpowered by a new and intimidating opponent. Nikki Pietrangeli did his best to contain Olmedo for a couple of sets but the score tells the story – 5–7, 10–8, 6–0, 6–1 to The Chief. It was also 5–0 to the US and the alarm bells were ringing in the Australian camp by the time the Americans arrived in Brisbane for

1958

the 1958 Challenge Round with an Australian, Dinny Pails, hired as trainer and Jack Kramer hovering on the sidelines as a sort of senior coach. Even after his success in Perth, it seemed that Olmedo's selection for the big one was not a foregone conclusion. Ham Richardson, who had been released from his work as assistant to a Louisiana Senator because the USLTA had said they could not win without him, had assumed he would play. Kramer actually favoured another youngster, Earl 'Butch' Buchholz who would later found the Lipton Championships. But Jones was captain and Olmedo played. Richardson, or more especially his wife whose expenses were being paid for by the USLTA, had a fit when he heard the news and went off to the racetrack instead of practising with the team. Later he issued a statement saying he would only play doubles 'for his country and not for the captain.' It sounded like a team in disarray but it turned out to be one that even the old fox could not hunt down.

Hopman had every reason to feel that Cooper and Anderson, back in front of 17,800 Queenslanders, would be good enough to do the job against MacKay and a rookie straight out of college. But Anderson began nervously against Olmedo and went down 8–6 in the fourth. Cooper levelled the tie by overcoming MacKay on a slippery court but Richardson joined up with Olmedo to beat Anderson and a newcomer whose name would eventually become synonymous with the Davis Cup, Neale Fraser. Richardson gave proper vent to his anger by playing brilliantly but an outside influence helped the American cause. 'I give Pancho Gonzales credit for helping us win the doubles,' says Olmedo who has been tennis director at the Beverly Hills Hotel for the past 30 years. 'He was up in the booth broadcasting but raced down to the locker room during the interval. The Aussies had been returning great and we were just hanging on after losing the first two sets. Pancho came storming in and said, "You stupid guys! You've let them get in a groove, returning cross court all the time. Use the tandem formation and force Fraser to go down the line." '

Olmedo laughed at the memory. 'So Ham and I looked at each and said OK. we'll try it. Ham was the Rhodes Scholar but the Mexican guy had come up with the winning idea! He had the eyes of a champ, that Pancho.'

It still wasn't that easy and Olmedo and Richardson had to labour through 82 games and four hours eight minutes before winning 10–12, 3–6, 16–14, 6–3, 7–5. But Olmedo wasn't finished. In the fourth rubber, he came in on Cooper's second serve and volleyed with an accuracy that spoke of instinctive court craft. When Olmedo seized victory 8–6 in the fourth to win the Cup for the United States, he clasped his captain in a great hug and then sobbed underneath his towel at court side. 'Perry Jones believed in me and I felt I had repaid him,' said Olmedo. 'And even though I had won the Cup for America, it made people proud back in Peru, too.'

By the time Hopman took his team on the road in search of the Cup in 1959, Cooper and Anderson had been whisked away by Kramer and so, finally, after five years as a loyal reserve, Neale Fraser stepped forward to take his place as front man for Australia. The son of a Melbourne judge, Fraser came from a somewhat classier background than most of his team mates but that, of course, did him little good in the Hopman pecking order. He had worked hard, toed the line, bided his time and now came the reward.

'Yes, it had been a long wait but when the chance came I felt I deserved it,' says Fraser whose status in the game is now so exalted that he carries the title of 'Davis Cup Ambassador'. 'You had to be

1959

RIGHT: NOW AN OFFICIAL DAVIS CUP AMBASSADOR, NEALE FRASER HAD TO WAIT BEFORE MAKING HIS MARK AS A DAVIS CUP PLAYER ON COURT.

able to get through stuff in the gym. Seven or eight months of the year we were in there doing the double knee jumps and the sit ups and then the long distance running. But Hop kept us going, kept pushing us and although he was something of a martinet we all respected him.'

The other player brought forward to fill the vacated singles spots was the scrawny one, the one with the red hair and freckles and a left arm like Popeye. They must have fed him spinach back on the cattle farm at Gladstone because he gave the ball a hefty whack for a comparatively small kid who was still only 20. Rod Laver was raw but ready. Consistency was something still to be attained but he came up with the big win Australia needed in the first rubber of the Inter-Zone Final which was played in that historic setting of the Germantown Cricket Club in Philadelphia. Facing the talented Pietrangeli, Laver won in four sets and Fraser then disposed of the giant Orlando Sirola before teaming with Emerson to beat the two Italians, now recognised as one of the best pairs in the world, 9–7 in the fourth. But Emerson and Fraser were soon to become one of the most effective doubles team of their era and, of course, it was Hopman who had brought them together.

'I had been playing with Coop a lot,' Emerson recalled, 'but one day Hop said "You and Frase could make a good team" and, of course, that was it. He had earmarked us as the next Davis Cup pair and as usual he was right. We didn't do too badly.'

Perry Jones was predicting a 5–0 whitewash as he moved his team into the Waldorf Astoria in New York in preparation for the Challenge Round at Forest Hills. But if thick carpets and chandeliers impressed his players, they did little for their form on grass. Fraser, seizing his opportunity, confounded Olmedo with a new spin serve and beat the new Wimbledon champion 8–6 in the fourth. Fraser's left-handed game was built on one of the best serves of all time. A very low ball toss made it impossible to read and when he mixed speed with spin on a fast court, he became almost unplayable. Laver could not handle MacKay's explosive deliveries but Australia regained the lead on the back of Fraser's serving in the doubles and then, in a fourth rubber that was interrupted overnight at one set apiece, the Melbournian took full advantage of the double fault virus that shook MacKay's game and, at match point, hoisted a winning lob to send the Cup back Down Under after just a year away.

1960

In 1960, the first crack in the dominance of the grass court nations appeared when Italy fought their way through to the Challenge Round, thus becoming the first European nation to do so since Britain in 1937 and, in terms of a continental clay court nation, the first since France in 1934. It was also the year that saw the emergence of three players who, in later years, would wield more influence off court than they ever did on it. Jan Leschly, a talented left-hander who is now CEO of SmithKline Beecham, was given a run in a dead rubber after France had taken a winning lead over Denmark in Paris; Eric Drossart, who has developed the television arm of Mark McCormack's IMG for the past several years, made the first of numerous appearances for Belgium in a 5–0 defeat by Britain on grass at Scarborough and the Italians themselves gave a youngster called Sergio Tacchini another chance to establish himself when he played the fifth match after Italy had made certain of a fine victory over Sweden at Bastad.

All seemed set for a familiar scenario when the United States, who were alternating between Missouri's Butch Buchholz and another young man from St Louis, Chuck McKinley, swept past the Philippines in Brisbane in the first of the two Inter-Zone Finals. But it all went horribly wrong for the Americans in Perth when, against all the odds, considering this was grass they were playing on, the Italians fought back from 2–0 down after Buchholz and MacKay, who had replaced McKinley for this tie, had won their singles on the first day. Then came a marathon doubles which Pietrangeli and Sirola grabbed after Buchholz and McKinley had lost a break in the fifth when McKinley hit the net while putting away a routine volley. At the end, McKinley lived up to his name by chucking his racket high over the stand and clean out of the arena. Inevitably it landed in the middle of a group of Italians and McKinley was suspended by the USLTA for a while as a result. Playing one of his best grass court matches given the circumstances, Pietrangeli then beat Buchholz in five sets before Sirola played the singles match of his career to beat MacKay 9–7, 6–3, 8–6. Sirola had known more nerve racking moments in his life – he had fought with the Yugoslav partisans at the end of World War II – but he had never served so consistently at such an important time. It was a battle of giants between the two biggest men in the game but Sirola had the edge throughout and ensured that the US would not feature in a Challenge Round for the first time since 1936. The Italians had been helped in their grass court strategy by their new coach, Jaroslav Drobny who had not only won innumerable Davis Cup ties for Czechoslovakia before his defection in 1950 but had conquered the grass at Wimbledon four years later. He was also a master tactician although, as he told me at the time, part of his duties centred around trying to make sure not too many Australian girls got their hands on his suavely handsome players. Early, celibate nights were not enough, however, for the Italians to produce any further heroics when faced with Australia at White City. Fraser defeated Sirola; Laver ripped past Pietrangeli in straight sets and Fraser and Emerson ended the Italians' unbeaten Davis Cup record in four sets. Nevertheless the pattern had been broken and suddenly the Challenge Round was no longer an Austro-American preserve. In fact from 1960 to 1972 these two nations met in the Challenge Round just twice, with Italy, for a second time, Mexico, Spain twice, Romania three times and West Germany all proving that players raised on clay courts really could succeed on grass. At least up to a point. None of those countries actually succeeded in winning the Cup during those years.

1961

The most significant event of 1961 occurred off court. The new US captain David Freed was obviously a man with a broader view of the world than some of his colleagues and pointed out that, whereas his team had played the Philippines in front of a handful of spectators in Brisbane, the same tie staged in Manila would have created enormous interest. The Davis Cup Committee finally saw the point of this argument and from then on Inter- Zone finals were staged on a rotating home and away basis, with cement being recognised as a permissible surface for the first time. It was a much fairer system which, ironically, did little for America's fortunes that year or, indeed, in the years ahead. Instead of meeting the Italians on grass in Australia, the US team found itself playing in front of several thousand screaming Romans at the Foro Italico. In what was surely the finest performance of his career, a young college football star called Jon Douglas, who now has his name emblazoned all over Los Angeles as one of the California's leading realtors, found a way back from two sets to love down against Fausto Gardini to win in five as the Milanese tired in the heat. Then it was Pietrangeli's turn to recover from a two set deficit as he caressed his way back into the match against Whitney Reed whose stamina rarely matched his talent. Reed, one of the game's eccentrics, trained mostly by playing cards through the night but was so good by day that he later became the No 1 ranked American. He was not, however quite up to helping Donald Dell overcome Pietrangeli and Sirola and the Italians ensured themselves of a second appearance in the Challenge Round by winning the reverse singles. But once again they were mere grass court fodder for Hopman's men, this time played at Kooyong. Fraser was struggling with injury but it mattered little because Roy Emerson was bursting to get out of the starting blocks as a fully fledged singles player and proceeded to outpace and outhit Pietrangeli to win 6–0 in the third. Laver then took care of Sirola and there was no way back for the Italians.

Rod Laver had won his first Wimbledon in 1961 and, the following year, confirmed his greatness by joining Don Budge as the only man to achieve the Grand Slam. In Davis Cup it was going to be Australia's year again but the road to the Challenge Round was full of tortuous twists and unexpected turns as new personalities who would add life and laughter to the game in the years ahead started to make their mark. In the European Zone no nation made quicker strides than South Africa, now blessed with a team comprising Gordon Forbes, author, sleep-walker and *bon viveur,* Abe Segal; loud, left handed and robust in both physique and temperament and Cliff Drysdale, a young man exuding the utter confidence that goes with sinful good looks.

Their run towards the semi-final included an unlikely victory over the French at Roland Garros in the second round. Drysdale set it off with a superb five-set victory over Gerard Pilet that lasted three hours. 'It was a match,' wrote Forbes who was next man on, 'in which fortunes fluctuated amazingly so that while waiting in the locker room and trying to gauge when the match would end, I went through all kinds of agonies and premature preparations: like having lunch too early; then two bouts of tea to compensate; three warm-ups; a jog in the nearby woods and about 50 glucose tablets.'

When Forbes did finally get out to face Pierre Darmon, he felt 'full of fluids, irritations and sinking feelings.'

Like many players Forbes had absolutely no idea how he was going to play until he actually started hitting the ball on court but it soon became clear this was not going to be a good day. Darmon won in straight sets. Then Forbes and Segal turned the tie South Africa's way by beating Jean-Claude Barclay and Jacques Renevand who would soon be welcoming 'Tout Paris' in his nocturnal role as manager of Castel's, a famous discotheque on the Left Bank.

The omens did not look good when a South African Embassy official made a stupid gaffe at an International Club dinner given that evening by standing up and congratulating South Africa on having won. The captain, Claude Lister and his team were dumbfounded and embarrassed and Forbes felt a gloom descending on him. But his moods are never permanent and even though Darmon proved too good for young Drysdale, Forbes saved the Embassy further embarrassment by beating Pilet in straight sets. However the Ambassador, who was on crutches following a skiing mishap, was lucky to survive the party that followed. As one of the last to leave in the early hours, Segal was saying good night in his usual hearty fashion when he grasped the Ambassador's hand and gave him such a blow on the shoulder blades that his crutches fell away. 'He stood swaying precariously, like a nearly-knocked-over skittle,' Forbes remembered, 'and would have gone over for sure had Claude Lister not caught for him. By then, Abie, impervious, had moved on to kiss his wife.'

Life was like that with Segal around and frequently his opponents, too, were left swaying from the pounding volleys that he launched at them. The South Africans achieved another seemingly impossible victory in Berlin when Forbes, by beating Ingo Buding, and Drysdale with a last gasp win over the future Wimbledon finalist Wilhelm Bungert, eradicated Germany's first day 2–0 lead. In Bastad, Drysdale suggested more tales of the unexpected by beating Ulf Schmidt, who would go on to play 38 ties for Sweden, in the opening rubber. Then Jan-Erik Lundquist, a tall, flaxen-haired figure with the melancholy temperament of a character in a Bergman movie, handled both Forbes and Drysdale to bring South Africa's run to a halt by 4–1. The Swedes were a formidable team at this stage and Lundquist, who never did justice to his talents in the Grand Slams, proved what a devastating performer he could be by losing just ten games in the six sets it took him to destroy Pietrangeli and Gardini when the Italians visited Bastad in the Zone Final. Lundquist, however had tendencies towards hypochondria and I am sure he was fussing about all manner of things when Swedes had to travel to Mexico City. This destination was a surprise in itself because the United States had been expected to beat Mexico in the American Zone semi-final. But Mexico had unearthed a breathtaking talent in Rafael Osuna, a mercurial serve and volleyer with a great tactical brain and a very fast pair of feet. Although he lost to Chuck McKinley, he teamed with Antonio Palafox to win the doubles over McKinley and Dennis Ralston before beating Jon Douglas 6–1 in the fifth to give the Mexicans a 3–1 winning margin. Osuna was in tears as his supporters carried him from the court at the Chapultepec Club and no wonder. Never before had a Latin American nation beaten the United States in Davis Cup. Soon it would become less of a unique occurrence but that did not detract from the splendour of Osuna's triumph. The Swedes found it just as hard.

Lundquist did defeat Antonio Palafox in the first match but, in a great five-set battle in the deciding rubber, Osuna beat Lundquist to take Mexico a step nearer the Challenge Round. Even in Madras, where he grew up, the great Indian Ramanathan Krishnan could not stop Osuna. Tugging at his crucifix as he bobbed back to the baseline to serve, the all-action Mexican beat the local hero 6–4 in the fifth to set up an impressive 5–0 victory.

An appearance in the Challenge Round gave tennis south of the border a tremendous boost but the Australian public were becoming *blasé* about their tennis triumphs and the smallest crowd since the war, little more than seven thousand, saw Laver and Fraser complete a 5–0 sweep on a soggy grass court after Laver, who was on the verge of turning pro, had beaten Osuna in straight sets in the opening rubber.

In 1963, Emerson stepped forward to become the leader of Australian tennis. With Fraser forced to retire from singles play with persistent knee problems and Laver in the pro ranks, this former track star emerged as the fittest and fastest man ever to play for Australia. Even though this would not be his most successful year, Emmo, as the tennis world still knows him, would end up playing nine Challenge Rounds, just two fewer than Tilden, winning 11 of 12 singles and four out of six doubles. One of those doubles defeats was to come in the Challenge Round at Adelaide when the United States, under the astute captaincy of Bob Kelleher, a California judge who would go on to become one of the most enlightened of USLTA Presidents, seized the Cup after a long campaign. The crusade to the Challenge Round saw the USA beat Iran, having volunteered to play in Tehran; Mexico at the Los Angeles Tennis Club where Osuna had plenty of support from his pals at USC; Venezuela in Denver and Britain on a damp shale court at the West Hants Club in Bournemouth where the Judge pulled a surprise by nominating the lanky Frank Froehling for singles instead of Ralston. After McKinley had beaten Mike Sangster, whose superb serve was making Britain a force in the tennis world once again, Froehling crushed British hopes by beating their clay court expert, Billy Knight in four sets.

In the Challenge Round, Emerson was brilliant, staving off fierce onslaughts from McKinley and Ralston but he and Fraser were powerless to stop the Americans ruining their unbeaten doubles record. When the rookie, 19-year-old John Newcombe, was asked to hold on to the Cup by beating McKinley, the task, not surprisingly, proved beyond him. McKinley, whose muscular little legs made it look as if he was playing tennis on a trampoline, so much bounce did he get when leaping for smashes and diving for volleys, weathered a fine Newcombe rally in the third

RIGHT: ROY EMERSON, A GIANT AMONGST DAVIS CUP STARS, WAS ONE OF THE FITTEST MEN TO PLAY THE GAME.

set which went to 9–7 before putting some American shine on the Cup by wiping up the fourth 6–2.

For a while in 1964, it seemed that Hopman would have no players to mount a challenge for the Cup. Led by Roy Emerson and Ken Fletcher and soon supported by a whole range of men and women players, a revolt began against the restrictive practices of the Australian LTA which insisted on keeping its players in Australia for exhibition matches in the outback and suspending them if they left the country a day early or returned a day late. It was a system that no one was going to tolerate for long. Emerson and Fred Stolle were married men working for cigarette companies who sponsored much of their travel and wanted them playing in as many high profile international events as possible. It was an untenable position for the die-hard amateurs who ran the association but the President, Norman Strange, decided to ban the rebels. Alarmed at losing his team, Hopman worked out a compromise which required Emerson and Stolle to apologise, no doubt through gritted teeth, while Fletcher, Marty Mulligan and Bob Hewitt were allowed to pack their bags and find more amenable tennis pastures elsewhere.

Hopman, as we have seen, had not been convinced about Stolle at first. But Fred's

BELOW: ONCE BOB HEWITT LEFT AUSTRALIA, HE SOON TEAMED UP WITH FREW MCMILLAN AND HIS WHITE CAP TO GIVE SOUTH AFRICA A DOUBLES TEAM WORTHY OF FOLLOWING IN THE FOOTSTEPS OF ABE SEGAL AND GORDON FORBES.

willowy frame concealed a streak of steel that would emerge precisely when his captain needed it most. It was in Cleveland, on a wet and miserable afternoon at the Harold T. Clark Courts where the United States had decided to hold the Challenge Round. Stolle had lost to McKinley on the opening day and then he and Emerson had been beaten by McKinley and Ralston in the doubles. The US were 2–1 up and even though Emerson was expected to beat McKinley that would not matter if Stolle did not subdue Ralston first. The match was a roller coaster on a damp, grey clay court. Ralston fought back to level it by taking the fourth 11–9 after being two sets down. The momentum, and the crowd, were with the American. At break point against the Stolle serve in the third game of the fifth, Ralston scored with a deep volley into the corner. Even though it was a hopeless pursuit, Stolle chased after the ball and ended up wide of the court, looking straight into the eyes of Don Budge. The great Grand Slammer, quite naturally elated, leapt from his chair and shouted, 'Come on, Dennis, you've got him now.'

The words seared into Stolle. 'Certainly I could understand the emotion of the moment,' Stolle wrote later. 'I understand patriotism and the thrill of victory. But seeing the great Don Budge jump up, wave his arms and shout at Ralston, was one of those moments that gets locked in your mind forever. It was one of those slow-motion, freeze frame, split seconds where time seems to stand still and something happens to you. I seemed to be in the action and yet above it at the same time. I could see clearly and not let emotions get in my way. Running into Don Budge did that for me at that moment. I knew the match was not over yet.' At the change over, Hopman looked a little anxious. His man was now 1–2 down and Ralston had a look of fire in his eyes. 'Do you think you can handle this, Fred?' he asked. 'Well, I certainly hope so, Hop,' replied a suddenly composed young player. 'I'm going to break right back and even up straight away. Isn't that what I should do?'

Hopman looked a little taken aback. Suddenly realising that Stolle had become the battle-hardened fighter he had always hoped for, Hopman just reminded his player of the usual things. 'That's it,' he said. 'Relax. Keep calm. Hit for the lines. Ralston's going to get nervous before this is over.' And he did. Stolle did break back and, with a wobbly forehand volley that revealed his own nerves were not entirely under control, he sealed a victory by 6–4 that set Emerson up for the decider against McKinley which he completed the following day because of rain after losing the first set. Once again America's hold on the Cup had been brief.

The next three years saw Australia have little problem retaining the Cup as Spain, twice, (1965 and 1967) and India, in 1966, managed to battle their way to the Challenge Round. The Spanish thrust was, of course, led by the incomparable Manuel Santana, a ball boy from Madrid whose victory at Wimbledon in 1966, would liberate tennis from the confines of upper-class country clubs in Spain and make it a sport for the people. Throughout, Santana was supported by Juan Gisbert in the singles and Luis Arilla as a doubles partner and the team came of age as a Davis Cup force in the 1965 Inter-Zone Final at the Real Club de Barcelona. In front of a near hysterical crowd of Catalans, Gisbert beat Ralston and Santana top spun and drop shotted Froehling to defeat. Then he and Arilla overcame Ralston and Clark Graebner in the doubles. Froehling, who had been beating everyone in practice, may or may not have been the right choice for clay in Spain. Earlier that year, a young man from Richmond, Virginia had made his Davis Cup début against Canada in Ralston's home town of Bakersfield, California, beating Keith Carpenter in straight sets. It was just the begin-

BELOW: MANOLO SANTANA SHOWS HE CAN VOLLEY WHILE DEFEATING ROY EMERSON IN A DEAD DAVIS CUP RUBBER DOWN UNDER.

RIGHT: A PROUD SPANISH SQUAD PREPARES FOR THE 1965 CHALLENGE ROUND AGAINST AUSTRALIA – JUAN GISBERT, JUAN COUDER, LUIS ARILLA, MANOLO SANTANA, CAPTAIN JAIME BARTROLI AND THE MARQUIS DE CABANES, PRESIDENT OF THE SPANISH FEDERATION.

ning for Arthur Ashe who would go on to bring prestige and honour to the competition and, indeed, to the game world-wide with his classic bearing, caring attitude and swashbuckling style of play. By the time he had beaten Osuna and Palafox in Dallas in the next round, Ashe had played four ties and not dropped a set. But red clay was something else and yet another American captain, George MacCall, took the brave decision to drop him. Ashe, who had been brought up by his father and a mentor, Dr Johnson, never to give the white man any ammunition that could be used against him, did not complain. Even in private he rarely did.

Santana arrived at White City in Sydney in 1965 as the new US Champion so there was no doubting his ability to play on grass – a fact he proved by playing one of the longest opening rubbers in Challenge Round history before succumbing to Stolle 7–5 in the fifth after leading by two sets to love. When Stolle lost the second set 6–3, Fred looked up into the stands only to see his father walking out. What followed offered a little vignette of what sporting competition and, in particular, the Davis Cup, can do to people and their families. In this instance it nearly destroyed Stolle. 'There he was, after all the years of lecture about discipline and getting tough when it counted and he was walking out. He could not take the pressure. I felt terrible.'

Stolle goes on to recount how the match unfolded. 'At that stage of my career I was fitter than ever before and Manolo began to wilt under the Sahara-like sun. I took the third set 6–1 and, after encouragement from Hop and my mates in the locker room, I struggled through the fourth to take it 6–4. At that moment I looked up and saw Dad returning to his seat. The fifth was an emotional, ding-dong affair which I clinched 7–5 and afterwards, in the locker room, there was my father to congratulate me, his face beaming with uncontrollable pride and joy. He could not stop shaking his head and smiling. For that one moment, that one look of gratification on my father's face, everything I had ever been through was worth it.' Gisbert, however, was overwhelmed by Emerson, a mismatch which made the Spaniards yearn for the departed Andres Gimeno, a world-class performer, who had joined the Kramer tour. They could hardly complain that much however. Over 50 per cent of Kramer's troupe were Australian champions, any one of whom could have beaten Gisbert on grass.

1966

The following year it was the turn of Krishnan and his colleagues – not to mention their beautiful sari-clad wives – to add a splash of the exotic to the Challenge Round which was held at Kooyong. There was no doubting India's right to be there. After victories over Ceylon and Japan, they had taken on West Germany in Calcutta and clinched a 3–1 winning lead when Jaidip Mukerjea scored a fine four-set win over Wilhelm Bungert. That followed opening day victories for Krishnan over Bungert and Mukerjea over Ingo Buding – performances that put the Indians in good heart for the visit of Brazil to Calcutta shortly afterwards. Two of the great stalwarts of Davis Cup, Thomas Koch, who stands fifth in the list of those who have played most ties with 44 and Edison Mandarino who ended one with one tie less, made it a thrilling encounter by pushing it all the way to the deciding rubber in which Krishnan, amidst frenzied scenes, edged past Koch 6–2 in the fifth. Thomas was used to the heat of Brazil but it usually came with sea breezes. Calcutta was something else.

In Melbourne, Stolle, a lean Davis Cup machine by this time, paid scant heed to Krishnan's delightful touch play and won in straight sets. After Mkerjea had lost to Emerson, he and Krishnan ensured that the third day's play would hold some interest by beating Newcombe and Roche, a duo destined for better things in the doubles. But Emerson finished the job.

1967

With Americans failing again – this time in Ecuador where Pancho Guzman and Miguel Olvera were the heroes – Santana led his troops back to Australia in 1967 after getting the better of Drysdale in the deciding rubber against South Africa at Ellis Park in Johannesburg. The Spanish captain Jaime Bartroli replaced Gisbert with a sublimely talented left-hander called Manolo Orantes for Spain's second Challenge Round but it was all to no avail. Emerson clobbered Santana in the opening match and Newcombe was just as tough on Orantes. It was obviously going to require something special to end Hopman's astounding run of success, which had brought Australia 15 triumphs in 17 years. And it arrived in the shape of a new American captain.

CHAPTER TEN

DELL'S AMERICANS

Clay court woes overcome.... Dell bonds with his own generation....
Threatening Graebner and appeasing Pasarell.... Victory in Cleveland

DESPITE THEIR TEAM'S BRIEF SUCCESS IN 1963, supporters of American tennis were getting impatient with the frequency of defeats against nations previously considered inferior. But it was all part and parcel of the brave new world that had done away with the cosy grass court cartel and exposed fast court players to the teasing, frustrating rigours of clay.

Too often they were being sent south of the border, not merely down Mexico way, but far deeper into the inhospitable clay court regions of South America. There, wily campaigners such as Brazil's Edison 'Banana' Mandarino, Pancho Guzman of Ecuador and the magical Mexican Rafael Osuna were lying in wait to ambush those damn Yankees. The crowds were raucous, partisan and frequently hostile. The rhythms of the samba and salsa may have been great for the locals, but the Americans always struggled to find the beat and got hopelessly entangled on the cloying clay.

Between 1960 and 1967, United States teams suffered three humiliating defeats in South America at the hands of Mexico, Brazil and Ecuador to go alongside losses to Italy on neutral ground at Perth, as well as in Rome. Even the more conservative elements in American tennis realised that something radical had to be done. So they turned to a brash, radical young man who was already carving out a career for himself in fields far removed from a tennis court.

In 1968, Donald Dell was working for Sargent Shriver at the Office for Economic Opportunity in Washington DC as well as managing Senator Robert F Kennedy's campaign for President in five states. He was a young lawyer not long out of Yale whose amateur tennis career was winding down after a few years of travel on the circuit and the odd appearance for the States as a Davis Cup player. Yet, sensing the possibilities that lay ahead in marketing and managing tennis players – as Mark McCormack was already beginning to do for golfers – Dell had kept in touch with the new generation of American stars who were emerging from college campuses during the 1960s. Arthur Ashe and Charlie Pasarell out of UCLA; Stan Smith and Bob Lutz at USC and others like Clark Graebner and Jim Osborne – these were the youngsters Dell earmarked as the future of American tennis after he was persuaded to take on the job of captain.

It was a radical choice because Dell himself was young; only a few years older, in fact, than the players he would lead.

'I was asked what was wrong with American tennis,' he recalled. 'I said nothing that a bit of winning wouldn't change.'

It was this bold, gung-ho spirit that Dell brought to the job and it was his over-the-top leadership qualities that enabled him to become one of the most successful and inspirational Davis Cup captains America has ever known. It was a brief reign but, after two years, he retired unbeaten, leaving American tennis in a completely different frame of mind.

He did it by what would now be called bonding. Accentuating the sameness of the generations between himself and his players – former captains had, traditionally, been a great deal older – Dell asked the veteran pro Pancho Gonzales to stand down as team coach and, in his place, appointed Dennis Ralston who had been the linch-pin of the team throughout the early 1960s.

'Although I had all the authority I needed in an age where the players were basically still amateurs, we travelled the world together as a bunch of young guys who naturally became very close,' Dell recalled with nostalgia. 'We had some memorable times and some trying times. As you remember, 1968 was not the easiest of years.'

It was, in fact, a nightmare for anyone who valued freedom and democracy in America. First Martin Luther King was assassinated and then came the shots in the pantry of a Los Angeles hotel and Bobby Kennedy lay dying. Those who understand American politics know that the odds were heavily in favour of JFK's younger brother becoming the next President of the United States in succession to Lyndon B. Johnson. Dell would have been a prime candidate for a senior White House post. A friend died and, for Donald, a career went with him.

It was with a sense of relief that Dell was able to concentrate on something that also meant a great deal to him but was, in the context of the tragedy he had been part of, comparatively frivolous. Not that Dell was able to view it that way. A fierce competitor to the core of his being, this son of middle class parents from a nice home in Bethesda,

Maryland flung himself into the job of reviving America's tennis fortunes as if it were a personal crusade. Favoured by the luck of the draw, Dell's team steamrollered a succession of teams that were forced to meet on Dell's chosen courts under Dell's chosen conditions. The British Caribbean, represented by two Jamaicans, Richard Russell and Lance Lumsden, were swept away 5–0 at Richmond, Virginia. Then there was revenge against two of those South American countries forced, this time, to travel north of the border – Mexico was thumped 5–0 at Berkeley, California, and Ecuador 5–0 at Charlotte, North Carolina. In the Inter-Zone Finals, Spain and India were the next to feel the new power and energy of the Americans under new leadership. Both were defeated 4–1 which meant that Donald took his boys Down Under for the Australian season – and the Challenge Round – with a win loss record of 23–2 after five rounds.

BELOW: GENE MURPHY WAS A POPULAR TRAINER OF DONALD DELL'S VICTORIOUS DAVIS CUP SQUAD. HERE HE GETS A LAUGH OUT OF ARTHUR ASHE, CHARLIE PASARELL, CLARK GRAEBNER, DENNIS RALSTON, DELL, STAN SMITH, JIM OSBORNE AND CLIFF RICHEY.

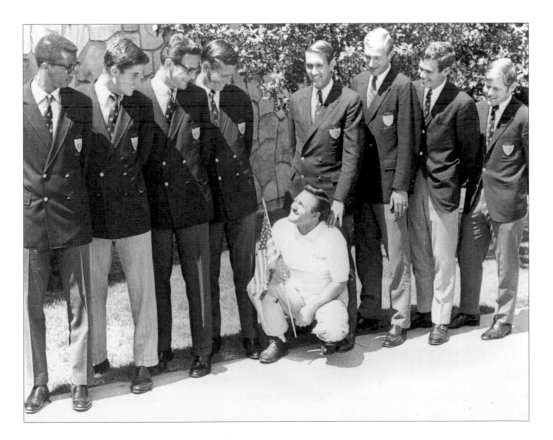

With Osborne in support, Ashe and Graebner had been handling the singles duties while Smith and Lutz, destined to become one of the world's longest serving and most successful doubles combinations, had taken care of the doubles rubbers.

In was symptomatic of a simpler age that when Dell felt there needed to be a rule change concerning the way Davis Cup squads were selected and changed, he merely went to his opposite number, Harry Hopman, a few weeks before the two nations were due to meet and talked about it.

'I wanted Hop to accept a rule change that would allow us both to change one player from the originally selected squad four days before the tie,' Dell explained. 'He agreed and we didn't bother about committees. We just did it.'

By the time the team had been playing the Australian circuit for a few weeks, Dell was becoming concerned about Graebner's attitude. Although possessed of a great physique, good looks and a broad sense of humour, Clark was also capable of coming across as a spoiled brat who found the team concept more difficult than the rest of Dell's players. When Graebner had virtually given up on a doubles match while partnering Pasarell in a tournament a couple of weeks before the Challenge Round, Dell's relatively short fuse blew. He remembers it all very clearly.

'I called Clark into my room and told him, "We're going to Adelaide and you're going home." There was no question I had the authority to do that and he knew it. He pleaded with me to let him stay with tears in his eyes. He was afraid of the disgrace and afraid of what his father would say, too. He swore that he would practise his guts out and do everything he could to force his way back into the team. So I relented and let him come with us. Clark was as good as his word. Although I had announced the team with Pasarell chosen to play singles in his place, Graebner worked like the devil and started hitting the ball really well. As the tie drew closer it was obvious he was playing better than Charlie so I took a decision that broke my heart. I dropped Charlie and put Clark in. Dennis Ralston thought I was mad.

'My main concern was breaking the news to Charlie, who had become a very close friend. I didn't want to tell him in front of the others so I suggested we go for a run in that big field behind the courts in Adelaide. It soon started to rain and we went on running and then took shelter under a tree. We were standing there soaking wet and I was trying to pluck up sufficient courage to say something. Eventually Charlie gave me a curious look and said, "Donald, what are we doing out here under a tree in the rain? You're going to tell me you're playing Graebner aren't you?" So I admitted it and soon

ABOVE: THE PRIZE AWAITS … ARTHUR ASHE IN PLAY AGAINST ROMANIA AT THE HAROLD T
CLARK COURTS IN CLEVELAND DURING THE 1969 CHALLENGE ROUND.

I couldn't tell whether it was tears or rain streaming down his face.'

Dell's decision was vindicated when Graebner went out and won both his singles 6–1
in the fifth against Bill Bowrey and Ray Ruffels. It wasn't Australia's strongest team –
Emerson and Fred Stolle had joined the list of contract pros who were still banned in
'68 despite the advent of Open Tennis that year – but when the Americans reclaimed
the Cup by a 4–1 margin, tennis in the USA had recovered a measure of pride.

The next year, with the USA sitting back while the rest of the world fought it out for
the right to play them in the Challenge Round, Dell had time to set about founding
his management company Pro Serv which would handle the financial affairs of Ashe,
Smith, Lutz, Marty Riessen and a few others until the end of their careers. He wanted

1969

171

one more triumph before handing over the captaincy and it came in the most decisive fashion. Surprisingly it was Romania, enjoying the first flush of success with its two new stars, Ion Tiriac and Ilie Nastase, who made it to Cleveland, having beaten Great Britain on grass at Wimbledon despite the inspired play of Graham Stilwell who won both his singles.

The 1969 Challenge Round at the Harold T. Clark Courts in Cleveland was significant for a variety of reasons – Tiriac's spirited display in leading Smith by two sets to one before going down 6–4 in the fifth; the crazy antics of Nastase that were just a preview of an act that would become familiar to tennis audiences the world over and the fact that the tie was refereed by Philippe Chatrier, shortly to become elected President of the French Tennis Federation and later the ITF. Although the incident has been largely forgotten, it was Chatrier who defaulted Tiriac for some misdemeanour at the end of the dead fifth rubber against Ashe. By then Dell's Americans didn't have to care. The default simply rubber stamped the extent of their superiority, enabling the USA to win the Challenge Round 5–0, giving Dell in his two years of captaincy a remarkable record of thirty-two rubbers won and three lost.

Dell, in fact, had been a member of the team that set America off on their successful run in 1963, helping to beat Iran in Teheran with two other eggheads, Eugene Scott, a Yale law student who is now publisher of *Tennis Week,* and Dr Allen Fox who was completing a psychology degree at UCLA. The conversation must have been riveting; the intellectual capacity possibly unsurpassed by any other Davis Cup squad.

CHAPTER ELEVEN

THE SEVENTIES

Davis Cup opens up to Open tennis.... The Battle of Bucharest....
Fraser's embarrassment of riches.... Amritraj's rage as India defaults
to South Africa.... Political clouds over the Cup

BY THE TIME THE SEVENTH DECADE OF DAVIS CUP PLAY BEGAN Herman David, chairman of the All England Club, had forced the hands of the national associations by courageously announcing that Wimbledon 1968 would be open to every category of player and the tennis world could lump it or like it – thus ensuring Open Tennis would become a reality. But it was still a painful one for those who yearned for the status quo despite the fact that the game had been hopelessly mired in shamateurism and hypocrisy. The Davis Cup, being still firmly under the control of the national associations, was slower to release itself into this brave new world than other departments of the game. In 1968 several nations decided that the Cup should still be a competition for amateurs only and they were vociferously supported by the Communist block for one simple reason. The Soviet Union and her acolytes regarded the Olympic Games as the moment when their dragooned and drug-induced young athletes could show the world that the Communist life style was best by winning more gold medals than the United States. And the Olympic Games was amateur. So, despite the fact that all Soviet athletes were subsidised in order to allow them to train full time – professionals, in other words, in everything but name – the living lie that they were amateur had to be maintained. Tennis had not yet been reinstated as an Olympic sport but all the major Eastern block tennis championships were 'amateur' so tennis players had to be seen to be amateurs, too. It was all a sad and sickly joke that became worse when the Kremlin started using the Davis Cup as a political football to suit its own purposes. It was, for several reasons, a dangerous time for Dwight Davis's competition. Had the Cup been chained to amateurism for too long or battered too heavily by evil political aspirations it could have withered and died. That it survived and eventually grew stronger was a testament to its own inherent strength as a sporting test that captured the imagination of all peoples across the globe and the fiercely determined work of such visionaries as Philippe Chatrier, Jack Kramer, Donald Dell, Bob Kelleher and the British ILTF delegate Derek Hardwick who ensured that the whole game evolved and grew into its new professional skin in a manner that allowed the Davis Cup to thrive along with the world's great championships.

———

1970

Two notable participants made their exits from the Davis Cup in 1970, one permanently and the other, to the Cup's detriment, only briefly. Harry Hopman, mourning the loss of his wife Nell and embarrassed at his failure to make a career on the Australian Stock Exchange, had stepped down as captain and emigrated to the States. It was an unhappy end to an incredible career in the service of Australian tennis but Hopman was too shrewd a judge of people's moods to stick around when he felt unwanted. He even withdrew voluntarily from the race to replace the reactionary Bill Edwards as President of the Australian LTA. He was being challenged by the young generation in the person of 30-year-old Wayne Reid who had played on the fringes of some of Hopman's Cup squads. Reid knew he had won when he felt a tap on his shoulder as he was buying a newspaper at the kiosk outside Earl's Court tube station in London during Wimbledon. Reid turned round to find his former captain facing him. 'I've decided to withdraw,' said Hopman. 'Good luck.' The old fox then literally disappeared underground until he re-emerged, after those years Port Washington, with his own club in Florida, new wife Lucy at his side and his reputation restored. But for Hop, there was no more Davis Cup. In 1970 Neale Fraser was appointed and a new dynasty would begin.

The temporary exit was made involuntarily by South Africa. For years, the issue of apartheid had created problems in various international sports but Davis Cup was becoming particularly affected, especially when the South African Government refused to grant Arthur Ashe a visa to play in Johannesburg. That led to a special meeting of the Davis Cup Nations in 1970 where the United States put forward a proposal that a committee be formed with the power to eject any nation whose participation endangered the competition as a whole. Blen Franklin, the South African delegate, argued that his national association had never refused an application from any qualified player to play in South Africa and that the actions of his government were outside his control. Franklin was a good man fighting an impossible corner and, when the committee was duly formed, a two-thirds majority voted to have South Africa stand down. Belgium, who had been drawn to play South Africa, were given a bye while Rhodesia, reading the tea leaves, withdrew voluntarily.

That still left 51 challengers of whom Germany, led by a couple of the last true amateurs to make any mark on the competition, emerged as surprise challengers to the United States. Wilhelm Bungert, who owned a sports shop in Dusseldorf and Christian Kuhnke, a lawyer from Cologne, made the most of the fact that the favourites, Romania, had fallen to the Yugoslavs when Zeljko Franulovic, a highly talented performer whose career was ruined by a shoulder injury after he had appeared in the final of the French Open, recovered from a two set deficit to beat Tiriac in Maribor. Yugoslavia, however, lost to Spain who then found themselves trying to handle the Germans on a specially laid, fast cement court in a Dusseldorf football stadium. The Germans had convinced themselves that it was worth the $15,000 it would cost to build it and break it up afterwards following their surprisingly decisive victory over India in Poona. There Bungert and Kuhnke had both scored straight set wins on a fast grass court over Jaidip Mukerjea and Premjit Lall respectively. Hence the decision to play to their strengths. The Spaniards were not happy at being thrown into such a makeshift setting and even less so when Kuhnke clinched the tie by beating Orantes in the fourth rubber. Despite all the efforts of von Cramm in the 1930s, Germany had never made it to a Challenge Round but, once there, they did not do themselves justice. With Dell concentrating on his management business, Ed Turville had become the US captain with Dennis Ralston as coach. Controversially they opted for the Texan firebrand Cliff Richey to support Arthur Ashe in the singles rather than Stan Smith who had played so well on this same arena in Cleveland against the Romanians 12 months before. But Richey, as competitive a man who ever played Davis Cup, did not let his team down. He totally dominated Kuhnke – the sleek, sophisticated Afghan to Richey's bug-eyed bull-dog – after Ashe had outserved Bungert. Smith and his regular partner Bob Lutz made short work of the doubles to ensure that the United States retained the Cup. The referee, a certain Harry Hopman, had a very restful weekend.

———

1971

For better or worse, politics was at the root of turning the clash between Czechoslovakia and the Soviet Union in Prague into the most extraordinarily dramatic tie of 1971. Bud Collins of the *Boston Globe*, who has seen a few sporting contests in his time, has described it as the most dramatic event he has ever covered. Having travelled to Prague with Bud that weekend, I would not quibble with that assessment. Seldom in the history of sport has one man been forced to endure the embittered wrath of an entire nation. But that was Alex Metreveli's lot in Prague. A Georgian by birth, Metreveli was unfortunate enough to be representing the Soviet Union when the Czech people were, once again, feeling the heel of an oppressor on their necks. It had been just three years since the Soviet tanks had rolled into Prague and only once since then – at ice hockey – had the two nations met in a sporting contest. Sport? Well, this could be termed sport, I suppose, but hardly as Dwight Davis had envisioned it. He would not have favoured his competition being used as a platform for political abuse but, looking at it in the best possible light, maybe it acted as a safety valve, offering the oppressed the opportunity to let off steam in a manner that their lords and masters in Moscow could just about tolerate.

Metreveli, who was to lose to Kodes in the 1973 Wimbledon final, showed amazing fortitude in beating the Czech No 1 6–3 in the fifth after trailing by two sets to one. The atmosphere on the little Centre Court was quite incredible. People booed every time Metreveli hit a winner and laughed when he slipped on the damp clay. Most memorably of all, suburban trains, which ran alongside one side of the court on an elevated track that passed within touching distance of the spectators in the back row of the stands, would slow down as the court came into view. The driver, like his passengers, would then grab the opportunity to add his kopec's worth of abuse, waving his fist and occasionally firing his whistle. There was a Czech film at the time called 'Closely Watched Trains'. This was closely watched tennis and quite as surreal as anything the Prague intellectuals dreamt up.

Frantisek Pala, a willowy figure, then showed his spine was strong enough to handle the tension by levelling the tie for the Czechs with a win over Vladimir Korotkov but the doubles was crucial. 'We have to win,' Kodes told me that evening. 'And I have to win singles, too. Somehow we have to do it. The country will not allow us to lose to the Russians.'

This tight-lipped, upright figure was hollow eyed with fatigue. Only the previous week he had gone the through the exhausting business of retaining his French Open title. And now this. Pressure is a vastly over used word in today's sporting lexicon but this was pressure of the most oppressive kind. Happily for the Czech people Kodes, with the massively-built Jan Kukal at his side, managed to recover from two sets to one down against Metreveli and Sergei Likhachev to win 6–3 in the fifth. Kodes produced one last explosive effort on the final day to trounce Korotkov and become a national hero. It was a magnificent achievement but I left Prague feeling very sorry for Metreveli.

The Czechs edged past Spain in the next round but could do nothing to silence the noise of the crowd nor the fighting qualities of the opposition in Porto Allegre where that formidable Brazilian Davis Cup duo of Thomas Koch and Edison Mandarino proved too good for Kodes and Pala. In Sao Paulo, however, the Romanians re-emerged as the competition's true challengers to American dominance when they fought back from 1–2 down to clinch another place in the Challenge Round when Nastase outwitted Koch and Tiriac, wielding his racket with that hammer-like grip, completely overwhelmed Mandarino 6–0, 6–2, 6–4.

The United States team hardly bore a look of invincibility. Ashe and Lutz had made themselves ineligible by signing with Lamar Hunt's World Championship Tennis and Cliff Richey, ever an independent soul, had stormed off the team when it was decided to hold the tie on grey clay at Charlotte, North Carolina, thus offering the Romanians

1972

BELOW: REFEREE RICKY MOREA, HIMSELF AN EXPERIENCED DAVIS CUP PLAYER FOR ARGENTINA, ATTEMPTS TO KEEP THINGS UNDER CONTROL IN BUCHAREST DURING THE INFAMOUS 1972 FINAL BETWEEN ROMANIA AND THE UNITED STATES. ION TIRIAC IS MAKING A PROTEST.

ABOVE: ERIK VAN DILLEN LUNGES FOR A BACKHAND VOLLEY WHILE STAN SMITH RACES TO
COVER DURING A TIE AGAINST ROMANIA IN THE CALIFORNIAN SUNSHINE AT WALNUT CREEK.

a surface they would be happier on than fast cement. The reason for the absence of
Ashe and Lutz now seems too stupid to contemplate. Before signing for WCT they had
been able to play Davis Cup because they were only considered quasi-professionals.
That meant they could accept prize money at certain designated tournaments but had
not quite gone the whole hog and signed up with a professional promoter. The idea of
real professionals playing Davis Cup was still one stage too far for the USLTA. It all got
sorted out in the end but it took a few more battles and one huge war at Wimbledon

in 1973 when 90 players boycotted the Championships before some sort of sanity was brought to the proceedings.

Controversially, Turville and Ralston opted to replace Richey with Frank Froehling rather than Graebner because of the clay. They were remembering Froehling's fighting performance against Britain at Bournemouth but that had been eight years before and it was asking a lot for this gangling athlete – a taller, Americanised version of Fausto Gardini in build and style – to pull it off again. But Froehling rose to the occasion against no less a competitor than the Bear from Brasov, Tiriac himself, in a match that needed to be finished on the second day with everything poised at six-all in the fifth set. Despite opening with two double faults on the resumption, Froehling held on and grabbed a dramatic victory in the next game by working his way round onto his forehand as he had done the previous day to finish off Tiriac with a mighty forehand winner. Even though Tiriac and Nastase – who had lost to Smith in the opening singles – beat Smith and newcomer Erik Van Dillen in the doubles, Stan became the man for America in the fourth rubber by defeating Tiriac 6–0 in the third set.

To the relief of all those nations who had felt intimidated and discriminated against by the Challenge Round system, Charlotte, North Carolina proved to be the last venue ever to stage one. It had been decided the year before that, after 1972, the champion nation should play through like everyone else and that the newly-styled Davis Cup Final should be held on an alternative home and away basis like most other ties. But in 1972, the draw would decide who would play where so as to start with a clean sheet. That, at least, was what was supposed to happen. But the USLTA President of the time, Bob Colwell decided a grandiose gesture was in order. The Americans had played Romania in Charlotte on the last occasion the countries had met so it would only be fair to play in Bucharest. The American captain, Dennis Ralston, was aghast. 'According to the draw we had the choice,' Ralston says, the indignation still ringing in his voice. 'My job was to see the United States retained the Cup and this was seriously going to damage our chances. We had a meeting on the porch at the West Side during Forest Hills to try and change people's minds but there was no way. We knew we were in for a tough time in Bucharest but even then we were not prepared for some of the things that went on.'

Of one thing there can be no argument – had the Challenge Round system remained in place, thus forcing Romania to play on American soil once more, the 1972 Final would have been very different in character, if not in outcome. As it was the clash between as a different a set of personalities as a sport has ever thrown together boiled up into one of the most exciting and, possibly, disgraceful contests in the history of the Davis Cup. On the American side there was the captain Dennis Ralston, the fiery temper of his youth quelled by his new-found Christian faith; Stan Smith, the tall, straight shouldered blond hero who could have appeared in a dugout alongside John Wayne in any war film you care to name; Tom Gorman, the epitome of all that is good about sporting life in America and Erik Van Dillen, a funny, highly strung and highly principled young man who was prepared to die for a cause. And then there were the Romanians, Ion Tiriac and Ilie Nastase, as perfect a pair of anti-heroes as any Hollywood script writer would ever dare offer MGM. Herbert Warren Wind, writing in the *New Yorker*, describes Tiriac thus: 'He has the look of a "heavy" all right. His hair is a mass of Brillo that droops in a sort of Transylvanian Prince Valiant style. Beneath beetle brows, his eyes slant downward, giving him a mien both dolorous and forbidding. The rest of his face is overpowered by a thick black Fu Manchu moustache. Tiriac comes from Brasov, speaks eight languages and is straight out of Eric Ambler.'

Nastase was a whippet to Tiriac's bear. As fast as his mentor was slow; wielding a foil instead of a crowbar, Nastase had ten times Tiriac's talent and only half his heart. They are both hugely generous human beings who are capable of mean acts and, in this memorable confrontation, neither were primed to present their nicer side to the opposition.

Nastase, in fact, was overwhelmed by the whole occasion and lost to a rampant Smith, who treated the medium paced clay at the Progresul Club as if it were grass, in straight sets. Gorman was the sort of man who would default on match point in the semi-final of the Masters – against Smith, incidentally – rather than deprive the Barcelona crowd of a final in case his chronic back would prevent him playing, as he was sure it would. Here he was presented with an opponent who translated sportsmanship differently. It is no use imposing Anglo-Saxon ethics on people who have seen Goths, Bulgars, Turks and Nazis rage through their land over the centuries. It is not a coincidence that Count Dracula lived in the Carpathian mountains. The Romanians have survived because they have a great sense of humour but an even greater instinct for what it takes to survive. Sometimes that is not pretty and certainly not fair. As Gorman was about to find out. Tiriac began orchestrating the hysterical crowd and pacing the match to suit his own needs. And those needs were considerable. Gorman had started brilliantly and led 6–4, 6–2, 3–2 with his serve to come. But Tiriac broke

ABOVE: EVEN BEFORE HIS MOUSTACHE GREW, ION TIRIAC LOOKED A FEARSOME FOE. HERE HE
PARTNERS ILIE NASTASE IN BUCHAREST.

back and the cacophony of sound rose to new heights. So did Tiriac's gamesmanship.
He would look down just when Gorman was ready to serve and protest every call he
didn't like. There were plenty of them and the Argentine referee Enrique Morea, a
tall, imposing figure to whom Davis Cup mayhem was nothing new, did well to impose
his authority on proceedings which could easily have spun out of control. Nodding
encouragement to linesmen who gave him the benefit of the doubt, Tiriac climbed
back into the match and levelled at two sets each. The American bench was going nuts
and once Ralston almost lost it. 'I was going to hit him,' Ralston admitted. 'I was so
mad! I yelled a few names at him as he walked by on the changeover but luckily he
ignored me and just kept on going.'

The fifth set was all Tiriac and he rattled off the last five games to win it 6–2.
Herbert Wind recorded the end: 'Stalling, protesting, grimacing, baiting, he ran out
the set to cap a thoroughly remarkable come back. Pandemonium. He was instantly
mobbed. Someone threw a gigantic white towel over his head and, covered like a tent,
the victorious gladiator left the arena to booming shouts of "Ti-ri-ac! Ti-ri-ac!".'

There was no respite for Ralston's team. Back at the Inter-Continental, the players were confined to 12th floor and not even allowed downstairs to eat in the restaurant. They were under the same kind of threat that the Australians would face in Madras the following year. There the terrorist group was called Black December. This was Black September. Different month, same problem. This was the group that had killed the Israeli athletes at the Munich Olympics just a few weeks before and, with two Jewish players on the squad, Brian Gottfried and Harold Solomon, no one was taking any chances. Twenty secret service agents were with them day and night for ten days. The tension was unrelenting.

But you would never have known from the way Smith and Van Dillen played in the doubles the following day. On previous occasions, Van Dillen had often been too excited to do himself justice but Ralston gave him a pre-match lecture on the need to keep himself under control and the result was a superb performance in which Erik played a full part in erasing the pair's loss to Nastase and Tiriac in Charlotte in no uncertain terms. Not even the linesmen could prevent a 6–2, 6–0, 6–3 rout.

On a colder Sunday morning, Smith faced Tiriac again and, as one might have expected, it was not so easy. Tiriac won the first set and then lost the next two as Smith imposed himself with his heavy serving. But Tiriac was always up to something and Ralston successfully had a linesman removed during the second set after a call that was even more outrageous than some of the others. Then this burly bear of a man started making inroads on the match again with his constantly changing pace and clever tactical manoeuvres that were both legitimate and effective. He levelled at

two sets apiece only to get blown away in the fifth as Smith, who was seething under his calm and haughty exterior, dragged every last ounce of power and will from deep within himself to win the fifth set, and the Cup, 6–0.

Ironically it was a Davis Cup issue that was used as the excuse for the showdown between the players and the ILTF,

LEFT: NIKI PILIC BECAME THE UNWITTING CATALYST FOR THE 1973 WIMBLEDON BOYCOTT AS A RESULT OF REFUSING TO PLAY IN THE DAVIS CUP FOR YUGOSLAVIA.

led by its then President, Allan Heyman, that erupted into the Wimbledon boycott of 1973. It was set up, in part, by the rational decision to allow contract pros to compete in the Davis Cup. That, however, led to scheduling problems for many of the players contracted to WCT. In particular, Niki Pilic, a stalwart of the Yugoslav team for the previous several years with Boro Jovanovic and Zeljko Franulovic, answered 'maybe' when his association, led by his uncle, asked him whether he would be available to play against New Zealand in Zagreb. When Pilic finally decided that the obligations lay with his WCT doubles partner Allan Stone and went off to compete in the World Doubles Finals in Montreal that week, his uncle found the warmth of family ties draining from his emotions. His mood was not improved when Yugoslavia lost to New Zealand in a tie they had been expected to win and he promptly suspended his nephew for nine months. In Rome, the natives in the locker room of the Foro Italico that week grew restive. In fact Cliff Drysdale, President of the Association of Tennis Professionals which had been formed at Forest Hills the year before, was surprised to discover how militant the rank and file were about this high-handed piece of amateur autocracy. Their mood was the inevitable consequence of the changing times in tennis. Players might have had little option to remain at the beck and call of their amateur associations prior to 1968, when there was no players' association, no ranking list and only under the counter payment, but all that had changed. There was no way that professionals, who were starting to earn serious sums of money, would put up with amateurs dictating where they could or could not play. The World Championship Tennis circuit, under the direction of Mike Davies, was strong enough to run three separate groups of 32 players each, culminating in a glittering showpiece for the top eight finishers in Dallas, but Wimbledon and, to a lesser extent, the other three Grand Slams were still the most famous and respected tournaments in the world. To be told you would be banned from playing in them because of confusion over a commitment to play in a Davis Cup tie was considered unacceptable. If Pilic was banned from Wimbledon, the players told Drysdale and Jack Kramer, who was their Executive Director, they would not play either. The details of how the ILTF deliberately chose Wimbledon as battleground because Heyman and other leading officials were convinced the players would never hold firm on a boycott of the world's No 1 tournament have been detailed elsewhere but, when the players proved them wrong, it suffices to say that the game was never the same again.

It was Australia's good fortune that their new President, Wayne Reid, was one of the game's progressives. A big man with big ideas, Reid had been given a freer run at changing attitudes in Australian tennis than he had expected when he received a phone call one day in 1969. It was Harry Hopman.

'I just thought I'd better tell you that I won't be able to be Davis Cup captain any more,' Hopman had said. 'I'm at the airport and I'm leaving for America – for good.'

'Oh, that's a bit of shock, Hop,' replied Reid, trying not to sound like a man being told his bank had just gone under. 'Who do you suggest we get to replace you?'

When Hopman mentioned Neale Fraser, Reid was relieved because it would have been his first choice. A fellow Melbournian with impeccable Davis Cup credentials and the stature of a Wimbledon champion would be just the man required to follow such a legendary figure.

'But it did come as shock,' Reid admitted recently on the eve of returning to Australia to run ATP Senior Tour events after a decade's exile in Monaco. 'Hopman and the Davis Cup had become synonymous and not having him around would take some getting used to.'

But Hopman had not been in favour of Open Tennis and, having him around might have hampered some of the futuristic plans Reid had in mind – like sponsorship. 'Ever since the beginning of the Hopman era, we had had a situation in which the Davis Cup had been making a fortune for Australian tennis,' Reid explained. 'But the national association had been giving it all to the States. The money hadn't been wasted because every State had built up its own tennis stadium – Milton, Memorial Drive, King's Park – but little of it had gone to junior development. I realised the only way we could keep money for ourselves to set up programmes was to raise it ourselves. So I went out and got A\$20,000 from Slazenger and Qantas and, a little later, Esso came in with A\$100,000 which was quite big money in those days.'

With sponsorship in place, Reid and his new captain felt a little more confident about going after some of the big names who had been unable to play for Australia during those early years of Open Tennis. Fraser, in fact, had been given a rough début; losing to India in Bangalore in 1970 and to Japan in Tokyo a year later. Even though Mal Anderson, Geoff Masters and Colin Dibley had gained some measure of revenge by defeating the Indians in Bangalore in 1972, Tiriac and Nastase had proved too much in Bucharest in the Inter-Zone Final and the pressure on the new team at the helm of Australian tennis to do something about this sudden run of failure grew.

'So we began tackling the players,' said Reid. 'We started with Newk at Wimbledon.

He was in the bath after one of his matches and we walked in and, putting my hand on top of his head, I told him, "Play Davis Cup for nothing or I'll push you under!" '

Reid laughed at the memory. 'Actually we had $2,000 each to offer Newcombe, Anderson, Laver and Rosewall and they all readily agreed to answer the call because, like their captain, they were all great Australians.'

The whole plan nearly went up in smoke when Australia found itself playing India in Madras is somewhat extraordinary circumstances in the Eastern Zone Final of 1973. Alan Trengove, who was there, describes what happened:

'The Australians had just arrived in Madras when they were informed by the police of a bomb threat against them made by a Pakistani terrorist group called Black December. The group was said to be trying to force the Indian Government to release some 90,000 Pakistani prisoners of war. Only a few days before it had blown up an airline office.

Fraser called an immediate meeting of the players – Newcombe, Anderson, Geoff Masters, Bob Giltinan and John Cooper – and the two writers travelling with the squad, Peter Stone and myself, to discuss whether to stay in Madras or leave immediately. The person most at risk was thought to be Newcombe because of his international fame. Both he and Anderson were married

and had children, and Masters, who was then single, nobly suggested that he and the other bachelors should stay and play the matches while Newcombe and Anderson departed. What finally determined everyone to stay was the personal guarantee of safety by the Madras assistant commissioner of police. Drastic emergency measures were enforced. All the Australians were moved onto one floor of their hotel, and when Wayne Reid, his wife and LTAA councillor, John Heathcote, subsequently arrived they were allocated rooms on the same floor. The players were confined to the hotel except for visits to the courts, when they were accompanied by a van full of armed police. Police with machine guns guarded the visitors day and night, checked all their meals and intercepted every letter or package addressed to them.

RIGHT: ILIE NASTASE SERVES FOR ROMANIA AGAINST THE UNITED STATES AT ALAMO, USA IN 1973.

In charge of the operation was one of the best sharpshooters in the Madras police force. Dressed in civilian clothes, he was never far from the players' sides, whether at the hotel or the courts. The sharpshooter always carried a sun hat. Inside it was concealed his revolver'

The actual tennis failed to live up to the drama. In what Vijay Amritraj described to me as the biggest embarrassment of his career, he and his brother Anand failed completely to produce their best tennis in front of their home town fans and both lost their opening singles in straight sets to Anderson and Newcombe. There was no way back.

The Inter-Zone Final against Czechoslovakia in Melbourne was made notable by the return to Davis Cup play of Rod Laver, after an interval of 11 years, and Ken Rosewall who had not played for 17. The Czechs were represented by Jan Kodes, the two-time French Open Champion and benefactor of that year's ATP boycott when he won Wimbledon. The mercurial but often unreliable Jiri Hrebec played second singles. Kodes, who twice reached the final of the US Open at Forest Hills, was a much better grass court player than some people gave him credit for but, in front of a packed crowd at Kooyong, Laver was inspired and beat him in straight sets. Hrebec then gave Fraser pause by upsetting Newcombe but Rosewall, who had made his début on this very court as a 17-year-old 20 years before, joined Laver in the doubles to restore Australia's lead and the next day Laver took Australia through to the final, but not before Hrebec had taken him to five sets.

The setting for the 1973 Davis Cup Final, the first final round ever to be played indoors, did not do justice to the splendour of the tennis. The memory is of a dark arena situated in downtown Cleveland. American inner cities were just starting to decay and visitors were told not to wander around the deserted streets at night. An atmosphere more removed from the open-air sunshine of Kooyong or White City could not be imagined. But that did not prevent Australia pulling off one of its most spectacular victories – a triumph that established Neale Fraser as a worthy successor to Harry Hopman, not merely because his team played so well but for the way he handled his embarrassment of riches.

The American captain Dennis Ralston was not so blessed. Confusion over Davis Cup eligibility had led Arthur Ashe to arrange a high-profile visit to South Africa – now trying to make amends by offering him a visa – the week before. Although he arrived on the eve of the tie, having flown 33 hours on the Pan Am milk run through Africa, he obviously could not play. Nor did Ralston feel inclined to pick Jimmy Connors, who

ABOVE: NEALE FRASER THREW THEM TOGETHER AS A MAKESHIFT DOUBLES TEAM BUT JOHN
NEWCOMBE AND ROD LAVER DIDN'T NEED THE HELP OF THE KOALA BEAR TO BEAT STAN SMITH
AND ERIK VAN DILLEN IN CLEVELAND IN 1973.

was just starting to carve his personality onto the fabric of the game with some astonishing tennis and equally astonishing attitudes. Connors had begun his Davis Cup career as he intended to continue it – ambivalently. He had told Ralston that he would not be available for the early rounds but could play the Final. It was an offer that would be repeated all too often down the years as far as American stars were concerned and Ralston rightly decided to stick with the team that had got him to Cleveland.

That it did not turn out to be good enough was not for want of trying. It was simply that Rod Laver and John Newcombe flicked the switch and went into orbit. The tennis they produced over the first two days was breathtaking. And yet this was no walk over. Stan Smith led Newcombe 3–1 in the fifth set of the opening rubber and had a point for 4–1 before going down 6–4 as the Australian hurled himself forward to outpower his tall opponent on the volley. Tom Gorman then made Laver work, too, leading by two sets to one after taking the first 10–8 but the Rocket was keeping his powder dry and, as Gorman began to tire, lit the fuse. The last two sets were Australia's in a blaze of stroke making, 6–3, 6–1.

That night Fraser had to make a decision and, as he freely admits today, it was the most difficult he ever had to make in his 20 years as Australian captain. He had to tell Ken Rosewall he wasn't going to play. 'I had a team of vastly experienced Grand Slam winners,' Fraser recalled. 'Mal Anderson was my fourth man and he had won Forest Hills. But even amongst that group Ken was a little bit different. He had answered the call at the age of 39 and was still as good as anyone as he proved by reaching the final of Wimbledon and Forest Hills the following year. But the performance Newk and Rod produced in the singles told me I had to go with them in the doubles even though they were not a recognised pair.'

Fraser's instincts were absolutely right. The fact that they had barely played with each other had no bearing on how they performed because these two great champions, each enjoying a purple patch of form, went out and basically played a game of singles side by side. Smith and Van Dillen did their best but were simply blown away. For the first time since the war Australia had won the Cup with someone other than Hopman at the helm.

It was the making of Neale Fraser. In the years that followed his teams were rarely out of contention in the latter rounds of the competition despite the fact that the well of talent at his disposal – with due respect to the players who produced so much for him – was no where near as deep as that which Hopman had been able to draw on. Only Pat Cash, the Wimbledon champion of 1987 could stand comparison with the Hopman generation and even he, beset by injuries, was something of a fleeting asset. But none of that prevented Fraser from winning the Cup four times in his 20 years as captain or finishing runner-up twice and reaching the semi-final or better every single year except 1974 between 1972 and 1988. He finished with a record of 55 ties won and 22 lost. Fraser would be the first to point out that, once again, grass played its part because there were years when Australia benefited from drawing tough European opposition at home and Fraser did not have to think twice about what surface to put them on. But that cannot detract from the consistency of performance that said a lot for his captaincy as well as the unwavering loyalty of Australian players. Playing for their country inspires them and, in turn, they inspire each other. Time and again the likes of John Alexander, Phil Dent, John Fitzgerald, Wally Masur, Mark Edmondson

ABOVE: THE AMRITRAJ BROTHERS, ANAND, LEFT, AND VIJAY, LED INDIA TO THE 1974 FINAL
BEFORE POLITICS THWARTED THEM. HERE THEY ENJOY A JOKE WITH ONE OF THEIR MENTORS,
THE GREAT PANCHO GONZALES WHOSE OWN DAVIS CUP CAREER WAS CUT SHORT BY THE NEED
TO TURN PROFESSIONAL.

and others proved that, as a united unit, they were greater than the sum total of their
parts. It was not always wine and roses and there were moments when Fraser found
himself at odds with certain team members but his record speaks for itself. Under the
circumstances, it stands comparison with that of Harry Hopman and 'Frase', as everyone calls him, could not ask for a better testimonial.

Having grown up under Hopman, Fraser was not afraid to inflict a similar kind of
regime on his players. 'I followed a lot of Hop's methods,' Fraser told me. 'Particularly
a lot of hard work on the practice court. Not so much extra physical activity, perhaps,
because I was dealing with top professionals which had not been the case early in
Hopman's career. I expected them to be fit and, mostly, they were. But we did a lot of
two on ones and I believed in making them fight for their places by playing each other
in practice. Even Cash. He had to prove himself time and again and some of the tennis we played amongst ourselves was outstanding.'

In many ways 1974 was the saddest in the history of the Davis Cup. South Africa
reached the final and India refused to play them. So the first time a nation outside the

1974

Big Four won the Cup it did so by default. It was the ultimate example of sport being unable to divorce itself from politics. In the opinion of millions, South Africa should not have been allowed to compete in international sport and therefore should not have been allowed back into the Davis Cup after its expulsion a few years before. The subjugation of 23 million people by a minority of six million was rather more important than any kind of sporting endeavour. But that did not make it any easier for the players to accept, especially the Indians.

Led by the Amritraj brothers, India had made it to the Final by finally gaining revenge for earlier humiliations at the hands of Australia by beating them on grass at the South Club in Calcutta. Fraser, however, had to do without his stars who were engaged in the WCT Finals in Dallas. Even though John Alexander got past Vijay Amritraj by the extraordinary score of 14–12, 17–15, 6–8, 6–2, Bob Giltinan, a droll Australian who raced pigeons, never quite found his way through the maze of Jasjit Singh's oriental game and went down by the equally extraordinary margin of 11–9, 9–11, 12–10, 8–6. But, in Calcutta's heat, they were just warming up. When Vijay and Anand took the court to face Alexander and the huge-serving Colin Dibley, the quartet were on the verge of making Davis Cup history. After a record number of 327 games had been played, Dibley was hobbling with cramp and the Indians had edged it 17–15, 6–8, 6–3, 16–18, 6–4.

Meanwhile Cliff Drysdale and Ray Moore, a young man who had entered into the spirit of the times and wore his long hair encased in a headband, aided by the burgeoning doubles combination of Frew McMillan and the Australian-born import Bob Hewitt had been scoring a series of remarkably one-sided victories all over South America. The Brazilians were swept aside 5–0, then, in Guayaquil, Ecuador suffered the same fate. Chile refused to play South Africa at home so the tie was moved to Bogota in Colombia and once again, with Moore and Hewitt playing singles, the result was 5–0. The Zone Final was also in Bogota but this time against the host nation who had scored a major upset in that city in the previous round by beating the United States – the clever clay court pair of Ivan Molina and Jairo Velasco proving too steady for Solomon and Van Dillen. Once again the South Africans proved themselves to be in a different class. Moore beat Molina in four sets while Hewitt needed only three to dispose of Velasco, and then joined with McMillan to settle the issue. For a non-South American team to tour that continent and rack up 18 victories in consecutive rubbers is an achievement that will, under the new system, never be challenged. It was a magnificent performance but one that, unhappily, was forgotten in the aftermath of the bitterness that followed. Quite unfairly as far as the players were concerned, their triumphs had been achieved under the apartheid flag and there was no answer to that.

India went on to beat the Soviet Union at Poona and the Amritraj brothers were in Sweden for the Stockholm Open in November when they picked up an *International Herald Tribune* and discovered their national association had defaulted the final and handed the Cup to South Africa.

'Although it did not come as that much of a surprise, we were still furious at the way it came about,' says Vijay Amritraj who, 14 years later, would be asked to address the United Nations' Special Committee on Apartheid. 'We were quite prepared to accept our Government's decision, whatever that might be, because we realised that they would be looking at the consequences from a higher level. But it turned out that our Association had taken the decision before any government edict was issued. That, we felt, was high-handed and premature.'

Leaving Ray Moore, Frew McMillan and Robert Maud with whom they were perfectly good friends in the hotel lobby, the brothers repaired to their room and phoned New Delhi. Anand, whose personality is, to put it mildly, more direct than Vijay's, ended up yelling at his Association President and was later required to apologise. But, of course, it did little good. The Final was never played and South Africa had won the Davis Cup.

Sadly, there was universal relief when the champion nation lost the Cup in Santiago in the semi-final of the American Zone in 1975. By then South Africa had caused havoc by its presence in that sphere of the competition. Both Mexico and Colombia had defaulted in earlier rounds rather than play them and there was much weeping and gnashing of teeth over Mexico's withdrawal, in particular, following their brilliant victory on American territory at the Palm Springs Racquet Club. Raul Ramirez, then 21, had been the architect of their triumph, beating both Smith and Roscoe Tanner in singles and teaming with Vicente Zarazua in a decisive doubles win over the scratch team of Tanner and Bob Lutz.

Had South Africa been at full strength the agony might have continued but, with Drysdale and Hewitt absent, the Chilean pair of Jaime Fillol, who was to follow in Drysdale's footsteps a couple of years later to become President of the ATP, and Patricio Cornejo proved too strong for Moore and Bernie Mitton and won 5–0.

However, the odour of politics clung to Dwight's silver bowl. Such was the state of

1975

the world that everyone seemed to have a grievance against someone else and it was doubly ironic that Chile, having rid the competition of one disruptive influence, should promptly become one themselves. They were due to play in Sweden next and activists in that left-wing nation immediately saw an opportunity to launch a protest against the right-wing junta that had ousted the socialist Allende regime a couple of years earlier. Fillol received a death threat and Chile requested that the tie be played on neutral ground. Only after the Swedish authorities promised maximum security at sleepy little seaside resort of Bastad did the tie go ahead. But that weekend it wasn't sleepy. Although few spectators ventured inside the arena, hundreds picketed the grounds and huge nets were erected to prevent missiles and fire crackers from landing on the court. Not that anything was likely to disturb the icy concentration of the game's new sensation.

Bjorn Borg was already a star by then, having cut his Davis Cup teeth at the age of 15 when he became the youngest player up to that time to win a Davis Cup match by beating New Zealand's Onny Parun at Bastad in 1972. Trained originally by Percy Rosberg and later by Lennart Bergelin, Borg would go on to become one of the most acclaimed and recognised athletes on earth. Six French Open crowns and five consecutive titles at Wimbledon, a feat which still leaves his contemporaries open-mouthed, left no room for argument when it came to placing him high in the game's pantheon of great players. But Davis Cup was never his true metier. A stubborn individualist, Borg was too often at odds with his association and never matched the commitment of his country's great Davis Cup players like Ulf Schmidt who played 38 ties or Sven Davidson and Bergelin himself who played 36. With just 21 Borg was not even close to Jan-Erik Lundquist, Stefan Edberg and Anders Jarryd, all of whom appeared 35 times for their country. But when Borg did decide to play, no one could doubt his worth or commitment to the team. In singles he won 45 matches and lost just 11 And 1975 was his finest year in Swedish colours.

Even Borg, however, could not do it alone and he was aided along the way in courageous fashion by one of the Cup's unsung heroes, Birger Andersson, a tall farmer with an agricultural gait and a temperament capable of weathering any storm. Twice on Sweden's road to the final, Andersson was handed the toughest of assignments – having to win fifth rubbers against highly accomplished opposition. In Berlin he managed it by beating the German No 1 Karl Meiler in straight sets and, in Barcelona, offered another performance of unflappable cool by defeating Jose Higueras 6–0 in the fourth. In Bastad, amidst the mayhem, Birger saved Bjorn the trouble of finishing off Chile by winning the fourth rubber against Cornejo and, unhappily for this noble servant of Swedish tennis, that was that. With perfect logic, Bergelin, now captain of the Swedish team, elected to play the final against Czechoslovakia, who had beaten a weakened Australian squad in Prague, on the fast tiles at the Kungliga tennishallen in Stockholm. Every Swedish player was familiar with the surface which was not to be found anywhere else on the international circuit. And as Borg's doubles partner was a towering, bearded giant with a massive serve called Ove Bengtson, Andersson, the clay courter, found himself on the bench.

The Davis Cup Final of 1975 was a great occasion for Swedish tennis and a forerunner of many more triumphs in the future. And although Finals in subsequent years would be played in the much bigger Scandinavium in Gothenburg, it was fitting that the first Swedish Final should be staged in the very special surroundings of the old Kungliga tennishallen, so redolent of matches involving King Gustav V and the young Bergelin practising with Baron von Cramm in the dark days of the war. It is a small arena, seating no more than 4,000 and it had always been packed for the Stockholm Open, which had been inaugurated with loving care by Hans-Ake Sturen in 1969. Sturen and his team of young blonds of both sexes had created a cosy, typically Scandanavian atmosphere that was duplicated during the Final. Small candles flickered on the tables in the players' lounge where those famous open-faced Swedish sandwiches were always on offer. And at night everyone tasted a little schnapps at Alexandra's discotheque. Even with grey-suited Czech officials hovering uneasily in the background, it seemed to be a family affair.

As soon as Borg snuffed out the threat of Hrebec in the opening rubber, losing just four games, the result was a foregone conclusion. True, Kodes beat Bengtson but Ove then got his serve in good working order for the doubles which he and Borg secured against Kodes and another big serving giant, Vladimir Zednik, to ensure that Bjorn only had to win his second singles to bring the Cup to Sweden. Against Kodes nothing was ever easy but Borg, blasting his ground strokes and getting in to volley when needed, won in straight sets and the party was on. It was still going by the time Bergelin got up on the table at the celebration dinner to disrobe and reveal his lucky underwear – long johns adorned with tigers – that he had been wearing, even in the heat of Barcelona, at every tie as his good luck charm. Over at the Czech Embassy, Zednik, who would later coach Petr Korda, was into his sixth schnapps and past caring. 'Look at them!' he exclaimed from his great height, sweeping a mighty arm in the direction of the Czech Communist Party officials crowding the reception. 'Dummies! They are all dummies!' Dear Zed. He was lucky not to get arrested.

Although Zednik was directing his evaluation of politicians at the Czechs in particular, his comments would have been echoed by tennis players across the world in 1976. Perversely, the Davis Cup's very prestige and prominence was threatening it with extinction. In the climate of the times, it was too juicy a target for those wishing to posture and pose. Governments could glean easy publicity for whatever cause or stance they were currently espousing by refusing its Davis Cup team to play against whatever nation it disliked. The Olympics was suffering from the same problem during these years but the Davis Cup was held every year and each hefty kick in its unwanted role as a prime political football left it more severely bruised.

Four nations had withdrawn for political reasons in 1975, seven in 1976 and four more would do so early in 1977. The Soviet Union would not play against Chile; Ireland would not play against Rhodesia and Kenya didn't want to have anything to do with New Zealand because the All Blacks still played rugby against the Springboks. Mexico withdrew for the second successive year. Of the tennis authorities, it was the United States which lost patience first. Reacting to Mexico's withdrawal, the Americans announced they would withdraw from the competition unless a rule was brought in automatically suspending a nation that pulled out for political reasons.

'Governments are making rules as to who will play whom at tennis,' commented Joe Carrico, chairman of the US Davis Cup committee. 'This is repugnant to us and frankly unacceptable.'

Fine sentiments except that, in the world of realpolitik they were useless. Governments, in Tilden's phrase, were going to play their own sweet game. Threatening to withdraw from the competition in 1977, as did the tennis associations of the United States, Britain and France, would have had no effect other than to ensure the death of the Davis Cup. Happily, a few of the more realistic tennis leaders recognised this and it was at an informal meeting in Monte Carlo in July 1976 that Pablo Llorens, President of the Spanish Tennis Federation, moved that 1977 be viewed as a neutral year in which everyone played as best they could while reviewing the future. Brian Tobin, the Australian President who would later succeed Philippe Chatrier as President of the ITF, supported Llorens and a crisis was averted.

Despite these dark political clouds, a record number of 53 nations entered the Davis

Cup in 1976 and some fantastic tennis was played across the globe, most of it involving the Italians who were now captained by their former star Nicola Pietrangeli. In every sense 1976 was Adriano Panatta's year. The handsome, doe-eyed romantic hero became the national heart-throb as he saved 11 match points in the first round against Kim Warwick at the Foro Italico before going on to win his national title and then saved another against Pavel Hutka in the first round of the French Open before claiming his only Grand Slam. And then there was the Davis Cup. After wins against Poland and Yugoslavia, Italy received their little piece of luck when Sweden had to go to the Foro Italico without Borg who had pulled a stomach muscle while winning Wimbledon. It must be said, however, that Panatta was the one man of that era who had the game to beat Borg on clay and proved it by being the last man to defeat the Swede before he started dominating Roland Garros. A clay courter with a big serve and volley game, Panatta was a formidable proposition and he did not lose a match in the early rounds.

BELOW: ADRIANO PANATTA BECAME AN EVEN GREATER IDOL IN ITALY THAN HIS PREDECESSOR NICOLA PIETRANGELI. HERE, IN SANTIAGO, PANATTA, WITH PIETRANGELI IN THE ROLE OF CAPTAIN, LEADS ITALY TO DAVIS CUP TRIUMPH.

ABOVE: A PACKED STADIUM AT CAMPO SANTIAGO FOR THE 1976 FINALS BETWEEN CHILE
AND ITALY.

Panatta was aided and abetted by a shorter, more phlegmatic player called Paolo
Bertolucci who was, in fact, blessed with more natural ability than his partner but,
unlike Caesar, lacked ambition. 'I like to hit beautiful shots,' he told me once. 'This
makes me happy. If I win, too, that is OK.'

It was an attitude that ensured Bertolucci never did himself justice in singles
although he and Panatta became one of the great doubles combinations of their day.
They met their match, however, on Wimbledon's No 1 Court when they came up
against John Lloyd and his formidably ambitious brother David. What kind of players
both John Lloyd and Bertolucci would have been had they possessed even a portion of
David Lloyd's burning desire to succeed can only be guessed at, but it was David who
took a memorable doubles encounter by the scruff of the neck and, literally throwing
himself about court in the most amazing display of defiance, turned a two-set deficit

into a loudly acclaimed five-set victory. It was only a temporary set back for the Italians, however, for the next day Panatta beat Roger Taylor, nearing the end of a fine Davis Cup career that saw him finish with a 26–9 singles record, to send Italy through to the Inter-Zone Final against Australia in Rome.

It had not been an easy year for Neale Fraser. Poised to beat New Zealand in Brisbane at 2–1 up with Newcombe waiting to play Brian Fairlie, the event had been hit by a cyclone. Such were the schedules of the players involved that the only way to finish was to stage the remainder of the tie on another grass court on the other side of the world – at Nottingham. Just about managing to keep his 32-year-old star's mind on the task in hand, Fraser shepherded Newcombe through a three-hour battle with the belligerent Fairlie who rivalled the future Wimbledon finalist Chris Lewis as New Zealand's finest player since Anthony Wilding.

———

If the Inter-Zone Final in Rome was not Newcombe's finest hour, it may well have been

BELOW: THE BROTHERS, DAVID LLOYD, RIGHT, AND JOHN LLOYD, WERE THE FIRST CHOICE DOUBLES PAIR FOR GREAT BRITAIN'S DAVIS CUP TEAM IN THE LATE 1970S AND EARLY 1980S.

ABOVE: ALITALIA BRING HOME PAOLO BERTOLUCCI, CORRADO BARAZZUTTI, CAPTAIN NICOLA PIETRANGELI, ADRIANO PANATTA – AND THE CUP.

John Alexander's. Revealing an unexpected ability to battle it out on clay, Alexander stunned the crowd by beating Panatta in straight sets after Newcombe had fallen to the unstylishly effective Corrado Barazzutti. Any hopes Newcombe and Roche had of pulling Australia back into the tie were blown away by a rare display of animation from Bertolucci who, possibly remembering David Lloyd, threw himself through the air at one point to make a backhand service return. Not even Boris Becker has tried that. Alexander produced another fine performance of aggressive clay court tennis to beat Barazzutti but Panatta was too strong for Newcombe whose fine Davis Cup career was eventually put to rest in the red dust.

So Italy were through to their third final with a long and, inevitably controversial, journey to Santiago awaiting them. 'We had a left-wing government at the time and the Prime Minister – who was it? who knows? Andreotti, perhaps – was against us playing,' recalls Bertolucci, now more involved than he has ever been, having succeeded Panatta as Davis Cup captain in the late 1990s. 'But we were determined to play. Just beat Chile to win the Cup? When would we get another chance like that? So, after playing a tournament in Buenos Aires, I went straight to Santiago and kept on sending radio reports back to Rome saying that it was all right, that the place was quite normal, that Pinochet's men weren't shooting people on the streets.'

So Paolo Bertolucci, always a little more committed than he appeared, played his part in ensuring that the 1976 Davis Cup Final took place. It was a big occasion for Chile, too, even though Jaime Fillol and Patricio Cornejo, two of the most popular players on the tour, had no chance of stemming the might that was Italian tennis that year. Panatta and Barazzutti won the opening singles and Panatta and Bertolucci wrapped it up in the doubles. The Davis Cup, for the third successive year, would find a new home, glinting under the huge marble statues at the Foro Italico a few months later when it was shown off with pride in the sunshine of a new Roman spring.

The year 1977 started well – Morocco refused to play Algeria. But, sticking to their promise to tiptoe through the political minefield, those nations that were allowed some freedom of sporting action by the governments produced another fascinating year of tennis. But even those ties that were played could not escape the political mood of the times. The new American captain Tony Trabert found himself in the thick of it when the United States met South Africa in Tucson, Arizona. Reacting as fast as Wyatt Earp, Trabert was out of his chair wielding a racket and striking out at two anti-apartheid protesters who rushed on court during the doubles to pour motor oil on the court. It did little for troubled waters, however, and there were more demonstrations and more retaliation from an enraged Trabert the following day. But by then the Smith-Lutz combination had ensured the Americans of victory following singles wins for Brian Gottfried and Roscoe Tanner on the opening day.

However, another trip south of the border for the Americans, proved fatal. No demonstrations, just Guillermo Vilas, the new star of Argentine tennis, proving himself virtually invincible on clay. Vilas had won the French and US titles that year and was at the height of his powers. He crushed Gottfried after Ricardo Cano had surprised Dick Stockton in the opening singles and although Sherwood Stewart and Freddie McNair kept the US momentarily alive, Vilas finished it off.

Australia were the next visitors to Buenos Aires, and even Vilas could not stop Fraser's men. John Alexander's 6-3, 6-0, 6-0 thrashing of Cano left the Argentine no. 2 in no shape to tackle Phil Dent in the reverse singles and Australia went through to yet another final.

Meanwhile, the Italians had been guarding their Cup jealously. Bjorn Borg helped them on their way by refusing to play Davis Cup that year, thus making Pietrangeli's life easier in Bastad where his team won 4–1. Then Barazzutti, having lost the open singles against Jose Higueras in Barcelona ensured that Italy beat Spain with a fourth rubber victory over Manolo Orantes. That left Italy with France standing between them and another Final. But it was too early for the French. Their true triumphs would come later. Pierre Darmon and the talented serve and volleyer Pierre Barthes had kept France competitive through the 1960s and early 1970s and now François Jauffret, Patrice Dominguez and Patrick Proisy were attempting to do the same. In 1977 they made a bold bid for further glory by beating Nastase and his Romanians at Roland Garros but Panatta and Barazzutti proved just too resilient on a dramatic opening day of the Inter-Zone Final, outlasting Dominguez and Jauffret respectively in long five set-ters. Panatta and Bertolucci clinched it. This time it was Italy's turn to go Down Under.

The Panatta-Bertolucci partnership, aided by a small group of flag-waving Italians, kept the Final alive by surprising Alexander and Dent in the doubles at White City. But then it was a do-or-die situation against Alexander for Adriano who had been beaten by Tony Roche's left-handed guile in the opening rubber. It was a blustery day but the wind did not diminish the drama. Panatta led by two sets to one and then, having lost the fourth, clawed his way back into the fifth from 3–5 down. But, back at 5–5, Alexander still had the advantage of serving first and, with clever use of the lob which exposed Panatta's overhead in the wind, J.A. as he is known, had the thrill of nailing down another Cup triumph for his country with a magnificent 6–4, 4–6, 2–6, 8–6, 11–9 victory. Alexander's success was magnified by the fact that he had proved himself at both ends of the earth, on both types of surface. Clay in Rome, grass in Sydney – nowhere could the Italians defeat this Alexander.

CHAPTER TWELVE

McENROE TO THE RESCUE

McEnroe commits.... NEC signs.... Format changes with World group....
Gothic horror show for Ashe in Gothenberg.... Becker and Edberg lead
European advance as the Cup spreads its wings

N 1977, A WILD-LOOKING YOUNG MAN from a good Irish family in the middle class New York suburb of Douglaston, reached the Wimbledon semi-final unseeded at the age of 17. In 1978, the selfsame John Patrick McEnroe made his singles début in the Davis Cup Final against Britain at the Mission Hill Country Club in Rancho Mirage, California. It wasn't the second coming but, for the Davis Cup, the arrival on the tennis scene of this blissfully talented left-hander was a blessing from heaven – even if his temper was not.

Nothing that has happened since has made me regret an assertion I made in *Open Tennis* in 1988 that John McEnroe saved the Davis Cup. I still firmly believe that, without him, there would have been a serious danger of the competition becoming second rate and, amidst the intensive commercial competition that has engulfed tennis throughout the last two decades of the century, that would have meant eventual extinction.

As we have seen, the Davis Cup was not only being buffeted by political storms but, more worryingly, it was being ignored by several of the world's leading players. Jimmy Connors basically wasn't interested in becoming a team man at anything; Bjorn Borg was also too individualistic and frequently at odds with his national association; Vitas Gerulaitis had his moments of patriotic fervour but they were not constant; Guillermo Vilas and the other great Argentine player of the era Jose Luis Clerc were also in conflict with the Argentine LTA over terms. Even Arthur Ashe could not claim a 100 attendance record. American captains, in particular, found themselves in the on-bended-knee position when asking increasingly rich young stars to represent their country. It was humiliating – but not when they talked to John McEnroe. Then the commitment was unconditional. 'I'll go anywhere, any time to play Davis Cup for the United States,' he announced to the world and he meant it.

'My parents brought me up to believe that it was an honour to play for your country and that Davis Cup was the way you did it,' McEnroe has told me on various occasions. 'And despite the problems that arose later, I hope I contributed something worthwhile. I just never understood why people didn't want to play and still don't. Right from when I was a kid it has always seemed a pretty exciting thing to do, being part of a team and representing your country.'

The importance of the most exciting new tennis star the world had seen in decades espousing those kind of sentiments towards the Davis Cup was monumental. It was not just a matter of prestige but rather one of survival in the hard commercial world. It had been clear for some time that the Davis Cup needed an overall sponsor, a top multinational company to come in with serious money so that it could compete for a professional's attention and time. McEnroe might have been willing to play for a pittance but there were not many McEnroes in the world and even players who were instinctively nationalistic would require proper remuneration. But for any multinational, the American market was paramount. And if American players were not interested in playing, public apathy would follow. So why fork out dollars for a dud? It would not have taken any Board of Directors long to pose that easily answered question. So it was of paramount importance that McEnroe was not only an exciting attraction and destined to become No 1 in the world but that he was American. For the equation, as I have said before, was simple: no McEnroe, no America; no America, no sponsor; no sponsor, no Davis Cup.

The very fact that McEnroe had rapidly established himself as a Davis Cup star was one of the main attractions for the Nippon Electric Company, or NEC, who were looking for worldwide exposure. In 1980 they came in with a sponsorship offer of $1 million dollars – the money to be split into prize money levels for each year's best performing nations – and the happy liaison has continued right through the last two decades.

So the début of the curly-haired youngster with the headband in the Californian desert at the end of 1978 was a significant milestone in the history of the Cup's development. That McEnroe started off with two straight-set victories came as no surprise. He had, after all, shown few signs of nerves when, partnered by Brian Gottfried, he had

LEFT: Iɴ ᴛʜᴇ ʙʀɪɢʜᴛ ᴅᴇsᴇʀᴛ sᴜɴsʜɪɴᴇ ᴀᴛ Mɪssɪᴏɴ Hɪʟʟs Cᴏᴜɴᴛʀʏ Cʟᴜʙ ɪɴ Rᴀɴᴄʜ Mɪʀᴀɢᴇ
Cᴀʟɪғᴏʀɴɪᴀ, ᴀ ʏᴏᴜɴɢ ᴍᴀɴ ᴡɪᴛʜ ᴀ ʜᴇᴀᴅ ʙᴀɴᴅ ᴍᴀᴅᴇ ʜɪs Dᴀᴠɪs Cᴜᴘ ᴅᴇʙᴜᴛ ɪɴ sɪɴɢʟᴇs
ᴀɢᴀɪɴsᴛ Bʀɪᴛᴀɪɴ. Iᴛ ᴡᴀs ᴛʜᴇ Fɪɴᴀʟ ᴏғ 1978. Jᴏʜɴ McEɴʀᴏᴇ ʜᴀᴅ ᴀʀʀɪᴠᴇᴅ.

ABOVE: ON THEIR WAY TO THE FINAL BRITAIN HAD DISTINGUISHED THEMSELVES BY BEATING
FRANCE AT ROLAND GARROS – DESPITE THE AIRBORNE EFFORTS OF ERIC DEBLICKER WHEN HE
MET BUSTER MOTTRAM.

made his first appearance in the doubles against Chile in Santiago in the previous round. No, the surprise was the opposition. Britain did not seem to have the firepower to make it all the way to the Final, certainly not at a time when Vilas was in his prime, Alexander and Roche were playing so well for Australia and Borg had decided that this would be one of his Davis Cup years. But Britain made it through on merit. Chile's Hans Gildemeister had got rid of the Argentine threat after setting up a 3–2 win in the American zone semi-finals by beating Vilas in the opening rubber. In the inter-zone finals, the Americans had taken care of the Swedes in Gothenburg with Ashe and Gerulaitis both beating Kjell Johannson and the Smith-Lutz duo taking care of Borg and Bengtson. In the other Inter-Zone Final, held in the unlikely setting of an indoor arena at London's Crystal Palace, the two men who were primarily responsible for setting Britain on the road to California, Buster Mottram and John Lloyd surprised everyone. Mottram, whose father Tony had been Britain's first post-war Davis Cup star, was a gangling young man whose galumphing gait masked a natural talent. In the opening rubber he abandoned his customary baseline game to attack Roche on the fast court and beat him 6–4 in the fourth. After a desperately nervous start, Lloyd then set about attacking Alexander's backhand. Finishing in a blaze of glory, Lloyd won 7–5, 6–2, 6–2. Before the Australians could recover from the shock, the British captain Paul Hutchins unleashed his pet rottweiler alongside Mark Cox in the doubles. David Lloyd, as usual, was straining at the leash and with a heavy-hitting southpaw at his side, he chewed up the 1977 Wimbledon champions, Ross Case and Geoff Masters, in four sets. Britain had won. The Australians were speechless.

At Mission Hills, a luxurious country club nor far from Palm Springs that was still being reclaimed from the desert and sported Frank Sinatra and Gerald Ford as neighbours – the fact that roads leading to the club were named after the singer and the

BELOW: THE CENTRE COURT AT MISSION HILLS COUNTRY CLUB DURING THE 1978 FINAL BETWEEN THE UNITED STATES AND BRITAIN.

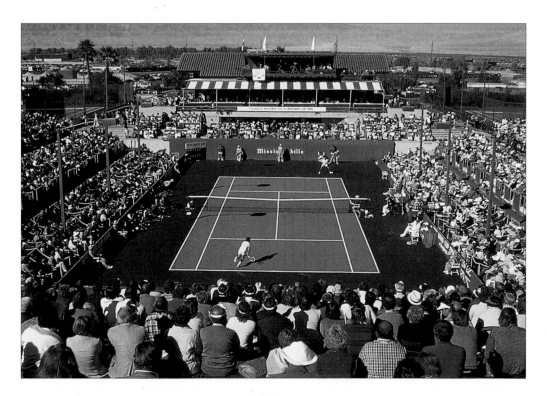

President sort of hinted at that – Britain knew that further glory could turn into a mirage. After the first rubber, John Lloyd didn't know what was real and what wasn't. He had been completely bemused by McEnroe's skills and admitted as much. 'I've never been made to look an idiot on court before,' he said. 'Not by Borg, not by Connors, not by anyone until I played McEnroe today.' The score was 6–1, 6–2, 6–2.

Mottram then restored British pride by playing the greatest match of his career. Two sets to love down against the solid Gottfried, he fought all the way back, saving a match point before he won it 6–3 in the fifth under the lights as icy desert air left small groups of spectators huddled around the Centre Court. Gerald Williams and Dan Maskell had to control chattering teeth as they commentated for BBC Radio on the exposed clubhouse roof. But it was all Britain could offer. Smith and Lutz mopped up the doubles and then Tony Trabert guided McEnroe through his reverse singles with Mottram, suggesting that he hit, rather than chip, his service returns so as to give Buster less time.

It had been a brilliant beginning by the 19-year-old who had been preferred to Ashe, who was then 35. 'John was my most coachable guy,' says Trabert. 'He would not only listen but had the skill to put whatever you suggested into practice. I just wish I could have controlled his behaviour.'

1979

So the Cup was back in the States and there it stayed through 1979. The Americans were saved from any dangerous sorties into Latin America and capitalised by using McEnroe and Gerulaitis to outhit the Argentines indoors in Memphis. They then had to travel to Sydney where Gerulaitis, who enjoyed his best year of Davis Cup play, put them on the path to a 4–1 victory by battling past the determined Mark Edmondson in five tough sets. In Europe, Britain's run had ended in Rome but not before Mottram had displayed his skills once more by beating Panatta in the opening rubber. Barazzutti, however won both his singles. That was more than he did in the Inter-Zone Final at the Foro Italico where the young Czech, Tomas Smid, beat him in five sets. However Ivan Lendl, also 19 years old and still raw, was no match for Panatta and the Italians came through 4–1 to gain the fourth Final appearance in their history.

The Final was staged indoors once more, this time in a cramped civic auditorium in San Francisco. The surroundings were more agreeable than Cleveland but the place was still unsuited to what should have been the pageantry of a Final. And, for the Italians, the omens had been bad from the start. The team was mourning the tragic loss of their captain, Umberto Bergamo, who had been killed in a car crash a few

ABOVE: Italy made it to the Final again in 1979 but this powerful team of Vitas Gerulaitis, captain Tony Trabert, Bob Lutz, Stan Smith and John McEnroe proved too good for them in San Francisco.

weeks before. With Smith and Lutz playing doubles as usual, McEnroe and Gerulaitis dominated the singles and Italy did not win a set.

———

The 1980s proved to be the decade that the Davis Cup changed irrevocably. For a start, 1981 saw the introduction of NEC's prize money as well as the World Group, consisting of the 16 best nations, with a play-off relegation system that would send teams back down into the Zonal Groups. The idea was the brainchild of the former *Guardian* tennis correspondent David Gray, a man of great charm and culture, who had become Secretary General of the ITF a few years before. Despite some embarrassing situations that have seen nations as seemingly powerful as the United States and Australia relegated for brief periods, most observers feel the system has worked well and remains a fitting testament to Gray's fertile mind. The 1980s was also the decade that saw Europe reclaim dominance of the competition for the first time since France and Britain held sway in the 1920s and 1930s. For six of the ten years the Cup was won by either Czechoslovakia, Germany, both for the first time, or Sweden.

It was the Czechs' turn first. They needed a little luck but who could begrudge them that. Deserted by the fickle Menzel when their country was overrun by the Nazis in the 1930s and unable to keep Drobny and Cernik after they had tried hard to bring home the Cup to their beleaguered nation, Czechoslovakia finally discovered a strapping athlete who, with some talented support, became capable of winning what was now styled The Davis Cup by NEC. It was a brave new world and Ivan Lendl was ready for it. Like Drobny, Cernik and Martina Navratilova, he would not stay forever but, unlike those great champions he was able to lift Czech hearts by bringing home the silverware before he left.

1980

The luck came in the form of injury and suspension for potential opponents. Nastase was undergoing one of those spells of suspension that came about periodically when even the Romanians felt his imitations of Vlad the Impaler became too realistic and so missed the Czechs' visit to Prague. Lendl and Pavel Slozil, with Kodes joining in for the doubles, raced to a 4–1 win. In the previous round France had gone to Prague without their new star Yannick Noah, who would later have such an impact on their fortunes. Noah was injured and France lost 5–0.

It was in Buenos Aires in the Inter-Zone Final that the Czechs really earned their spurs. The Argentines were cock-a-hoop after their fine victory over the United States which even McEnroe's presence could not forestall. Partnered by Peter Fleming, McEnroe had managed to win the doubles but, in a decisive fourth rubber, he went down 6–4 in the fifth to a triumphant Vilas. For Czechoslovakia, Tomas Smid was suffering from a back strain and was only played in the doubles, leaving Slozil to try and do the best he could against Vilas and Clerc. A two-set to one lead against Clerc was much as he could do and the tall, rangy Argentine who must rank as the best player never to have reached a Grand Slam final, ran out the fifth set 6–1. Lendl, however, was a different proposition. Immensely strong and capable of intense concentration, Ivan pounded the ball from the back court with unwavering weight and accuracy and, on this occasion, did so with too much power for Vilas. Beating Vilas 7–5, 8–6, 9–7 in front of Guillermo's own crowd was something of which Lendl could be truly proud. He and Smid then won the doubles in straight sets and Lendl completed an unexpectedly straightforward victory by defeating Clerc in four.

Meanwhile, the Australians were back in Rome, this time with a team spearheaded by the pair who had just won the Wimbledon doubles title, Peter McNamara and Paul McNamee. Both Macs had plenty of experience of European clay but Panatta was too strong and, despite McNamara's fine win over Barazzutti, the Italians were never likely to squander the opportunity of reaching the Final for the sixth time.

Frustratingly for their fans, Italy was also forced to play away again for the sixth time. Nor was snow-covered Prague in the dead of winter quite such an attractive proposition as Sydney. At least one Italian supporter probably regretted going anywhere near the place. It was a bizarre final, in many ways; partially because the matches were staged at in indoor ice rink and partially because of the amazing events that caused the proceedings to be halted while frantic diplomatic phone calls crackled between Prague and Rome. The trouble erupted when Smid started a courageous fightback against Panatta in the opening rubber after the Italian hero had won the first two sets. There were about 300 Italians supporters in the sold-out arena and they were not to be ignored. The decibel level ricocheted off the roof every time Panatta won a point and frequently they were on their feet, yelling their heads off. All this made the Czech police a little nervy. Foreigners seemingly on the verge of running amok were not amongst the listed set of contingencies in their manual on how to suppress the masses and when they came down the aisle to try and quieten one particularly vociferous individual by laying hands on him, an officer got his hand bitten. Oh, dear. The Czech police knew exactly what to do then. Take the culprit outside and beat him up in the snow. Normal procedure. What was not normal was the reaction of the man's friends.

'Stop the match!' they yelled at a startled Panatta. 'They've taken one of us away!'

Panatta, who looked as if he could do with a break, needed no further bidding and ceased to play. Impasse. Frantic conversations between David Gray of the ITF and various court officials became even more frantic when a phone call was received from Rome. The match was being televised live and the man who had been dragged out of the stadium had been recognised by his friends – his Communist friends. By some weirdly improbably irony, the police had hand picked the one person out of 300 who was a close friend of the leader of the Italian Communist Party. Faces can get redder but not much. Hurriedly dusting the snow off their victim, they released him back into the bosom of his fellow fans and, after a 40 minute hiatus, the match continued. But it only got worse for Italy. Smid, charging the net in his high stepping style, grabbed the fifth set 6–4.

ABOVE: TOMAS SMID, IVAN LENDL, PAVEL SLOZIL AND JAN KODES LINE UP BEHIND THE CUP BEFORE THE 1980 FINAL IN PRAGUE WHERE POLICE AND POLITICS INTERRUPTED PLAY.

LEFT: IVAN LENDL WAS DOING HIS MILITARY SERVICE AT THE TIME. DID THE UNIFORM HASTEN HIS DEPARTURE TO THE STATES?

Lendl then overpowered Barazzutti and teamed up with Smid to beat Panatta and Bertolucci in five sets to ensure that Czechoslovakia, a nation rich in tennis folklore, became the eighth nation to win the Davis Cup. The Italians, upset by some line calls, not to mention the behaviour of the police, declined to join in the victory ceremony. But no one could argue that the Czechs were deserving winners.

With NEC installed as sponsors, there would be $200,000 on offer for the winning team in 1981 with $100,000 to the runners-up amongst other prizes. In announcing the deal as well as the creation of the new World Group format, Philippe Chatrier, a visionary who had done so much for the modernisation of both French and international tennis, spoke of the need to preserve traditions while also keeping pace with the times. Chatrier had been a Davis Cup captain himself in the 1960s and, having dealt with players in good times and bad, knew how important it was to make the Davis Cup attractive to the new generation. This new look at the start of the 1980s with John McEnroe on board, went a long way down the track to achieving that goal.

Appropriately McEnroe led the United States to another triumph in 1981. The 16 nation World Group set up some fascinating early round matches that included Australia, inspired by McNamara, beating France in Lyon and then overcoming the Swedes in Bastad where Mats Wilander was still too young to handle either McNamara or McNamee. The Italians' dreams of another Final were thwarted in Brighton where Mottram once again came up trumps by beating Barazzutti in straight sets in the deciding fifth rubber. Hutchins then took his team around the world, beating New Zealand in Christchurch but failing to win a set in Buenos Aires. That victory put Argentina into the Davis Cup Final for the first time.

The Americans, meanwhile, had a new captain. After a major heart problem, Arthur Ashe had been forced to retire but his standing in the game made him an obvious choice to succeed Trabert as captain. By the time his team had beaten Australia 5–0 at Portland, Oregon, Ashe, outwardly the most phlegmatic of men, was ready to check into a stress clinic. He had been appalled by the behaviour of McEnroe as well as Peter Fleming who could also work up a good head of steam on court. The Australians were scathing in their comments afterwards. After McEnroe beat Edmondson, Tanner came through a tough five-setter against McNamara who, with McNamee injured, had Phil Dent as a partner in the doubles. This was where the explosion occurred. Riled by line calls and annoyed that Ashe didn't jump up and argue their case at every opportunity, McEnroe and Fleming worked themselves up into such a state of nervous tension that they were soon abusing the Canadian umpire, the lines judges and even Ashe himself. Two warnings were issued and, under the new rules laid down by the Men's Professional Tennis Council, a third would have meant disqualification. After the match had been won 8–6, 6–4, 8–6, Ashe apologised to the Australians and admitted that he had been close to disqualifying his team himself.

The problem between Ashe and McEnroe was one of mutual incomprehension. Ashe had been taught to keep all emotions under wraps as a deliberate defence against any white person being able to accuse him of misbehaving. McEnroe, as an Irish New Yorker, had never known the true meaning of emotional control. What was felt was revealed and what was felt to be true was said. But despite the inevitable problems that erupted between them, both recognised the goodness in each other and, later, when

Ashe was dying from the AIDS virus he contracted through contaminated blood, McEnroe was a constant source of support. 'If Arthur calls, I'm there,' said McEnroe who volunteered to take on some of Ashe's charity work.

But tensions were still simmering when the American team arrived in Cincinnati to play Argentina in the 1981 Final at the Riverfront Coliseum. What would turn out to be one of the most pulsating finals of the era could have been played in front of a mere handful of people had not a local businessman, concerned for his city's reputation, bought 10,000 seats and distributed them to his friends and associates. The 17,000 stadium was never full but enough partisan interest was whipped up to provide a suitable atmosphere for a tie that produced tennis of the highest standard and crackled with tension. Ashe had warned his team that he would disqualify them himself if they lost control and he must have been close to it on a number of occasions, especially in the doubles, when tempers flared between the two sets of players. Ashe, aided by the amiable trainer Bill Norris, had to physically get between McEnroe and Fleming and their heavyweight opponents, Vilas and Clerc, to prevent a brawl. The fact that the two Argentines did not like each other either only heightened the sense of drama but that did not prevent them playing the doubles match of their lives. In a match that last lasted 4 hours and 52 minutes, the Americans came through 11–9 in the fifth after Vilas had served for it at 7–6.

The stunning quality of McEnroe's service returns had thwarted Vilas but Fleming, supreme at returning off the backhand side, was an equal partner in a thrilling victory. Tanner had lost to Clerc on the opening day so McEnroe needed to beat Jose-Luis in the fourth rubber to ensure victory. He managed it but not before Clerc had revealed why he had climbed to No 5 in the world with some thunderous top-spin drives that enabled him to win the second and fourth sets. By the time McEnroe won it 6–3 in the fifth, the good citizens of Cincinnati were no longer in any doubt that the Davis Cup offered sporting theatre of the most dramatic kind.

The first taste of the joys and despair of relegation and promotion in the Davis Cup saw Switzerland, Brazil, Japan and South Korea go down to the Zonal groups after play off matches between the first round losers in the World Group and the Zonal winners – the system that was still in effect at the end of the century. Spain, the Soviet Union, Chile and India were promoted.

1982   Mats Wilander established himself as a world star in 1982 by becoming the youngest-ever winner of the French Open at 17, until he was replaced by an even younger

ABOVE: JOHN LLOYD, MARK COX, JEREMY BATES AND OUT IN FRONT A LEAPING PAUL
HUTCHINS CELEBRATE A DOUBLES WIN FOR JONATHAN SMITH AND ANDREW JARRETT AGAINST
THE ITALIANS IN 1981.

Michael Chang in 1989. Wilander then engaged McEnroe in what was to become the longest match in Davis Cup or any other kind of professional tennis, when the pair met in the deciding rubber of a tremendous quarter final World Group battle at St Louis, Missouri. By the time McEnroe, having ranted and raved his way through various contentious line decisions, finished it off 9–7, 6–2, 15–17, 3–6, 8–6, they had been on court six hours twenty-two minutes. After much calculation, it was decided, five years later, that the relegation match between McEnroe and Boris Becker at Hartford, Connecticut, had lasted six hours and twenty-one minutes, thus leaving the St Louis record fractionally intact. That McEnroe, for all his behavioural shortcomings, should have been involved in the two longest Davis Cup matches in history, spoke volumes for his commitment to the cause.

New Zealand was the surprise team of the year, pulling off the extraordinary feat of beating the Italians on their own red clay at Cervia. Chris Lewis, a finely-honed athlete who would reached the Wimbledon final unseeded the following year, beat Barazzutti on the opening day and a fading Panatta in straight sets on the third. As Russell Simpson had also beaten Panatta, their doubles loss didn't matter and the triumphant Kiwis were through to a semi-final against France at Aix-en-Provence where, once again, Lewis kept them in the tie by beating Thierry Tulasne after he and Simpson had upset Yannick Noah and Henri Leconte in the doubles. But Noah, who was developing into one of the most impressive athletes ever to play the game, was too strong for Simpson in the decider.

In one of his less successful moves, Fraser had decided to import a synthetic French court and lay it in the Perth Entertainment Centre for Australia's semi-final against the United States. McNamara had played well on it while helping beat France in Lyon the previous year and it was thought McEnroe might enjoy it less than grass. Wrong. The Americans won 5–0.

So the Final came down to two of the Cup's oldest antagonists, France and the United States, and Grenoble, somewhat surprisingly, was chosen as the site of the first Davis Cup Final to be staged in France since 1933 when Britain won at Roland Garros. The time of year dictated that the tie would have to be held indoors but, unlike Australia, the French decided to stick close to their roots and, at a cost of $50,000 became the first nation to lay clay at an indoors venue. The Swedes would make it fairly commonplace in the years that followed. Such was the skill of McEnroe and his new singles partner Gene Mayer, an unorthodox two-handed player of great ability whose father had been a coach in his native Hungary, that France could never take full advantage of the slower surface. Not that Yannick Noah didn't try. To some extent the altitude balanced the speed of the court and both players were able to rack up aces galore – 16 to McEnroe, 13 to Noah – but, throughout a first set that lasted 111 minutes, it was the young Frenchman who pressed most, six times coming within a point of breaking the American's serve. McEnroe eventually took it 12–10 but was swept away by Noah in the next two sets as the man whose father had played soccer for the Cameroons scored with every shot in the book including some amazing top spin lobs. McEnroe needed to regroup at the interval and, switching to a tighter racket, regained control of his shots and the match to win a wonderful battle that had the crowd in hysterics much of the time, 6–3 in the fifth.

Noah was to win the French Open the following year and cement his place in

ABOVE: As captain of the American team, Arthur Ashe accepts the Cup from his friend Philippe Chatrier, President of the International Tennis Federation, after France had been defeated in the 1982 Final in Grenoble.

French sporting history. But he came of age in Grenoble and, ironically, the captain of the opposing team could not conceal a small smile of satisfaction at the way Yannick had played. Arthur Ashe had discovered Noah. Like the best kind of adventure stories, it happened one dark night in Yaounde when, at Arthur's beckoning, Charlie Pasarell and I stopped to watch a coltish 11-year-old hitting with his uncle on a badly-lit court. Ashe arranged for Noah to go to France, where his mother lived, and the French Federation did the rest. It was one of the swiftest and best engineered development programmes I have known, based on two men's mutual respect. Ashe told Philippe Chatrier the youngster had the right potential and Chatrier responded instantly. The programme Chatrier had put in place to unearth talent all over France was also bearing fruit as this team in Grenoble showed. Henri Leconte and Thierry Tulasne had both come through the system and, although they couldn't prevent the Americans winning 4–1, they had already revitalised the game in France. McEnroe, incidentally, won

215

the hearts of the French public by playing a serious dead rubber against Leconte after Mayer had simply gone through the motions while losing to Noah. The capacity crowd appreciated that he had treated them, and indeed the Davis Cup, with respect.

1983

Predictably enough the United States lost the Cup in Buenos Aires, the following year. Vilas and Clerc exacted due revenge for Cincinnati with Clerc beating McEnroe 7–5 in the fifth in the opening rubber. But the fast courts of the Kungliga tennis hallen were too much for the Argentines in Stockholm and Sweden went through to the Final against Australia who had beaten the French in Sydney despite Noah's valiant first day victory over Pat Cash.

Fraser had blooded the 17-year-old Cash against Britain at Adelaide in the first round and it was clear that Australia had produced the class player it had been search-

BELOW: A FIRST FOR NEALE FRASER – THE FORMER WIMBLEDON CHAMPION LEADS AUSTRALIA TO ITS FIRST DAVIS CUP TRIUMPH SINCE THE HOPMAN ERA IN THE MELBOURNE SUNSHINE. PAT CASH, MARK EDMONDSON, AUSTRALIAN FEDERATION PRESIDENT BRIAN TOBIN, FRASER, PAUL MCNAMEE AND JOHN FITZGERALD GET TO FINGER THE SILVER BOWL.

ing for. Cash had an American mother and an Irish heritage and comparisons with McEnroe did not end there. In truculence if not always with the same decibel count, he mirrored some of the New Yorker's on-court behaviour and, on the eve of the Final, Fraser dismissed him from the practice court after Cash had bounced his racket so hard that it flew into the empty Kooyong stands. Fraser seriously considered dropping him from the team but a tough talk the next day brought him into line. Nevertheless Mats Wilander, understated in everything he did, even on a fast grass court, gave him a lesson in the basics by winning the opening rubber in four sets. John Fitzgerald, who grew in stature the moment he walked on court for Australia, then came to the rescue just as he had done against the French by beating Joakim Nystrom, also in four. An inspired performance by Paul McNamee who threw himself about at the net while Mark Edmondson took care of the percentages, gave Australia the lead over Anders Jarryd and Hans Simonsson. Cash then wrapped it up for Australia and Fraser had won the Cup for the first time since the last of Hopman's great assembly line of stars had driven off into the sunset.

Jimmy Connors, who was now under Donald Dell's management, decided he would like to play some Davis Cup in 1984 and, in retrospect, it would probably have been better if he had found something else to do. He helped McEnroe beat an ageing Nastase and his Romanians 5–0 in Bucharest; Argentina 5–0 at Atlanta and Australia 4–1 at Portland, Oregon. But then came the *débacle* in Gothenburg that would haunt American tennis for years and leave the great McEnroe debate festering as an open sore.

1984

The Swedes, with a youngster called Stefan Edberg playing doubles with Jarryd and another powerful young man, Henrik Sundstrom supporting Wilander in the singles, had proved too strong for Ecuador, Paraguay and Czechoslovakia in home ties and now had the chance to face the Americans in the vast Scandinavium at Gothenburg. Hopes were high but the Swedes are a realistic people and they did not need reminding that Ashe would be bringing one of the strongest Davis Cup teams in history to play them. The problem was, they were not a team. They flew in individually and late. Connors left rude notes for Jimmy Arias when there was a mix up over where they should meet for practice and Ashe was at a loss to know how to handle the massive egos bulldozing their way through the ethics and traditions of the game.

Connors set the temper of the tie by moaning over line calls in his match against the implacably composed Wilander and, after receiving a Code of Conduct warning and being docked a whole game as a penalty for obscene language, completed a shocking display by shaking the umpire's chair in fury at the end. The referee, Alan Mills, came close to disqualifying him from the reverse singles but ended up by accepting an apology and fining him $2,000.

Connors, normally such a doughty fighter, had won only seven games. McEnroe did better than that but, after a year of relentless brilliance that had seen him win Wimbledon and the US Open and lose only two matches, he was rusty after six weeks out with injury and found himself outplayed by a very determined Sundstrom who smothered his ground strokes with top spin and hit deep with relentless accuracy on the specially laid clay. Sundstrom, etching his name on to the list of outstanding achievements in Swedish sport, beat the man who was incomparably the best player in the world that year 13–11, 6–4, 6–3. Even then the tie was not over – or shouldn't have been – because Ashe had at his disposal the unbeaten Davis Cup pair of McEnroe and Fleming. After a duel that was highlighted by the brilliance of Edberg, who unveiled the true splendour of his backhand volley for a world audience, they were unbeaten no longer. With the feisty Jarryd playing the anchor role, the Swedes won 7–5, 5–7, 6–2, 7–5 and could barely believe that they were holding the Cup for a second time after beating such a potentially powerful team for the loss of just one set.

The repercussions in America were long and loud. The Louisana Pacific Corporation, which was sponsoring the U.S. Davis Cup team to the tune of $300,000 a year, threatened to withdraw its backing unless the players signed a letter agreeing to show 'courtesy and civility to competitors, officials and spectators at all times.' Connors, who didn't really care whether he played Davis Cup again or not, refused to sign it and so did McEnroe, for rather different reasons. He was still unable to understand why people did not appreciate his commitment to something that meant so much to him. The fact that many people at the USTA never wanted him to represent them again, left him aghast. It took him years to understand the depth of embarrassment and resentment that his behaviour caused and, with some reason, he felt especially aggrieved that he was being tarred with the Connors brush for what happened in Gothenburg. Unlike Connors, McEnroe had made a point of shaking hands with everyone in sight after his loss to Sundstrom and had only lost the diplomatic plot when he criticised the less than wonderful clay court in terms that seemed quite reasonable when compared to the criticism unleashed on the conditions at the Longwood Cricket Club by H. Roper Barrett 84 years before.

It meant that McEnroe did not play Davis Cup in 1985 or '86 even though the new

RIGHT: A YOUNG BORIS BECKER PLUCKS THE STRINGS WHILE FORMER WIMBLEDON FINALIST WILHELM BUNGERT WAS STILL CONDUCTING THE ORCHESTRA. BUT NOT FOR LONG. NIKI PILIC SOON TOOK OVER THE CAPTAINCY AND BECKER BECAME THE BRASS BAND OF GERMAN TENNIS.

captain Tom Gorman wanted him on the squad. Gorman's request was flatly refused by the USTA President Randy Gregson and it was not until the more forgiving figure of Gordon Jorgensen took over as President that Gorman was allowed to pick the team he wanted. But by that time, the United States were in the embarrassing position of having to beat Germany to stay in the World Group after a first-round loss to Paraguay of which more later. To leapfrog our story briefly, McEnroe tried his best to provide a rescue act – his best being that wildly exciting, flag waving six hour twenty-one minute losing marathon to Becker at Hartford – but it was too late. So the following year, after Gorman's team had survived a trip to Peru, McEnroe answered the call again when a victory in Argentina was required for them to regain the dignity of a place in the World Group.

'I'll play,' McEnroe told Gorman. 'I just want to win one match in Buenos Aires before I die!' And he did. After a five-hour battle in front of chanting crowds, he overcame the persistence of Guillermo Perez-Roldan in five sets to allow his new team-mate, Andre Agassi to set America on the winning path by beating Martin Jaite. So the United States were back after just one year in the Zonal regions. Each year spent outside the top echelon would have cost the USTA millions in potential revenue. The man they didn't want had rescued them again.

In 1985 Boris Becker hit the tennis world like a flame-haired comet. Winning Wimbledon at the age of 17 was just the start of a career that would give professional tennis another star whose fame would transcend the confines of the game. Quite simply, Becker became one of the two most famous Germans on earth and one suspects he will still be on every German's lips long after they can't remember Chancellor Kohl's first name. He welded himself to German hearts by leading his nation to the 1985 Davis Cup final and, at the Olympiahalle in Munich, did the best he could to snatch the Cup from Sweden by winning both his singles against Wilander and Edberg. But Michael Westphal, who was to die at a tragically young age from a rare disease, could not beat either of the Swedes and when Wilander and Nystrom beat Becker and Adreas Maurer

1985

in the doubles, it proved the decisive blow. Sweden were Cup holders for the third time. They lost it at Kooyong the following year despite a cameo performance by Mikael Pernfors that will live in the memory. The 1986 Final was played once again in the kind of Christmas sunshine that used to epitomise the old Challenge Round. Only this time there were Swedish students with faces painted blue and yellow to cheer their team and Pernfors, an offbeat character who had that priceless ability to establish an instantaneous rapport with a crowd, kept them in fine voice by beating McNamee in straight sets to level the tie after Cash had come through

LEFT: BECKER TRIUMPHANT.

BELOW: MUNICH 1985 WAS THE START OF A LONG RIVALRY BETWEEN SWEDISH AND GERMAN PLAYERS. ALL IN GOOD SPIRIT, HOWEVER, AS MATS WILANDER AND BORIS BECKER SHAKE HANDS WHILE THE WINNING CAPTAIN HANS OLSSON, JOAKIM NYSTROM, STEFAN EDBERG AND ANDERS JARRYD LOOK ON.

ABOVE: SWEDISH CELEBRATIONS INCLUDE THROWING THEIR PLAYERS INTO THE AIR. IT'S PROBABLY A VIKING THING. HERE STEFAN EDBERG GETS THAT FLOATING FEELING.

a titanic battle with Edberg 13–11, 13–11, 6–4. Cash and Fitzgerald then gave Australia a 2–1 lead but Pernfors did his utmost to bring things back to parity by playing two spellbinding sets of grass court tennis to leave Cash trailing 2–6, 4–6. Splay-footed and aggressive, Pernfors bounced around the famous Kooyong Stadium Court like a kangeroo on heat and it says everything about Cash's determination and resilience, fuelled by Fraser's cool captaincy, that the Australian was able to quell this inspired invader and win it 6–3 in the fifth.

Fraser had done it again but, the following year, his team suffered the most unexpected of defeats at the hands of India on their own courts at White City. Managed by P.J. Reddy, one of the greatest servants of Indian tennis, and captained by Vijay Amritraj, India's team was completed by Anand Amritraj and Ramesh Krishnan, son of Ramanathan who, with his colleague Jaidip Mukerjea, is tied in sixth place on the list

1987

221

ABOVE: BORIS BECKER AT FULL STRETCH IN THE GERMAN CAUSE.

LEFT: DAVIS CUP SUPPORT NOW COMES IN FULL COLOUR.

of players who have represented their country in the most number of Davis Cup ties (43).

By beating Fitzgerald, Krishnan had added to Vijay's victory over Wally Masur to give India a 2–0 lead. But the captain was under no illusions as to Australia's capacity to fight back and was well prepared for a fifth rubber decider with Krishnan needing to beat Masur. It was a nerve-wracking prospect and when it arrived, Krishnan was, indeed, nerve-wracked. Like many people, his reaction to nervous tension is to go stiff. Arthur Ashe reacted in a similar fashion. Only people who knew him well would recognise the signs. His legs would go as stiff as stilts. Krishnan, not such a graceful mover as Ashe, suffered the same way and Vijay exhausted himself trying to loosen Ramesh's limbs.

'Exaggerate your movements,' Vijay told him when Masur took a 4–1 first set lead. 'Follow through all the way on each stroke.'

'Mmm,' replied Krishnan whose vocal chords tended to go stiff as well.

'Move your feet,' implored Vijay. 'Jump up and down when you receive serve. Move, loosen up. Go for it!' Amritraj never knew which one of them was more exhausted at the end but Krishnan got everything moving in time to unleash enough of his silkily smooth shots to win 8–6, 8–6, 6–4. In his autobiography *Vijay!* the Indian captain reveals what Davis Cup means to the people who play it.

> *'Against all the odds known to man, a team with a 33-year-old part-time actor as captain, a semi-retired 35-year-old as his doubles partner and one top class singles player who was not, even then, ranked in the world's top 30, had beaten Australia on their own turf. My mind was full of so many emotions as I leapt from the captain's courtside chair to embrace Ramesh, Anand and P.L. Reddy, that it is difficult for me to isolate the main sources of the happiness engulfing me. Like hot springs spurting from rock, they came from deep within, but in the madness of the moment were soon to dissolve into a spray of champagne as we celebrated in the locker room. Of course we were happy. And it did not require the amazing sight of little Ramesh, normally the picture of modesty and decorum, standing there with Dom Perignon trickling down his face to realise that this was more than a victory – it was the realisation of a dream, the culmination of a career, the fulfilment of a lifetime.'*

Amritraj was under no illusions that a visit to Sweden would bring the dream dramatically closer to harsh reality but that didn't matter. His team from Madras had made the whole of India proud and a 5–0 loss to Wilander and Jarryd at the Scandinavium did little to diminish the sense of achievement.

Sweden had now won the Cup three years out of four and everyone was starting to get complacent. The 12,000 capacity Scandinavium was not sold out for the visit of Germany for the 1988 Final and when Carl-Uwe Steeb, a steady baseliner from Stuttgart, fought his way past Wilander 8–6 in the fifth set in the opening rubber, the Swedes awoke from their complacency too late and Germany, thanks to the ever-dominant Becker, became the ninth nation to add its name to the plinth supporting Dwight's little pot. In 1989 Becker was rampant back in Munich and, with one of his greatest displays, overpowered both Wilander and Edberg in straight sets to give Niki Pilic, the former Yugoslav who had settled in Germany and become a citizen, his second triumph as captain of a powerful team.

1988

1989

CHAPTER THIRTEEN

DRUMBEAT IN ASUNCION

Heroics from Krickstein…. Prayers for Pecci and Paraguay….
Chapacu an unlikely hero…. President tries to knobble Nielsen

ARON KRICKSTEIN KNEW WHAT WAS GOING TO HAPPEN. They were going to come over the top. Over the flimsy railings that were separating Victor Pecci and himself from 5,000 near-hysterical Paraguayans and onto the court to engulf their hero and do heaven knew what to him. No tennis player, in the entire history of the game, has had greater cause to go into a blue funk, to cut and run and just get the hell out of there than this boyish looking 20 year-old from the opulent Detroit suburb of Grosse Point, Michigan. Had Krickstein ever strayed into the ghettos of his home city, he could have found an atmosphere only marginally more intimidating than the one he faced here in this newly built stadium on the banks of the River Paraguayos – a little cockpit of mayhem and noise that epitomised, nay exceeded, everything one had ever heard about playing Davis Cup in South America.

The situation in the match was, from the Americans' point of view, a disaster. Tom Gorman's team were going to lose. To have suggested that when the teams returned to a sunlit stadium on a hot Sunday afternoon with the USA leading by two rubbers to one would have risked accusations of madness. But, from the Americans' point of view, lunacy had arrived with the dusk and, by the time it was all over, the big moon sat up above, wearing a lop-sided but very South American grin.

In this fifth and deciding rubber, Krickstein was down by two sets to love and there was no way back. As he looked up at the stands, illuminated by the yellow glare of floodlights on this steamy evening, all he could see were faces flushed with the expectation of victory and, at one end of the stadium, the specially erected stand that was occupied by the thick-set figure of the country's notorious dictator, President Alfredo Stroessner. Behind the iron-fisted ruler stood eight plain-clothes bodyguards with suit vests bulging, and around the stand itself, a platoon of militiamen, rifles at the ready, the lights glinting off the top of their helmets. Never, in 40 years of covering international sport, have I experienced an atmosphere more intimidating than this.

And then there was the noise. There were two bands, seemingly orchestrated by one conductor, who brought his baton down in unison with the server's arm so that the music stopped the instant the ball was put into play. That, at least, allowed the points to be played in relative quiet, but as soon as the rally ended, the cymbals clashed, the drums rolled and the rhythms of the pampas echoed out into the night and across the river into Argentina as the crowd danced and chanted and willed their players to beat the damn Yankees.

But Krickstein did not crack. Maybe, somewhere in his mind, was the wild thought that he could still pull off the impossible. An apparent miracle had occurred, after all, in the previous singles when little Hugo Chapacu, an Argentine brought into this expensively assembled, multinational team to offer support to the national hero, Pecci, had fought back from 1–5 down in the fifth set against Jimmy Arias. At 1–5 in the fifth a player is down amongst the dead men with Davy Jones and there seemed every likelihood that little Hugo would have been dumped in the river had he lost. Mercenaries are only any use when they win you the war and Stroessner was not renowned for his forgiving nature. Chapacu certainly looked close to death as he hauled his bedraggled body towards the chair after losing his serve a second time in the fifth. But, even if it seemed as if the spirit had drained from him, neither the crowd nor his captain were going to let him buckle. Screaming into his face and shaking his shoulders till the bones rattled, Gross Brown, the Paraguayan captain, urged his man to 'Fight! Fight!', and threw a pale-faced Hugo back into the fray. Incredibly, Chapacu responded. The wiry clay courter had little to offer other than to run and fight and chase so that Arias, who prided himself on similar qualities, suddenly found himself being outmanoeuvred by a mirror image. The difference was the crowd and the increasing pressure Arias found himself under as Chapacu refused to surrender. Three match points came and went for America – points that would have ensured the USA of a winning 3–1 lead. But Arias could not put the ball away and, as his huge lead shrank point by point, the bands got louder and the screams of the delirious Paraguayans touched a new pitch.

Arias, of Spanish parentage himself, was staying remarkably calm amidst the bedlam and courageously insisted on a 'play two' decision after his first serve was disrupted by a shout from someone in the crowd. It was one of those acts of defiance that seemed like a good idea at the time. But, after a three-minute hiatus, during which time all hell broke loose, Chapacu, taking deep breaths to calm his nerves, seemed fired by an even greater sense of determination and saved the first of three match points with a great cross-court backhand.

Hanging in there, Chapacu reduced the arrears to 3–5 but he was on the brink again in the ninth game when Arias reached 15–40 on his serve – two more match points, either one of which would take the United States through to the next round. Once again the drum roll was silenced by the leader of the bands and, amidst the momentary calm, Arias made a mess of a high forehand. On the next point he was pushed back onto the defensive as Chapacu found a nagging length and angle on his forehand and eventually forced an American error.

At 5–4, Arias served for the match again and got as far as 30–0. But Chapacu, with Brown and Pecci up out of their seats after every point goading, coaxing and screaming, delved ever deeper into his reserves of resolve and found still greater accuracy and penetration on his ground strokes. Arias ran and parried as best he could but suddenly fatigue flooded through his body as an inspired opponent forced him to reach and lunge again and again during baseline rallies that pushed both men to the limits of their endurance. Chapacu broke back only to lose his own serve for 7–6, giving Arias the chance to serve for the match a third time. Still it was not enough as Chapacu struck boldly for a couple of passing shots that left Arias dead at the net. The American was dead on his feet, too, and deaf in the head as the noise engulfed him. Has anyone measured the effect on the nervous system given the certain knowledge that, if you miss this forehand or net this volley, a cacophony of sound, of drums, of cymbals, of high pitched roars of delight and derision, will assault your ear drums? How exhausting and debilitating is that? How much of it could any of us stand?

For Arias, gallant to the last, the answer was: no more. Chapacu broke to lead 8–7 and, after Arias had double-faulted, won it on his second match point. The crowds spilled over onto the court, dancing, cavorting, crying and screaming with delight.

Overreaction? A dispassionate observer might think so. But then listen to the man who told me in all seriousness, 'Beating America could be the greatest thing that ever happened to this country.' And he wasn't talking just about sport. Or look into the eyes of the woman who admitted that, during the previous day's doubles match, she had returned to her hotel room for a moment to light a candle and pray. Dwight Davis may not have envisaged this when he offered his little pot for international competition.

And so it was two-all. If Krickstein had a sinking feeling going into the deciding battle on the banks of the Paraguayos, few could have blamed him. Quite apart from the crowd, he was facing easily the most talented performer on either team in Victor Pecci. It would have been difficult in Detroit, but here…

And so it was that young Aaron found himself trailing 6–2, 8–6, 7–7, knowing the cause was beyond recall, knowing that no matter how hard he fought the end result was already written large in the night sky. And yet still he fought, blocking out the scenes that he knew would engulf him, concentrating, in the time-honoured manner, on the next point, the next stroke. That was courage of the highest order. But often, in battle, courage is not enough. It was way past the midnight hour when Pecci, slicing his returns and charging into the net, broke Krickstein for the last time to unleash the delirious hordes. While Krickstein made a wild dash for the exit, Pecci, showing an incredible amount of faith in his countrymen, simply lay flat on his back and allowed the mob to pick him up and carry him around the stadium.

Meanwhile Ken Flach, a hero of the doubles with his partner Robert Seguso, was clutching his wife in an attempt to shield her from the crowds that swirled about them. The vast majority were too happy to be a threat but, inevitably, there were some nasty-minded thugs amongst them and, with the militiamen doing nothing to protect the Americans, Flach admitted to being in fear for his life when a small group advanced towards them shouting anti-American obscenities.

Unhappily, there had been a more insidious threat to America's hopes during the Chapacu-Arias match when the Danish referee Kurt Nielsen suddenly felt the presence of the Paraguayan Tennis Association President Alejandro Velazquez Ugarte behind his chair. By then, Nielsen had started to get very picky with the letter of the law as a result of some outrageous attempts by line judges to foot fault American players and was instructing the umpires to overrule any decisions they deemed to be unfair. The Davis Cup Committee is lucky to be able to call upon men of Nielsen's stature and bearing for this difficult job. It takes more courage than one might imagine to make decisions against the home team in situations like this but Nielsen, the only man to have twice reached a Wimbledon final unseeded, had never been afraid of fighting the odds and, in own his view, was simply doing his duty. President Velazquez Ugarte saw it somewhat differently.

'You obviously want the Americans to win,' he hissed into Nielsen's ear. 'I must warn you that you will be jeopardising international relations by your actions.'

Nielsen's florid features turned a deeper hue of pink and his moustache twitched.

Aghast and infuriated at this deliberate attempt to intimidate him, he told the President to get back to his own seat and leave him to referee the match.

'I could not believe what he was saying to me,' Nielsen said afterwards. 'I will mention it in my report.'

And so it was that Philippe Chatrier, President of the International Federation, came to read a report that confirmed his worst fears about the state of tennis in Paraguay. He had seen for himself how his own French team had been treated two years before when the tie was played indoors on the fastest court imaginable to aid the power serving of Pecci and his Puerto Rican-born colleague Francisco Gonzales. The conditions then had been dire and now, with further evidence of malpractice from Nielsen, Chatrier urged the Davis Cup committee to slap a ban on Paraguay, forbidding them to play any more ties at home that year.

Yet those of us who had been neutral observers at this unforgettable tie urged otherwise. We asked Chatrier to take into account certain factors that had changed since his visit. The venue had changed with the erection of the new stadium and the completion of the elegant Golf and Racket Club Paraguayos had offered the Americans luxurious hospitality. And the Paraguayan team had also been blameless. Gross Brown had been no more partisan than any other captain while Gonzales had sat next to the main band during some of the singles matches, ensuring that they stuck to their promise of not banging drums during the points. That, at least, made life easier on the players than had been the case the previous year when the United States had suffered similar humiliation against Ecuador in Guayaquil. There the crowds had grunted in unison every time an American player struck the ball – a distraction of appalling proportions.

Chatrier listened to this plea and became more convinced of the Paraguayans' sincerity when Richard Kent, part owner of the Paraguayos Club and some of his allies, including Pecci, agreed to stage a coup to oust Velazquez Ugarte. This was done and not long after President Stroessner was gone, too – a double score for freedom. As a result Paraguay's Davis Cup team would have been allowed to play its third round at home had it managed to beat Spain in a tie switched to neutral ground in Caracas, Venezuela. But the Spanish were too strong so Pecci and his colleagues were denied the opportunity to take full advantage of a truly memorable victory – a triumph that Tom Gorman categorised correctly when he said, 'Our defeat was not about bad line calls or intimidation. We were beaten by a better team.'

CHAPTER FOURTEEN

THE NINETIES

*Noah lionised in Lyon…. Borotra says merci…. Fraser's Aussies keep
on going…. Drama as Moscow stages back-to-back Finals…. Boetsch holds
on to win longest-ever Final in Malmo*

T HE TENTH DECADE IN DAVIS CUP HISTORY has been a story of modernism matching poorly with tradition. Inappropriate stadia have been selected to stage some of the most exciting and emotional confrontations the competition has ever known. Less correctable is the disparity of interest in Davis Cup play between the United States and other nations, a worrying state of affairs that would have brought a wry smile to the face of the Cup's founder. Dwight Davis created the competition to envelop the world

*BELOW: THE NINTH DECADE OF DAVIS CUP PLAY BEGAN WITH A HAPPY REUNION OF SOME OF ITS
GREATEST STARS AT THE WHITE CITY IN SYDNEY. VIC SEIXAS, TONY TRABERT, MERVYN ROSE,
REX HARTWIG, LEW HOAD AND KEN ROSEWALL SURROUND THE CUP.*

ABOVE: AMERICA'S LONGEST SERVING CAPTAIN, TOM GORMAN, FLANKED BY ANDRE AGASSI, MICHAEL CHANG, TRAINER BOB RUSSO, AND JIM PUGH CELEBRATE BEATING AUSTRALIA IN THE 1990 FINAL AT ST PETERSBURG, FLORIDA.

RIGHT: PAT CASH – TEMPORARILY UNHAPPY WITH THE WAY THINGS WERE GOING AGAINST ARGENTINA IN SYDNEY.

and spread goodwill through sporting endeavour. In that respect, he succeeded far beyond expectation. But he would have been saddened that, as the century neared its end, neither his own country's leading players nor its public placed the Davis Cup on quite the same pedestal as France, Russia, Chile or Germany to name but a few.

1990

The first three years of the 1990s provided all too clear examples of what was happening. In 1990, the Final offered the traditionally classic match up between the United States and Australia. Yet few will remember it. The tie was staged at the vast Suncoast Dome in St Petersburg, Florida, and the Americans, having laid a red clay court that certainly contravened the spirit if not the letter of the stipulated rules of court selection, won the first three rubbers to win the Cup for the 29th time. The crowds were good but, with the nations' sports editors preoccupied with football and other domestic competitions, American sports fans were not exactly talking tennis that week.

Twelve months later, a still impressionable Pete Sampras was shaken to the core by the passion which poured out of the 8,300 people cramming the Palais de Sport in Lyon as Yannick Noah led France to Davis Cup triumph for the first time in 49 years. A nation was in tears and Gallic joy unbounded.

Yet in 1992 the Final was back in the antiseptic setting of the Tarrant Country Center in Fort Worth, Texas where the presence of Marc Rosset and Jakob Hlasek, worthy veterans of Swiss teams over the years, did not exactly stampede the cattle. It did, however, bring forth a stinging riposte from one of the best guardians of America's tennis soul, Eugene Scott, whose column in his New York publication *Tennis Week* rarely allows ineptitude or wrongdoing to pass unnoticed. Having quoted one player's disgust over the fact that the 1992 semi-final between the US and Sweden, featuring stars as big as Andre Agassi and Stefan Edberg, did not receive any kind of television coverage in the States, Scott then turned his attention to the chosen venue for the Final.

'Did I mention the final was slated for Fort Worth? Where? This column has nothing against the place, but the game's historic showcase cannot be staged in Fort Worth. The Davis Cup Championship deserves to be in a major media capital… The players and captain Gorman have done their job. The rest of the job should be turned over to new (USTA) leadership. A television blackout for the first session of a Davis Cup semi-final is a black eye for tennis. A Fort Worth final is the last straw confirming that fresh thinking is in order.'

Fresh thinking did come in although not always to Scott's liking. However no one could suggest that promoter Bill Dennis had erred when he persuaded the USTA to return to a traditional tennis venue in a risky city – Caesar's Palace in Las Vegas – for the semi-final against Sweden in 1995. On courts that had staged the Alan King Classic back in the seventies, Todd Martin led the Americans to victory in front of sun-drenched capacity crowds that fully justified the gamble. But, generally, the American team had to go abroad to taste the real atmosphere of Davis Cup – a fact that would have saddened those pioneers at Longwood.

The French victory in 1991 was very much a captain's triumph. Yannick Noah is an inspirational figure in build, style and personality and it was his ability to inspire as well as corral the wayward skills and fragile temperaments of his talented team that enabled him to bring off a sensational victory against the United States in Lyon. The run to the

1991

final had been comparatively straightforward. Guy Forget and Henri Leconte were far too good for the Israelis in Rennes and Fabrice Santoro helped out in Nimes where the little double-handed clay court expert was required to beat Wally Masur in the fifth rubber after Richard Fromberg, Fraser's laid-back Tasmanian with a liking for clay, had won both his singles. Then, while the US were beating the Becker-less Germans in Kansas City, France took care of Yugoslavia, a team that was starting to be torn apart by the effects of civil war, 5–0 in Pau, without the services of the two Croatians, Goran Ivanisevic and Goran Prpic, who would never play for Yugoslavia again.

Santoro had done well but on an indoor carpet in the final, Noah knew he would have to turn back to his two big serving left-handers, Forget and Leconte, despite the fact that Henri was still short of match practice following a back operation. Both, for years, had been amongst the most talented players in the game and both had failed to match up to their potential. In personality they were about as similar as David Niven and Jerry Lewis but both needed good direction. Noah provided it. Tom Gorman was not that kind of leader but he had become an experienced and successful captain over the years and was well liked by his players. His mistake, however, was in not having John McEnroe on his squad. Even if he had not played – and a doubles berth should surely have been there for him – McEnroe's charismatic presence in the locker room would have done much to counter the bewildering pressure cooker of tension and excitement that the Americans had to deal

LEFT: The Pete Sampras serve prepares to inflict more damage but not enough to prevent France upsetting the United States in Lyon in 1991.

with. Andre Agassi, a showman who has rarely been intimidated by a big stage, came back from losing the first set against Forget in the opening rubber to win with ease. But, incredibly, that was the last wave of the Stars and Stripes. Pete Sampras, at 20, was not ready for what he had to deal with, as he now admits. He looked confused and over-whelmed as the flamboyant Leconte strutted to a straight-set victory to level the tie. Then the two southpaws went to work on the experienced doubles pair of Robert Seguso and Ken Flach who had been through more intimidating experiences but rarely against such inspired opposition. With Noah all over them at changeovers, Forget and Leconte won it 6–2 in the fourth.

Now Forget had to beat Sampras, already a winner of the US Open, to bring the Cup back to France. Up until that year, Forget had no reputation as a crunch player. Despite his beautiful flowing game and stinging serve, the Frenchman had never won a title outside his native land until he picked up the New South Wales title that January. He followed that with Brussels and finished up with six in all for 1991, including Bercy, where he also proved himself before a French crowd. So, finally, he knew he could do it. But this was still different. This was Davis Cup. And not just Davis Cup but the pivotal rubber in the Final. It is the sort of match that, quite literally, changes a person's life. You know, deep down, that whatever happens, you will walk from the court marked for forever – a success or a failure. For Sampras that did not apply. He had his career in front of him and there would be many more opportunities for glory. But for Guy Forget, this was it. Agassi was favourite to beat Leconte in the fifth rubber and so it was now or never. Sampras played better than on the opening day and only lost the first set on the tie break. Then he broke to grab the second 6–3 and the match was on a knife edge. It was Noah who drew blood. He roared Forget back into action. He

ABOVE: THE FIRE IS STILL THERE AS JOHN McENROE REJOINS THE US TEAM FOR THE VICTORY OVER SWITZERLAND IN FORT WORTH.

LEFT: McENROE AND HIS FLAG.

lifted his man, stared into his eyes and made him believe. Serving up a storm and volleying brilliantly, Guy regained control of the match and swept through to a victory 6–4 in the fourth. That set off an emotional cloud burst of near hysteria that reduced Leconte to floods of tears and saw Noah lead his team in a conga procession around the arena. And then, the most poignant moment of all. Jean Borotra, sprightly but frail, came up to Noah and, clasping his hand, said, 'Thank you, thank you. I don't know how much longer I could have waited.' Borotra was 93.

In 1992 McEnroe was back on the team that defeated Switzerland in Fort Worth. Marc Rosset beat Jim Courier to give the Swiss a point but the crucial match was, as ever, the doubles. This time Gorman called it right and paired Sampras with the maestro. After losing the first two sets against Rosset and Jakob Hlasek on tie breaks, McEnroe inspired Sampras by personal example, throwing every last drop of his talent, experience and passion into a performance that enabled the Americans to win it 6–2 in the fifth. 'It was a great feeling to win that one,' McEnroe said later. 'When Pete turned to me at the end and said "I love you" that was the ultimate for me. It made you feel wanted.'

It was McEnroe's last hurrah that left him with a 41–8 record in singles and 18–2 in doubles. That he had offended cannot be denied but no one could suggest that he had not served his country well.

Michael Stich emerged as the Davis Cup hero of 1993, grabbing the opportunity left to him by Boris Becker's decision to concentrate on trying to regain his No 1 world ranking. Just for once, Stich stole the limelight. Aided by Carl-Uwe Steeb in Moscow and by the tall Marc Kevin Goellner against the Czechs at Halle where Germany made full use of a grass court, Stich displayed his versatility by switching surfaces again in Sweden to lead the Germans to a surprising 5–0 win against a team that included Stefan Edberg.

Neale Fraser's Australians made it through to the final once again after Wally Masur and Mark Woodforde had disposed of a weakened US team represented by Brad Gilbert and David Wheaton in the first round in Melbourne. Woodforde was now a major force in doubles with his partner Todd Woodbridge and they remained unbeaten in the early rounds as Australia progressed against Italy in Florence and India in Chandigarh. But, in Dusseldorf, where Ion Tiriac, now a promoter of influence and imagination had turned the Dusseldorf Trade Centre into a tennis complex

RIGHT: THE 'WOODIES' – MARK WOODFORDE AND TODD WOODBRIDGE – HAVE GIVEN AUSTRALIA A SIGNIFICANT ADVANTAGE IN THE DOUBLES DURING THE 1990s.

ABOVE: IN DUSSELDORF IN 1993, BECKER'S ABSENCE DID NOT PREVENT MICHAEL STICH, SURROUNDED HERE BY CAPTAIN NIKI PILIC, CARL-UWE STEEB AND PATRIK KUHNEN, FROM DEFEATING AUSTRALIA.

complete with vast hospitality areas, the Woodies, as they are known, could not prevent Stich and Patrik Kuhnen restoring Germany's lead. On the opening day Richard Fromberg, with Tasmanian *sangfroid,* had beaten Goellner 9–7 in the fifth after saving three match points and taking the last ten-minute break in singles following the third set in Davis Cup history. The tradition was abolished in 1994. Stich then beat Fromberg to win the Cup for Germany for the third time in its history – and for the first time without Becker.

For Switzerland the year offered a cruel contrast to the one that had gone before. Beaten by India in Calcutta when Krishnan outmanoeuvred Hlasek in the fifth rubber, the 1992 finalists then lost to Israel, for whom the talented and devoted Amos Mansdorf won both his singles, at Ramat Hasharon. This was the relegation battle and, from the mountain peak, the Swiss discovered themselves slithering all the way down the slope into the Zonal valleys.

There followed two Davis Cup Finals in Moscow in consecutive years – Finals that celebrated the arrival from the East of a major new talent in the person of Yevgeny Kafelnikov who was to become the French Open champion of 1996. Russia, playing now as its own entity without the help of satellite States, reached the final in 1994 with a surprisingly decisive victory over Germany in Hamburg while their opponents, Sweden progressed by beating France in Cannes on a brutally hot Riviera weekend that was marked by the death of Jean Borotra. Now only René Lacoste remained of the Musketeers. The Swedes then recovered in dramatic fashion after trailing the U.S. 0–2 in Gothenburg. The doubles pair of Jan Apell and Jonas Bjorkman kept Swedish hopes alive, and when Sampras had to retire with a hamstring injury against Edberg in the fourth rubber the tie was level. Magnus Larsson then successfully completed the comeback by beating Todd Martin.

Despite the fact that Sweden ended up with the Cup for the fifth time in their history after just three rubbers, the Final at the vast Olympic Stadium in Moscow where 18,000 people filled every available seat, was more dramatic still. Edberg had to stave off match point against Alexander Volkov, whose nerves and concentration might have been in a better state had not President Yeltsin decided to bluster his way to his seat surrounded by bodyguards and aides in the middle of a point. The distraction this caused was considerable, which surprised presidential watchers because Yeltsin is a genuine tennis fan who usually attends the Kremlin Cup which is played in the same stadium every year. Volkov, with his deceptively casual style, battled on but could not prevent Edberg grabbing victory 8-6 in the fifth. It was the magnitude of the occasion rather than any presidential presence that caused Kafelnikov's attack of stage fright against Magnus Larsson, and he managed only two games in the opening two sets. After that, the Russian did well to push Larsson to five before succumbing.

The doubles could hardly have been closer, either. Kafelnikov and the veteran Andrei Olhovskiy

RIGHT: PRESIDENT BORIS YELTSIN, A GENUINE TENNIS FAN, ATTENDS THE FINAL AGAINST SWEDEN IN MOSCOW.

took the new ATP World Doubles champions Jan Apell and Jonas Bjrokman to 8–6 in the fifth before succumbing and leaving Russia with the unwanted record of being the only team in history to have won as many as six sets in the first three rubbers of a Final and lost.

During the Final against Sweden, the rather forlorn figure of Andrei Chesnokov turned up in the lobby of the Penta Olympic Hotel. He had fallen out with the Russian captain Vadim Borisov but just couldn't stay away. 'This is such an important time for my country,' he said, 'I felt I had to be here.'

Loyalty was rewarded. By the time Russia staged its second consecutive Davis Cup Final 12 months later, Chesnokov was a national hero. Restored to the team by the new

1995

LEFT: PETE SAMPRAS AND ANDRE AGASSI WRAP UP IN THE CHILL OF PALERMO WHERE AMERICA PLAYED ITALY IN 1995.

BELOW: CAPTAIN TOM GULLIKSON, SECOND FROM LEFT, AND HIS SUPPORT TEAM RUSH TO AID STRICKEN PETE SAMPRAS IN THE 1995 FINAL AT MOSCOW'S OLYMPIC STADIUM.

RIGHT: AFTER SAVING NINE MATCH POINTS AGAINST MICHAEL STICH IN MOSCOW, ANDREI CHESNOKOV SCREAMS IN DELIGHT AT HAVING WON THE TIE FOR RUSSIA.

captain Anatoly Lepeshin, who just happened to be Kafelnikov's coach, this tall, droll man with a wonderful line in dry humour, was asked to perform the unfunny task of beating Michael Stich to win the semi-final of the 1995 competition against Germany. This had started as the full German team, Becker and Stich united, but after Kafelnikov and Olhovskiy had pulled Russia back from 0–2 down by winning the doubles 7–5 in the fifth, Becker injured himself, blaming the watered court, and replacement Bernd Karbacher was unable to put up much resistance against Kafelnikov. So it was all up to Chesnokov. In front of an increasingly excited crowd of 18,000 Muscovites yelling for their native son, Chesnokov took the match into the fifth set and then started to perform heroics. Nine times poor Stich reached match point to take Germany to the final and nine times, including a few double faults, he failed to clinch it. Chesnokov, giving Stich baleful Russian stares from the other end of the court, clung on and eventually grabbed the glory awaiting the winner 14–12.

It was a remarkable performance but more was to come. The Americans, now captained by Tom Gullikson after Tom Gorman's worthy eight-year reign had come to an end, had survived a trip to Palermo where, in chilly conditions, they had beaten Italy 5–0 and then, in the warmth of Las Vegas, had overcome the Swedes 4–1. In Moscow it was not as easy. Pete Sampras, knowing the importance of beating Chesnokov first up, laboured long and hard in his country's cause against a man whose popularity had soared since the semi-final. On the soft clay court, which had only been laid a few days before, Sampras battled on and eventually completed a victory that had required every ounce of his courage, skill and stamina 6–4 in the fifth. So much so that Pete collapsed at the end with cramps and had to be literally dragged from the court for urgent attention in the locker room. Although Kafelnikov beat Jim Courier, Sampras and Martin won the doubles and then Pete finished off his finest performance in American colours by beating a nervous Russian No 1 in the fourth rubber in straight sets.

In 1996, the longest, closest and most dramatic Davis Cup Final of all time ended in triumph for Yannick Noah and his Frenchmen in a converted automobile factory near the Malmo docks that was barely worthy of staging such an historic encounter.

But the poverty of the setting was forgotten as France hung on to beat an heroic Swedish team 3–2 after Cedric Pioline, who had led by two sets to love and 5–2 in the fifth, had been thwarted by Thomas Enqvist and Nicklas Kulti, a brave understudy for the injured Stefan Edberg, had missed three consecutive match points against the ultimate hero, Arnaud Boetsch. Enqvist's 3–6, 6–7, 6–4, 6–4, 9–7 victory over Pioline had lasted four hours twenty-five minutes while Boetsch's decisive 7–6, 2–6, 4–6, 7–6, 10–8 clincher over Kulti kept us all gasping for four hours forty-eight minutes.

Those were the bare bones of an exhausting, emotional and unforgettable final day that produced nine hours and thirteen minutes of the most remarkable tennis which ended up re-writing the Davis Cup record books.

Incredibly, the ultimate round of Davis Cup, be it Challenge Round or Final, had never before gone to a fifth set in a live fifth rubber. Not since it all started in 1900 had the outcome taken so long to be decided. The previous closest encounter had also involved France but less successfully – Perry defeating Merlin 7–5 in the fourth set of that fifth match at Roland Garros in 1933.

Since the new 16-team World Group format was instigated in 1981, only one other final had gone as far as a live fifth rubber and that, ironically, involved Edberg who would have been playing the decider in Malmo had he not twisted his ankle in the sixth game of the first set against Pioline on the opening day. That had occurred in Munich in 1985 when Edberg beat the late Michael Westphal 6–3 in the fourth.

This tie was supposed to be all about Edberg, too. It was to be the very final curtain call after a year of farewells. When the draw was made and we saw how Stefan would be playing the fifth match all manner of romantic endings were written in the imagination. But fate is cruel and unjust. After a career so remarkably free of serious injury – back problems had never stopped him competing in a record number of 54 consecutive Grand Slams – Edberg moved to his right at the net in that first set against Pioline and then tried to push back as the Frenchman passed him down the backhand side. One sensed immediately that it was serious. Histrionics have never been part of the Swede's repertoire and the expression on his face spelt out the worst. He had his ankle strapped and played on but it pained him every time he pushed off on it and Pioline was playing much too well to allow him to get into the match. France soon had a 1–0 lead in their pocket, 6–3, 6–4, 6–3. There was nothing the matter with Arnaud Boetsch – except Thomas Enqvist. Edberg's successor as Swedish No 1 was simply too big, too powerful and too good for Boetsch who was never allowed to settle.

So everything was nicely poised after a first day that offered little hint of the drama that was to come. 'It was a strange atmosphere out there,' Noah told me that evening. 'It was as if we had all gathered to say goodbye to Stefan and nothing really caught fire. Although our supporters were great. They are mostly friends of ours, ex-players and staff from the Federation so it was wonderful to have them there.'

The French supporters had, in fact, saved the day. With their pom-poms and flags; weird hats and bright red and blue wigs and endless enthusiasm they had added a large splash of colour to the drab little hall that made up part of this sprawling building that had once been a Saab factory. Five thousand eight hundred seats had been squashed into an arena whose metal walls, painted a dirty yellow, had not been allowed to be covered for security reasons. It was a place that no self-respecting High School in the States would dream of using for anything other than a storage depot. But it was the site of the Davis Cup Final and if the Swedish crowd was sombre to the point of silence perhaps it was because they were embarrassed to be entertaining their chic French guests in such shoddy surroundings. Happily the drama soon made the stage immaterial.

As usual, the doubles was pivotal. 'Where else' asked Noah, 'does doubles take on such importance, except in Davis Cup?' Where else, indeed, and the nerves were showing in the early stages of a roller coaster match that saw Guy Forget, the veteran of the French squad, and Guillaume Raoux get away to an impressive start against Jonas Bjorkman and Nicklas Kulti only to lose the second set 6–1.

For the Swedes to have capitalised on that sudden flash of form Bjorkman would have had to have served better and he couldn't. 'I don't know what happened,' he said. 'The rhythm had been perfect all week in practice and then suddenly I lost it. In the middle of a match it is very difficult to get it back.'

With Forget shepherding Raoux through some erratic patches, even the excellent Kulti couldn't cover for his partner and it was sad to see the normally assertive Bjorkman being forced to play second fiddle. The final score was 6–3, 1–6, 6–3, 6–3 and still there was no news on Edberg.

Rumours circulating around the spacious and well run press room on the Sunday morning suggested that Stefan had been encouraged after a practice session and still might play. 'Wrong,' said Tony Pickard, Edberg's long-time coach, later. 'He asked me to come and watch the practice and I urged the Swedes to really test him. Once he tried to push off properly behind a serve, he knew it was useless. You can't play a match like that less than 80 per cent fit.'

But there was no confirmation of that when Enqvist and Pioline started the fourth rubber. The pair had never played before and Enqvist quickly discovered how awkward Pioline is to play. The backhand creates deceptive side spin and the flowing, heavily topped forehand kicks off a court like Plexipave. Enqvist admitted it was a style he did not enjoy and his displeasure seemed to be about to translate itself into defeat when the Frenchman served for the match at 5–3 in the fifth.

Did Pioline try too hard or was it just nerves? Either way, two bad errors in the first three points allowed Enqvist to get his foot in the door and that was all the invitation he needed. After Pioline had put another backhand long, Enqvist stepped forward to pound a service return and the chance was gone. Pioline had been broken to 15. Sadly, it was a double fault at 7–7 that enabled Enqvist to keep Swedish hopes alive and, despite having to beat off a break point against his own serve with a typically robust forehand winner down the line, closed it out triumphantly.

By then the Swedish sections of the crowd had come alive and there was much flag waving when Boetsch and Kulti emerged to play a historic fifth rubber – Kulti having been publicly confirmed as Edberg's stand-in only minutes before. They had met twice previously with the Frenchman winning both matches on clay but this court was fast enough to suit Kulti's heavy hitting, go-for-broke game and Boetsch was somewhat fortunate to survive a blistering first set and grab it in the tie break 7–2. The second and third, however, belonged to the Swede, 6–2, 6–4. Kulti's career had included three ATP Tour titles, one on grass at Halle and two at Adelaide, but he had never kicked on from there, remaining one of those players of unfulfilled potential that litter the middle echelons of the game. But fate had thrown him a lifeline to glory and he knew it. He also knew that the only way he was going to grab it was to play his own game so Boetsch, who likes to give the ball a hefty whack himself, especially off his classic backhand, continually found himself bombarded with booming first serves and pounding ground strokes.

However, with Noah keeping him relaxed and focused at changeovers, Boetsch battled on and one of those superb backhands, clipping the line, deprived Kulti of a service point for 4–3 in the fourth set breaker. A point later and the Swede was suddenly in trouble. Cramps. He limped towards the chair to seek assistance but referee

ABOVE: ARNAUD BOETSCH ON HIS KNEES AT THE END OF THE LONGEST, CLOSEST DAVIS CUP
FINAL IN HISTORY. FOR THE SECOND TIME IN THE 1990S, FRANCE WERE CHAMPIONS.

Ken Ferrae was off his chair like a jack rabbit to inform the umpire that no time-outs
were allowed for cramps – a rule that had only just been rescinded on the ATP Tour
after road manager Weller Evans watched Shuzo Matsuoka writhe in agony for several
minutes on the burning Stadium Court at Flushing Meadow – a potentially life-threatening situation.

There was nothing life-threatening about Kulti's condition and, under ITF rules he
simply had to get on with it. Bravely, he did so, winning a couple of points on his serve
before Boetsch levelled the match 7–5.

'Yannick warned me that Nicklas would get better and he did,' said Boetsch.
'Cramps come and go and although I tried to move him around, I didn't make a very
good job of it at first.'

That could have been perceived as something of an understatement when Boetsch, having been hit by two enormous power blows off the forehand by Kulti, found himself 0–40 down at 6–7 in the fifth. Yes, Kulti had got better and yes, this was triple match point for the whole thing – the set, the match, the very Cup itself. The French were slumped in their seats; the Swedes being quieted by the umpire. Kulti played true to form. Boom and a backhand cross court service return flew wide. A blocked backhand service return was in the net. Another backhand mishit. He'd gone for it and he'd blown it. Before anyone realised what had happened Boetsch was back at that little sanctuary called deuce and two points later it was 7–7.

For the second time that day, a match was way past its fourth hour and it was becoming as exhausting for the crowd as the players. Kulti moved ahead 8–7 with an ace but the cramp was returning and when he cried out in pain right in front of the bank of cheering French supporters, Noah sprung out of his chair and doused their ardour. Obediently they accepted the reprimand from a man who feels sport has no meaning unless it is sportingly played and Kulti was allowed to fight his increasingly helpless battle with just the roars of his own people ringing in his ears.

He encouraged them, too, cleverly giving himself precious seconds to recover until they allowed play to continue. But he was swinging wildly now, like a man who knew he could run no more and after one huge, defiant blow which saved a second match point from 0–40 at 8–9, it was all over and Arnaud Boetsch, who had brought France back from 0–2 by winning the fifth rubber in the semi-final against Italy at Nantes had gone one better, all the way into the history books, doing something no one had ever done before. He had won a Davis Cup final in the fifth set of the fifth rubber.

Not even the Four Musketeers had done that. But Yannick Noah, a mystical sort of man, was sure they were up there watching. He was remembering them, especially René Lacoste who died only weeks before, but he remembered, too, the man whose party this was supposed to have been and, being Yannick, ran over at the end to lift Stefan Edberg on his shoulders. Sport, one felt, should be like this more often.

But then that is the Davis Cup. Despite celebrated and lamentable lapses, it tends to bring out the best in people and, without question, it offers the participants some of the most intense and memorable moments of their lives. It also, as Dwight Davis wished so deeply, brings them together. In recent years, especially, this has been so. The end of apartheid allowed South Africa back into the fold and, in 1995 Frew McMillan, who was captain at the time, took his team to Dakar to play Senegal in African Zone tie. 'We were overwhelmed by the hospitality we received,' said McMillan.

ABOVE: FRENCH CELEBRATIONS IN MALMO IN 1996.

RIGHT: TYPICALLY, YANNICK NOAH FOUND TIME TO RECOGNISE
STEFAN EDBERG'S CONTRIBUTION TO THE DAVIS CUP AMIDST
FRENCH EUPHORIA IN MALMO.

'Like our cricket team in India, we were amazed at
the warmth of the welcome. It didn't seem to matter whether we were black or white.' Sport, as
President Nelson Mandela was so quick to recognise, is the fastest healer of all.

The 1997 campaign was hardly into its stride
before France were in need of field dressings.

1997

Cruelly, the Cup holders had been drawn against Australia and no one was going to
win any prizes for guessing which surface the Australians, now led by the former doubles team of John Newcombe, as captain, and Tony Roche, as coach, were going to
choose. Grass at White City was the venue and the Cup was dashed from French lips in
just three rubbers. But not, however, before Patrick Rafter had responded to

ABOVE: STILL PACKING THEM IN – SYDNEY'S WHITE CITY IN 1997 WITH THE ONE GRASS COURT
IN THE STADIUM STILL IN USE.

Newcombe's first piece of inspirational captaincy. The young Queenslander found himself trailing Cedric Pioline by two sets to love in the opening rubber before Newcombe reminded him that nothing is over in tennis until match point is won. Rafter proved it by winning 6–4 in the fifth. He credited that turnaround to setting him off on a year that saw him become US Open champion. Pioline, too, seemed to benefit from the experience by becoming the first Frenchman in 51 years to reach the Wimbledon final a few months later.

Sampras and Michael Chang, another American who has blown hot and cold over Davis Cup commitment, cheered all those politicians who enjoy tennis by ending Australia's run at the semi-final stage in Washington DC. It was a well-staged occasion in front of a sell-out crowd and was burnished by fine displays from Sampras and Chang who won both their matches against Rafter and Mark Philippoussis, leaving the Woodies to salvage some Australian pride in the doubles. In the other semi-final in Norrkopping, Jonas Bjorkman led Sweden to a 4–1 victory over the Italians who had caused the upset of the year by beating the highly fancied Spanish team 4–1 on carpet in Pesaro. This time with Omar Camporese and Renzo Furlan as their leading lights, the Italians were, once again, proving that world rankings mean little in the Davis Cup cauldron.

So for the United States it was back to Gothenburg to meet the Swedes for the third time in four years. The result was not quite such an embarrassment as that suffered by McEnroe and Connors in 1984 but it was close. Bjorkman, startled to find himself plastered on billboards all over the city, lived up to his new found fame as the world No 4 by beating Chang on a medium paced carpet at the Scandinavium 6–3 in the fourth. Sampras then hurt his ankle at a set all against Magnus Larsson and had to retire. American commentators were disappointed to see that the world No 1 did not reappear the next day to support his team-mates as Todd Martin and Jonathan Stark went down to Bjorkman and Nicklas Kulti in

RIGHT: YANNICK NOAH TRIES TO COOL DOWN CEDRIC PIOLINE IN THE SYDNEY HEAT AS FRANCE STRUGGLE VAINLY TO HOLD ON TO THE CUP IN THE FIRST ROUND OF 1997.

BELOW: A FULL-THROATED RENDITION OF 'WALTZING MATILDA' FROM TODD WOODBRIDGE, MARK WOODFORDE, AND CAPTAIN JOHN NEWCOMBE AT WHITE CITY.

straight sets. Sampras's leg was heavily strapped and he would have needed to use crutches. Nevertheless team morale did not seem to be everything that captain Gullikson would have wanted.

The Swedes had a somewhat different concept of the Cup. Their captain, Carl-Axel Hageskog, was thrilled to have won the trophy for his small nation for the sixth time in Sweden's 11th appearance in the Final. It made Sweden easily the most successful Davis Cup nation after the Big Four. All this looks great in the record books but it is people who create statistics and it is their personalities that tend to be remembered long after the numbers have been consigned to history. The Davis Cup is fortunate to have been rich in personalities of all shades and sizes – Brookes and Wilding, Tilden and Cochet, Perry and von Cramm, Hoad and Trabert, McEnroe and Borg. How different these men were yet how united in their ability to add a lustrous sheen of drama, excitement and bravery to one of the greatest sporting competitions yet devised by man. For 100 years it has been captivating us and the next generation seem set to carry the Davis Cup's fascination with them into the next century. They will do so because of deeds great and small. One of the smallest, perhaps, was to be witnessed outside the Scandinavium on that cold December night after little Sweden had beaten the great United States for the third time in that very stadium. Yet somehow, I don't think this was of total insignificance because it said a lot about generosity of spirit and the passing of generations. Standing on the sidewalk as light snowflakes fell, one found Magnus Larsson, still in his track suit, encumbered with racket bags, with his arm round the shoulder of a young admirer who had asked to have his picture taken with this new star of Swedish tennis. The man he had asked to take the photograph was duly obliging, making sure he was pressing the right buttons on the boy's little instamatic. The boy will have a nice picture of himself with Magnus Larsson. What it won't show is that the picture was taken by Stefan Edberg. Big stars making small gestures. Dwight Davis would have approved.

BIBLIOGRAPHY

Vijay Amritraj with Richard Evans, *Vijay!* Libri Mundi, London, 1990

John Barrett (ed.), *World of Tennis* 1995, CollinsWillow, London,1995

Gianni Clerici, *Five Hundred Years of Tennis,* Octopus, 1976

Bud Collins & Zander Hollander (eds.), *Bud Collins's Modern Encyclopedia of Tennis,* Gale
    Research Inc., Michigan (1994)

Jean Couvercelle and Guy Barbier, *L'Année du Tennis,* Calmann-Levy, Paris, 1991

Mike Davies, *Tennis Rebel,* Stanley Paul, London, 1962

Frank Deford, *Big Bill Tilden,* Victor Gollancz, London, 1977

Jaroslav Drobny, *The Autobiography of Jaroslav Drobny,* Hodder & Stoughton, London,
    1955

Richard Evans, *McEnroe: Taming the Talent,* Bloomsbury, London, 1990

Richard Evans, *Nastase,* Aidan Ellis, London, 1978

Richard Evans, *Open Tennis,* Bloomsbury, London, 1988

Gordon Forbes, *A Handful of Summers,* HarperCollins Publishers, London, 1978

Jack Kramer with Frank Deford, *The Game,* G.P. Putnam's Sons, New York, 1979

Nancy Kriplen, *Dwight Davis: the Man and the Cup,* Ebury Press, London, 1999

S. Wallis Merrihew, *The Quest of the Davis Cup,* American Lawn Tennis, New York, 1928

Paul Metzler, *Great Players of Australian Tennis,* Harper & Row, 1979

A. Wallis Myers, *Memory's Parade,* Methuen, London, 1932

A. Wallis Myers, *The Story of the Davis Cup,* Methuen, London, 1913

Fred Perry, *An Autobiography,* Stanley Paul, London, 1984

Edward C. Potter, *The Davis Cup,* A.S. Barnes, New York, 1969

Fred Stolle & Kenneth Wydro, *Tennis Down Under,* National Press, Maryland, 1985

Michel Sutter, *Vainqueurs/Winners 1946-1991,* Rosay, Vincennes, 1991

Ted Tinling, *Tinling, Sixty Years in Tennis,* Sidgwick & Jackson, London, 1983

Alan Trengove, *The Story of the Davis Cup,* Stanley Paul, London, 1985

Herbert Warren Wind, *Game, Set and Match,* E.P. Dutton, New York, 1979

1998 Media Guide, Davis Cup by NEC, The International Tennis Federation, London,
    1998

1998 Player Guide, ATP Tour, 1998

INDEX

ACKNOWLEDGEMENTS

The author and publishers would like to thank the following for their kind permission to reproduce the photographs in this book and apologise if any credits have been inadvertently omitted.

Russ Adams 205, 207, 215; Allsport 216; Allsport/Hulton Deutsch 82 left & bottom, 84, 111 bottom; Allsport/Scott Halleran 230 top, 232 top; Allsport/Olive Mason 239; Allsport/Doug Pesinger 235; Allsport/Mike Powell 6, 234 top; Allsport/Gary M. Prior 1, 23, 236, 238 left, 245 top; Amritraj Collection 189; Ron Angle 248; Gianni Ciaccia 232 bottom, 243; Michael Cole Camerawork 197, 204, 233; Richard Evans 10, 178, 210 left; Féderation Française de Tennis 83;

Arne Forsell 237; Ray Giubilo 229, 230 right, 246, 247 right & bottom; Max Peter Haas 127, 134; Tommy Hindley 221; Jenny Hoad Collection 135, 140, 143, 147, 149; Hulton Getty 44; International Tennis Hall of Fame 34, 53, 61, 64 top & left, 73, 74 top, 77, 86, 97, 101, 165, 169, 171; Longwood Cricket Club Archives 37, 39, 40, 42, 59, 67, 69, 78; T. Macarschi 181; Professional Sport 213; Prosport 238 bottom; G. Riebicke, Berlin 113, 114; Schroeder Collection 122-123, 123 right, 124 top & left; Rémy Steinegger 222 left; Angelo Tonelli 195, 196, 198, 210 top; Wimbledon Lawn Tennis Museum 17, 27, 31, 36, 47, 96, 110, 111 right, 116, 148, 155, 161, 164, 182; Paul Zimmer 219, 220 left & bottom, 222 top, 234 left, 245 right.